LEADING PEOPLE AND TEAMS IN EDUCATION

Leading People and Teams in Education

The companion volumes in this series are:

Effective Educational Leadership, edited by Nigel Bennett, Megan Crawford and Marion Cartwright

Strategic Leadership and Educational Improvement, edited by Margaret Preedy, Ron Glatter and Christine Wise

All these readers are part of a course Leading and Managing for Effective Education (E849) *that is itself part of the Open University Masters programme.*

The Open University Masters Programme in Education

The Open University Masters Programme in Education is now firmly established as the most popular postgraduate degree for education professionals in Europe, with over 3,000 students registering each year. The Masters Programme in Education is designed particularly for those with experience of teaching, the advisory service, educational administration or allied fields.

Structure of the Masters Programme in Education

The Masters is a modular degree, and students are, therefore, free to select modules from the programme which best fit in with their interests and professional goals. Specialist lines in leadership and management, applied linguistics, special needs, and lifelong learning are also available. Study within the Open University's Advanced Diploma can also be counted towards a Masters Degree, and successful study within the Masters Programme entitles students to apply for entry into the Open University Doctorate in Education programme.

OU-Supported Open Learning

The Masters Programme in Education provides great flexibility. Students study at their own pace, in their own time. They receive specially prepared study materials, supported by tutorials, thus offering the chance to work with other students.

The Doctorate in Education

The Doctorate in Education is a part-time doctoral degree, combining taught courses, research methods and a dissertation designed to meet the needs of professionals in education and related areas who are seeking to extend and deepen their knowledge and understanding of contemporary educational issues. The Doctorate in Education builds upon successful study whthin the Open University Masters Programme in Education.

How to apply

If you would like to register for this programme, or simply find out more information about available courses, please write for the *Professional Development in Education* prospectus to the Call Centre, PO Box 724, The Open University, Walton Hall, Milton Keynes, MK7 6ZW, UK (Telephone 01908 653231). Details can also be viewed on our web page http://www.open.ac.uk/courses

LEADING PEOPLE AND TEAMS IN EDUCATION

Edited by
Lesley Kydd, Lesley Anderson and Wendy Newton

The Open University   in association with   Paul Chapman Publishing

First published 2003

Paul Chapman Publishing
A SAGE Publications Company
6 Bonhill Street
London EC2A 4PU

SAGE Publications Inc
2455 Teller Road
Thousand Oaks, California 91320

SAGE Publications India Pvt Ltd
32, M-Block Market
Greater Kailash - I
New Delhi 110 048

Library of Congress Control Number: 2002105578

A catalogue record for this book is available from the
British Library

ISBN 0 7619 4059 6
ISBN 0 7619 4060 X (pbk)

Typeset by Pantek Arts Ltd, Maidstone, Kent
Printed in Great Britain by Cromwell Press,
Trowbridge, Wiltshire

Contents

CONTENTS

Acknowledgements

The editors and publishers wish to acknowledge the following for permission to use copyright material:

J. Reeves, C. Forde, B. Morris and E. Turner for material from their BELMAS Conference paper, 'Investigating the impact of the Scottish Qualification for Headship: Social processes involved in using work based learning as a vehicle for leadership and management development' (2001).

Elsevier Science for permission to reprint material from *Futures*, Volume 33: 6, pp 519–530, B. Garvey and G. Alred, 'Mentoring and Tolerance of Complexity' (2001).

H. Busher 'Principals and Headteachers as Chief Executives' (1997) in Ribbins, P. *Leaders and Leadership in the School, the College and the University* (1997) by permission from Continuum International Publishing Group Ltd. The Tower Building, 11 York Road, London, England.

SAGE Publications Ltd. for material from *Educational Management and Administration*, Volume 28: 1, pp 47–62, H. Timperley and V. Robinson 'Workload and the Professional Culture of Teachers' (2000), and *Educational Management and Administration*, Volume 29: 3 pp 291–306, I. Evans, 'Delving Deeper into Morale, Job satisfaction and Motivation among Education Professionals. Re-examining the Leadership Dimension' (2001). http://www.sagepub.co.uk

Paul Chapman Publishing for material from J. O'Neill, 'Managing through teams' (1997) in Bush, T. and Middlewood, D (eds.) *Managing People in Education* (1997).

Taylor and Francis for material from *International Journal for Academic Development*, Vol. 5: 1, pp. 42–53, S. J. Marshall, M. J. Adams, A. Cameron & G. Sullivan 'Academic's Perceptions of their Professional Development Needs Related to Leadership and Management: What can we Learn?' (2000), and *Educational Research*, Volume 42: 1, pp 13–27, M. Coleman. 'The Female Secondary Headteacher in England and Wales: Leadership and Management Styles' (2000), and *School Leadership and Management*, Volume 21: 1, pp 43–57, M. Clement and R. Vandenberghe 'How School Leaders Can Promote Teachers Professional Development: An Account from the field' (2001), and – *British Journal of Sociology of Education*, Volume 21: 3. pp 331–353, G. Troman, 'Teacher Stress in the Low–Trust Society' (2000). http://www.tandf.co.uk/journals

R. Harrison for 'Learning for Professional Development' (2002).

J. Aubrey-Hopkins and C. James for material from their BELMAS Conference paper, 'The influencing role of subject leaders in secondary schools' (2001).

Triangle Journals Ltd for material from *Research in Post-Compulsory Education*, Volume 7: 1, pp. 63–78, A.R.J. Briggs, 'Facilitating the Role of Middle Managers in Further Education' (2002),

'Creating a Team in their Own Image', M. Wallace and L. Huckman (1999) in M. Wallace and L. Huckman *Senior Management Teams in Primary Schools* (1999), Routledge.

F. Vogt for material from a BERA Research Student Conference paper, 'New Managerialism and Primary Teachers' Collegiality and Teamwork' (2000). The author would like to thank the Swiss National Science Foundation and the Overseas Research Student Awards Scheme for their support in funding this research.

Swets and Zeitlinger Publishers for material from *School Effectiveness and School Improvement: International Journal of Research, Policy and Practice*, Volume 10: 3, pp 269–295, D. Fink, 'The Attrition of Change: A Study of Change and Continuity' (1999).

Every effort has been made to trace the copyright holders but if any have been inadvertently overlooked the publishers will be pleased to make the necessary arrangement at the first opportunity.

Introduction

Lesley Kydd, Lesley Anderson and Wendy Newton

People and teams in organisations need to be led and managed – otherwise the organisation would fail to function. This book is about a leadership approach to managing people and teams – taking the lead on the strategy to be adopted and setting the tone and culture of the organisation. It seeks to provide leaders with insights into how they can take the lead in managing people – in other words, how they adopt a strategic approach. The key to leadership is that it is value-driven and, therefore, in taking a leadership approach to managing people and teams, the leader needs to be clear about his or her own values and how these are demonstrated through the culture and the management practices of the organisation.

The words 'leading' and 'managing' are the subject of much debate. These debates are concerned with the relationship between leading and managing – whether managing is a fundamentally different activity from leading or whether the two are really inter-changeable. The questions 'do leaders manage' and 'do managers lead' are at the heart of the debate. We take the view that leading is about vision and strategy and providing the inspiration to the people working in the organisation so that the aims of the organisation can be achieved. Managing is about putting the vision into practice and enabling the organisation to function.

Managing people and teams is not the same as managing any other resource. Managing people involves recognising and dealing with the range of human nature, life choices and, importantly, feelings and emotions. In this respect there is an affective dimension to leadership and the exercise of leadership and management skills. There are important underlying issues of motivation and relationships; questions of managing information; and questions of power and trust. These are underpinned by the values and ethics held by individuals and expressed in the way in which the organisation is managed – in other words, its culture.

Taking a leadership perspective to managing people and teams does not necessarily mean that the exercise of leadership is undertaken by only one person in the organisation – although we all know or have known autocratic leaders. Leadership may be dispersed throughout an organisation and thereby vested in a variety of individuals and teams. Leadership roles may be fluid in that individuals or teams may take on the mantle of leadership for a particular purpose or time. In these ways leadership may be described as time bounded and situated. Teams may be specially created and carefully selected for a specific purpose. More commonly in organisations, teams are formed according to organisational hierarchy and structure. Teams may, therefore, be constituted by post-holders and this provides a particular challenge to leaders who may not have selected the people who make up those teams.

Two important parts of the external context in which educational organisations are located are, first, the relationship between government and education professionals and, secondly, changes in the nature of learning resulting from developments in technology and electronic communications. The external environment presents a situation of continuous change and challenge to leaders and managers within the educational system. Leading people in the context of these changes is critical to the successful management of organisations. For educational leaders, there is the challenge of selecting from a myriad of policy directives those which help further the vision and aims of the organisation. For educational managers, there is the challenge of managing the multiple policy changes.

One of the key aspects of a leadership approach to managing people and teams is that of self-management in terms of preparation for leadership. This involves knowing oneself and, in particular, one's own value system as a leader and engaging with ongoing professional development. In the educational field leadership development has traditionally taken place through both formal and informal means and through various types of what might be described as 'work-based learning'. Work-based learning is important in the induction and development of leadership and leadership qualities.

The chapters have been selected to provide analytic frameworks that can be used to assist the reader in understanding a leadership approach to managing people and teams. We hope that you find them helpful in reflecting on both your own leadership and management practices and those employed in institutions known to you. The book has been structured so that it begins with an overview of the field of leading and managing people and teams in education. It then moves on to look at the professional learning of leaders. Leading and managing people and teams is located within the context of organisational structures and cultures, and Part 3 considers some of the operational aspects of managing people. The last part provides a single longitudinal case study of what might be described as leadership in action. It demonstrates both the successes and failures of leading in an organisation.

In Chapter 1, Lesley Anderson opens the book by providing an overview of a leadership approach to managing people in educational organisations. Its purpose is to introduce the reader, in broad and general terms, to these complex activities and the theoretical perspectives associated with them. The chapter identifies themes and raises issues that are considered in more detail later in this volume. In doing this, it also explains terms and enables the reader to become familiar with language used throughout the book.

Part 2 has the central theme of learning to lead. We are all familiar with the phrase 'born leader' but most would subscribe to the notion that there are aspects of leading which we can learn through formal training, through the exercise of leadership roles and through our own experience of working with those with such responsibilities. A key aspect of learning in educational organisations is that of professional learning. How do professionals learn and what do they need to learn, not only before they take on leadership roles but also throughout their working lives?

Roger Harrison in Chapter 2 looks at the issue of professional learning. Leaders and managers are themselves professionals but, at the same time, they are also responsible for the professional development and learning of others. This raises two questions – 'what is professional learning?' and 'how does it take place?' Harrison examines the growth in popularity of the notion of reflection on practice – how does this influence learning? He also looks at professional learning in relation to practice and how theory is applied in practical settings.

Moving on in the area of professional learning, in Chapter 3 Stephen J. Marshall, Moya J. Adams, Alison Cameron and Gavin Sullivan examine how academics at Macquarie University, Sydney, perceive their professional development needs as leaders and managers. They identify several dimensions on which leaders and managers in higher education institutions need to develop knowledge and skills – professional identity, strategic leadership and management; operational leadership and management; financial and physical resources management; human resources management; information management; and academic leadership and management. In particular, the study highlights the differences in perceptions between those in academic and those in administrative roles.

Another way in which professionals learn is through formal qualifications. In recent years there has been a move towards providing specific qualifications for those who aspire to be headteachers in the UK and also for those who are already heads. Such qualifications are usually built round a framework of standards. Jenny Reeves, Christine Forde, Brian Morris and Eileen Turner (in Chapter 4) examine the impact of the Scottish Qualification for Headship on both the practice of individuals and their institutions. The findings may provide a challenge to individualistic and rational cognitive models of professional learning. The researchers found indications that changing practice is bound up in a network of socio-political processes within and, in some cases, beyond the school.

In Chapter 5, Bob Garvey and Geof Alred look at learning in the workplace. They consider mentoring in the light of complexity theory and the importance given to knowledge in organisations. While the organisations they describe are not educational organisations, their arguments resonate well with experiences in the educational sector. School and colleges are complex organisations characterised by ever-changing working and learning environments. Complexity, the pace of change and the very real needs of people in organisations are difficult challenges for educational leaders and managers.

In the context of changing roles and responsibilities within education, Chapter 6 by Hugh Busher considers educational leaders as the chief executive of their organisation as opposed to the more traditional view of them as the leading professional. Drawing on empirical data generated through individual conversations with nine heads of different kinds of educational institutions, he addresses four questions: 'what are their educational and leadership values?' 'What is their leadership style?' 'How do they manage people and resources?' 'How do they understand their accountability?' Through this analysis, Busher provides another perspective on the relationship between leading and managing people in education and the way these activities are carried out in practice.

The final chapter in this part by Marianne Coleman (Chapter 7) deals with the issue of female headship. Debates about gender tend to polarise around whether women bring different 'feminine' qualities to leadership or whether, once in leadership roles, they adopt what are seen as 'masculine' leadership qualities. This study found that there is continuing discrimination against women who are in senior management positions in education. However, it also shows that the majority of respondents identify ways that being a woman leader freed them from the stereotypes of masculine leadership; that most women choose to manage their schools in ways that can be clearly identified as consultative and people orientated; that they give added importance to teamwork; and that they are concerned to give 'power to' rather than 'power over'.

Part 3 looks at leadership approaches to the management of people and teams in organisations. It begins by considering issues connected with the nature of teaching – with professional development as well as morale and motivation; with the professional culture of teachers and teacher stress. While this part is not intended to provide comprehensive coverage of all the aspects of leading and managing people and teams in organisations, these chapters deal with issues which profoundly affect the ways in which educational professionals view and undertake their jobs and their role in society. If leaders and managers do not understand these broader issues, how can they be effective?

In Chapter 8, Mieke Clement and Roland Vandenberghe look at how school leaders can promote the professional development of teachers in the workplace. Their study goes beyond the structures and conditions which leaders put in place to promote the professional learning of their staff and considers the processes which contribute to successful learning in the workplace. As we said earlier, such learning is crucially important to the development and well-being of staff in schools.

Linda Evans, in Chapter 9, looks at the issues of teacher morale, job satisfaction and motivation. She points out that in the earlier stages of her research she took the view that the relationship between morale, job satisfaction and motivation was straightforward and directly linked to educational leadership. More in-depth analysis of her findings leads her to conclude that the relationship between educational leadership and teachers' attitudes to work is much less straightforward.

In suggesting the adoption of a leadership approach to managing people we recognise the implication that there is a hierarchical relationship between leaders and those who follow. Chapter 10 by Helen Timperley and Viviane Robinson uses a case study to consider issues of workload and the professional culture of teachers in a way which challenges teachers to look carefully at their own levels of responsibility. Their findings suggest that many of the problems associated with increased workload can be attributed in part to the ways in which teachers organise themselves. They suggest that the traditions of teacher autonomy, collegiality and what they term 'bounded systems thinking' (which implies that teachers often do not think in a 'whole school' way) inhibit the decisions which would lead to a reduction in workload.

Geoff Troman in Chapter 11 uses qualitative data from a study of primary teachers' stress to examine staff relationships in primary schools. He considers the view that some causes of teacher stress are in the intensification of work which has come about through government policies which promote managerialism. His research leads him to argue that, while the intensification of teachers' work is involved in eroding positive staff relations, it is also changing the trust which shapes those relationships. This leads to what he calls the 'relations of low-trust schooling' which have a negative impact on teachers' physical and emotional well-being and their professional relationships.

The next two chapters move on to look at the important area of middle management. The first of these (Chapter 12 by Judith Aubrey-Hopkins and Chris James) focuses on the influencing role of subject leaders in secondary schools. The researchers conclude that subject leaders influence their departments in a number of ways – for example, through the use of symbolic power, the establishment of norms and expectations and through the routines of departmental practice. They also used a wide range of strategies to ensure the legitimacy of the norms and commitment to them. This study draws attention to the importance of middle managers in terms of carrying 'people with them' in the organisation and in the creation of organisational culture.

Ann R. J. Briggs reports in Chapter 13 findings from her research into the perceptions of a range of middle manager roles in the further education sector from the point of view of staff at three levels of college hierarchy. She examines what she calls the 'environment' for management, which she means the management systems of the college and the management styles within which the middle managers operate. (Readers wishing to follow up the outcomes of Briggs' research should consult academic journals for forthcoming reports.)

The next set of chapters moves on from considering individuals and groups of managers to considering teams in educational organisations. John O'Neill (Chapter 14) provides a challenge to widely disseminated theories of team formation and team development drawn from general management theory. In his view, normative conceptualisations do not take account of the complexity of educational organisations nor of the nature of the key roles of lecturers and teachers. While a team model potentially provides a supportive means of enhancing *management* practice, including teaching-*related* activities of curriculum design, assessment and evaluation, its appropriateness is contested in the domain of individual teaching practice and classroom autonomy. Interesting questions are raised about the contribution of conflict to teamworking and about the ways in which team approaches can help challenge conventional management structures. In particular, he highlights feminine management styles and distributed leadership.

Mike Wallace and Linda Huckman in Chapter 15 report on research undertaken with senior management teams (SMTs). Their case studies underline how heads are central in creating and developing team approaches and expressing the transformational aspect of their leadership. They were all keen to develop a shared culture of teamwork which did not predate the adoption of a team approach. While these senior teams' positions of authority gave them access to key resources for promoting team development, such as being able to make a major contribution to selecting other members or holding responsibility for the school's in-service training budget, these were not enough for teamwork necessarily to follow. Other members also played a crucial part, having recourse to influence over how far they might enter into the spirit of teamwork as advocated by the head, or whether they might offer minimal compliance or even open resistance.

In Chapter 16 Franziska Vogt explores primary schoolteachers' perceptions and practices of teamwork in the context of new managerial policy change and identifies possible shifts in the meaning of collegiality for the teaching profession. These reflections are based on an ongoing ethnographic research project, involving English and Swiss primary schools, into teachers' perceptions and experiences of policy change, teamwork and organisational culture. A comparison between English and Swiss case studies helps to explore the interplay between an internationally employed discourse of managerialism and the culturally specific reforms, practices of implementation and patterns of resistance. In England, the numerous reforms of recent years have led to some changes in patterns of teamwork. In Switzerland, managerialism is linked to a call for teachers to intensify their teamwork. In both countries, however, managerialist policies potentially undermine teamwork by emphasising management and individual performance in the introduction of performance-related pay. These two consecutive chapters raise important questions about what is conceived as teamwork and whether without the informal 'stuff' of teams – the social gel – formally constituted teams can be really effective.

The final part of the book comprises one chapter (Chapter 17) by Dean Fink. This is a single case study of the creation of a new school – Lord Byron High School, Ontario. The chapter considers issues to do with leading in practice and what actually happens in a school over a long period of time. The school moves through a number of phases in its existence from being a highly successful school to a failing school in danger of being closed. The staff then implement changes which lead to the school becoming successful once more. What are the leadership issues which led it through these phases?

All leadership and management activities are about encouraging and persuading people to act in the best interests of those who work and learn in the organisation. We hope this book makes a contribution to that aim.

Part 1

Leading People and Teams in Education

1

A Leadership Approach to Managing People in Education

Lesley Anderson

People – the Key Resource

Without people, organisations would not exist. Indeed, without them, there would be no need for leaders or for leadership. People are not, of course, the only resource of interest to organisations but without them, and without organisations, there would be no need for either the other resources or for the management of them. It is people themselves who create a need for leadership and management, both of people and other resources such as finance, time and premises. This is because, as individuals, people have drives and needs, values and beliefs: all of which influence the way they behave and respond to one another. Moreover, it is recognised (Everard and Morris, 1990, p. 256; Foreman, 1998, p. 18) that an organisation without vision, without direction, without order and without discipline is one in which people's performance varies and where individuals may not fulfil their full potential. This is not only detrimental for the organisation as a whole but affects each person. Thus, people are integral to both leadership and management. Furthermore, it follows that, in order to understand the nuances of effectively leading and managing, it is necessary to understand people in organisations – how and why they behave and react as they do, both as leaders and managers and as those being led and managed, and, relatedly, how individuals become successful leaders and managers.

As the series title and that of this chapter indicate, this book and its sister volumes are concerned with *educational* organisations – schools and colleges and other establishments providing education and/or training. Generic theories of organisations, leadership and the management of people apply to educational organisations in the same way as those with other purposes, but the focus on

---

Source: Commissioned.

organisations specialising in education creates an additional dimension to the discussion. Leading and managing people and teams in educational organisations is not only about applying these functions to the staff and volunteers who work within the organisation, it is also about leading and managing the learners who are registered with the educational establishment. Although, on the one hand, learners can be regarded as the customers or the clients of the organisation (Simkins, 1997, pp. 26–29), on the other they are a significant part of its operation. Without them, there would be no educational organisation. Furthermore, many people involved in education view their work as more than just a job. They often hold strong values and beliefs about education, the ways in which schools and colleges should operate and how they want to carry out their work. Thus, leading and managing people and teams in educational organisations are specialised activities and require careful consideration.

This opening chapter sets the scene for the rest of the book by introducing the key issues associated with a leadership approach to managing people and teams in educational organisations. It identifies themes for effective leadership and management and raises related matters that successful organisations address as part of their practice. Many of these themes and issues are also considered in later chapters of this book.

Understanding the Terminology

As with any communication, it is important there is shared understanding, as far as it is possible, about the meaning of the words used – whether they be written or spoken. Four key words are used throughout this book and, to ensure clarity throughout the volume, their meanings in an educational context are considered.

The word 'people' is used carefully because, as indicated above, learners as well as staff need to be considered in organisational planning. This is clearly evident in conventional educational settings such as schools and colleges where the learners – or students – are physically present in the buildings. They have to be managed as a group in terms of a timetable for teaching and use of facilities. They also need to be led and managed in their learning. Of course, these more personal aspects of leading and managing students apply equally to those people studying in a less conventional way, for example, by distance learning or through electronic media. The word 'student' also includes a wide range of professionals who are undertaking study and/or training as part of their continuing professional development (CPD). Leadership and management are required to support the dual role such people take on.

Turning to the other group of people of interest here, it has already been indicated that the intention is not to limit the term to teachers or lecturers nor, indeed to paid staff. There are a numerous people who, in adopting different roles, contribute to the functioning of educational organisations and all these people need to be led and managed. Of course, the group includes teachers, lecturers, tutors and trainers as well as classroom assistants who are increasingly deployed in school classrooms in the UK. However, it also includes administrative, technical and operational staff such a caretakers and cleaners. Moreover, there may be volunteers who contribute to the work of the organisation, for example, in schools and in prisons.

The next word that needs consideration is 'teams'. What makes a group of people into a team is considered in detail in other chapters of this book. It is, therefore, sufficient to say here that the purpose of a team is to achieve a shared outcome or outcomes and that it is usual to expect that they do this as effectively as possible. The team may consist of any of the people identified above. It may be a permanent team or one that has come together for a particular purpose and whose existence is planned to be short term. The individual members may be selected with the team in mind or they may have come together for historical or other reasons.

Moving on to the word 'leading', it is important to make it clear that because the activity itself and the important related areas of leadership and leaders are extremely complex, the comments that follow can only be superficial. Again, these issues are discussed in later chapters of this book although it should also be made clear that, as topics in their own right, they are not intended as the substance of this book. It is suffice to say here that research suggests leadership is a key factor for effective educational organisations (Sammons *et al.*, 1997) and this finding has resulted in a wave of interest in the topic, especially in the context of school improvement. In turn, there has been a wealth of literature published that explores leadership and the characteristics of leaders from every conceivable angle and in every setting (see, for example, Riley and Seashore Louis, 2000; Gunter, 2001; Bennett *et al.*, 2002). Thus, the provision of effective educational leadership has gained immense importance in the last twenty years or so and is well exemplified by the establishment of the National College for School Leadership (NCSL) in England in 2000 for the purpose of transforming school leadership.

In this chapter, three definitions of leadership are highlighted. The first, provided by Hodgson (1987), describes leadership as 'path-finding', implying movement towards an endpoint or goal. The next one – 'doing the right things' (Bennis and Nanus, 1985) – is, in many ways, similar because the implication is that in 'doing the right things' the 'unit' being led is taken towards the desired endpoint. Thus, there is still evidence of movement within the definition. The third definition, Bryman's (1986) 'focus on the creation of a vision about a desired future state', differs in that it is static in its implication. However, like the others, it looks forward to a changed condition in the future that it is reasonable to assume is better than the present. Thus, together, these definitions convey the idea of identifying a future state that is desired for the organisation as well as ways in which it can move forward to this point and, in doing so, improve.

The final word, 'managing', is about the actual process of moving the organisation along the path towards the identified vision. It involves putting plans, structures and procedures in place and, then, enacting them through the people within the organisation to achieve improvement. Helpfully, each of the three groups of writers above offers a definition of management that contrasts with their version of the meaning of the term leadership and, in this way, demonstrates the relationship between the two concepts. Their definitions of management are as follows:

■ Path-following (Hodgson, 1987).
■ Doing things right (Bennis and Nanus, 1985).
■ A preoccupation with the here-and-now of goal attainment (Bryman, 1986).

Hence, theoretically, a clear distinction between leading and managing is suggested. However, as is often the case, in practice it is not so straightforward (see Crawford, 2002). Law and Glover (2000, p. 13) point out that the terms tend to be used interchangeably and that leading is frequently seen as an aspect of management. Moreover, the nature of educational organisations, such as the number of staff employed in many primary schools, means that it is often necessary for leaders also to undertake management activities and, inevitably, this means that styles of management influence styles of leadership, and visa versa. For example, a manager who adopts an open, collegial approach that involves sharing resources is likely to lead in a similar way while, for a manager who adopts a hierarchical approach, decision-making and leadership tend to be located at the apex of the organisational hierarchy. Whatever definitions of leadership and management are used, it is clear that there must be a bridge between the two activities. The effective leader must not only have the ability to identify the appropriate developmental path for the organisation to take but also have skills that enable him or her to encourage or persuade the people to follow that route, to do the right things and to focus on here-and-now goals. Thus, the two functions are considered side by side in this volume.

Leading and Managing People for a Purpose

It is reasonable to assume that all organisations exist to succeed whatever criteria are used to assess that success. In most private organisations, the overall success criterion is likely to be linked to profit. In the public sector, it is usually determined through measures that consider the relationship between inputs and outcomes, in other words, organisations in the public sector are held accountable for their effectiveness (Riches, 1997, p. 15). Although the exploration of issues such as effectiveness is beyond the scope of this chapter, for the purpose of this discussion an effective organisations is taken as one that 'produces' the highest-quality product or service. In turn, part of the purpose of leadership and management is to enable the organisation to achieve such outcomes. The corollary to this statement is that a quality product or service is dependent upon the performance of the people working in various ways to achieve it. There are, therefore, various aspects to the purpose of leading and managing people.

To begin with, there is an obvious requirement that suitable people are 'in place' to undertake the work and to be led and managed. These people have to be recruited and selected. Furthermore, in order to be 'suitable', they require relevant knowledge, understanding, skills and abilities to carry out the work. Of course, appointing 'suitable' people is an important aspect of the manager's role in relation to staff although expecting to find a person who 'fits perfectly' on every occasion is unrealistic. It is, therefore, anticipated that people new to a post will often require training and/or support initially in terms of the details of their actual role and responsibilities. In addition, there is another important part to the induction role for managers. This is in helping new appointees become familiar with, and understand, the culture of the organisation in which they are now working.

However, the developmental role of the leader and manager does not end here. The *ongoing* development of people, especially those working in educational organisations, is important for a variety of reasons. These include the significance of the rapidly changing climate in education and, hence, the importance of ensuring that the people undertaking the work are able to adapt their thinking, understanding and working styles in relation to change – both internally and externally. Hence, there is an important leadership task in setting the vision and ensuring a strategic approach to staff development, including planning for people to take on new and different responsibilities as others move on – in other words, succession planning. Moreover, leaders also fulfil their role by leading by example so that the effective leader will demonstrate good practice by being the 'lead learner' and participate actively in CPD. Finally, in order for an organisation to achieve its overall success criteria, the leaders and managers also require knowledge of individual performance as well as providing feedback and opportunities for development.

These purposes are achieved through a range of activities that can be described as 'functional' – in other words they are a necessary part of the day-to-day management of people in organisations. Using the different developmental stages in the lifespan of a 'worker' as a framework, the key areas can be summarised within a cycle as follows:

- Recruitment and selection.
- Induction and mentoring.
- Performance review and appraisal.
- Staff development.

It is, however, essential to point out that, in practice, managers deal with these different tasks concurrently and on an ongoing basis. Once again, there are numerous sources of guidance in the literature about 'how to undertake' and 'good practice in' these various functional aspects of leading and managing staff (for example, for sources relating to organisations in general, see Hunt, 1986; Goss, 1994; Thomson and Mabey, 1994; Graham and Bennett, 1995; Megginson and Clutterbuck, 1995; for those concerned with educational organisations in particular, see: Paisley, 1985; Southworth, 1990; Wilkin, 1992; Smith and West-Burnham, 1993; Bush and West-Burnham, 1994; Craft, 1996; Glover and Law, 1996; Bush and Middlewood, 1997; Tomlinson, 1997). A detailed discussion of these functions is, therefore, not included in this chapter.

However, as already indicated, there is more to successful leadership and management of people than ensuring that the functional tasks are carried out successfully. Effective leaders and managers are sensitive to a range of other issues that affect the way people perform at work in order to get the best from them. Therefore, the focus of the rest of this chapter is on these matters. In the next section the issue of leading and managing people as *human resources* is considered.

■ Leading and Managing Human Resources

The shift towards self-managing, public sector educational organisations in many countries in the 1980s and 1990s brought with it the need for these workplaces to take responsibility for matters relating to staff where, previously, a separate 'personnel' function had often been provided at a district or regional level. Individual schools and colleges were now encouraged to plan strategically (Davies and Ellison, 1999), including an integrated approach to the management of staff. As part of this development, a change in language occurred and the expression *human resource management* (HRM) was imported from mainstream management in the commercial world (O'Neill *et al.*, 1994). Further evidence for this point is readily available by glancing at the titles and terms used for books, chapters and articles towards the end of the twentieth century (for example, Riches and Morgan, 1989; West-Burnham, 1990; O'Neill, 1994; Seifert, 1996).

The question then arises about the significance of this change. What differentiates HRM from the personnel models that were previously used to support publicly funded schools and colleges? Middlewood and Lumby (1998, p. 9) attribute the move towards HRM to a range of issues that relate to the nature of 'traditional, specialist personnel provision'. These include the latter's bureaucratic nature, its unsustainable 'cost' in financial and human terms as well as the way it threatens the relationship between line manager and subordinate. They also point out that 'old' personnel functions in education were reliant on, and perpetuated the mystique of, the perceived expertise of personnel specialists rather than focussing on the development of line manager capacity (ibid.). They go on to list typical features of HRM approaches and describe the theory as predicated on the principles of 'concern for the quality of relationships, a desire to reduce unnecessary bureaucracy and a concern to see staff management issues as the routine preserve of the line manager, to be addressed in the workplace' (ibid., p. 10). Drawing on Riches and Morgan's (1989, pp. 2–3) definition of HRM, Hall (1997, p. 141) highlights what she considers to be a useful aspect of this change in that HRM recognises the 'links between managing staff and achieving the organisation's strategic objectives'. Thus, HRM is seen as highly normative, proactive and strategic. Furthermore, it is claimed that it provides a backdrop that enables rapid and complex change to be managed effectively by addressing organisational and individual needs together rather than allowing situations to occur where the latter could clash with those of the former. Although, in these ways, HRM strategies may be regarded as appropriate and relevant for educational organisations in the twenty-first century, it does not have universal support (see, for example, Bottery, 1992).

The significance of the shift to HRM in recent times also highlights another important factor for leaders and manager in education. This is the relevance of the context or external environment in which the educational establishment operates. Factors such as government legislation and economic prosperity impinge on all aspects of the organisation which, inevitably, means they affect the people that are associated with it. For example, schools in the UK have been subjected to a constant stream of innovation and changes in legislation over the past twenty years or so which has resulted in significant increase in teacher stress, ill health and resignation from the profession.

Approaches to Leading and Managing People

Returning to the theme that organisations are, in fact, just groups of people working together, it is appropriate to consider people's behaviour. One of the ways in which people are marked out from other living beings is, of course, because human beings have feelings and emotions and live and work in a context that is driven by values, beliefs and attitudes. These attributes are acquired throughout a lifetime and are unique to each person. They influence the individual's personality, what he or she strives to do in his or her life and how he or she goes about it. Riches (1997, p. 26) describes individuals as having a 'unique pattern of motivations . . . [which they] are striving to satisfy' while, according to Whitaker (1993, pp. 8–9), 'in the end our behaviour will depend on the ways in which our intentions . . . are empowered into action'. It follows that behaviour depends on the way in which people believe they, as an individual, are treated as a worker, as a member of a team and as part of an organisation.

People working in education are no different. They bring to the educational context their own set of values and beliefs about the purpose of education and rights to it which, in many instances, may have been influenced by their own experience as a learner. For people in educational leadership and managerial positions, these individual characteristics are demonstrated through their decisions and actions that, in turn, affect all the people working in the organisation, including the learners. Educational leadership, in particular, is values driven. As Grace (1995, p. 14) points out in the school context, 'headteachers . . . use the moral authority of their role to advance and propagate particular values to constitute the ethos of a school'. Grace (ibid.) cites 'traditional Christian values, innovative Christian values and relatively secular values to do with community, cooperation, fraternity and solidarity' as examples of the types of values headteachers may draw on and promote from their position of leadership. However, although these descriptions are useful, they do not explain how personal values are interpreted and acted out on a day-to-day basis. Discussing the way in which educational organisations operate, Bottery (1992, p. 6) suggests that approaches range from one that treats 'human beings as resources to be manipulated' and another that regards people as 'resourceful humans'. These are the two extremes: at one end there is the manager who is driven to achieve the task at all costs while, at the other, there is the person who is motivated by concern for the people involved in the process.

Various conceptualisations are used to model these contrasting perspectives within the literature. Goss (1994) distinguishes between them in terms of how people conceive the strategic potential of HRM and defines the two approaches as 'instrumental' or 'humanistic'. He describes (ibid., p. 10) the first as being rational and concerned with outcomes in its approach to HRM that is 'driven and derived directly from corporate, divisional or business level strategy, and geared almost exclusively to enhancing competitive advantage'. In comparison, the other model emphasises the 'reciprocal nature of the relationship between strategic management and HRM and the latter's role in ensuring that competitive advantage is achieved by people, but not necessarily at their expense' (ibid.). Storey (1987) adopts a similar approach in his use of 'hard' and 'soft' normative models of HRM. The former is concerned with the 'ends' rather than the 'means' while both are important in the latter. Riches (1997, p. 20) points out that 'people are employees and performers with legal and moral rights: they are to be treated as ends and not only means to an organisational end'. Like Bottery (1992), he goes on (1997, p. 20) to argue that 'there are conflicts inherent in the view that people are semi-mechanical human resources to be assessed in quantitative, calculative terms as assets in an organisation'. He describes the latter as 'a "hard" variant of HRM'. Focusing on education, Hall (1997, p. 144) highlights that *people* are actually both the 'means' and the 'ends', a fact that emphasises the importance of effective leadership and management in education. Using Storey's model, Hall (1997) suggests ways in which approaches to leading and managing people can contrast according to different individual philosophies (see Table 1.1). Although Hall is at pains to

Table 1.1 *Hard and soft models of HRM*

Hard	Soft
Systems-led/market-led	People-led
Cost effectiveness	Effective learning
Improbable goals	Diverse goals, 'visions'
Periphery workers = variable costs	All workers important
Selection to 'fit'	Something to offer
Targeted development	Development for all
'Accountable' appraisal	'Development' appraisal
Human resources	Resourceful humans
People – means to an end	People – ends in themselves
Control, compliance, 'fit'	Consensualism, mutuality, commitment
Training for now	Development for the future
Strategic concern	Excellence ethos
Mechanistic	'Organic'
Uniformity	Flexibility

Source: Hall (1997, p. 145).

point out the oversimplification in this model, particularly in the assumption that 'soft' approaches are less controlling than 'hard' ones, it is useful in that it highlights the fact that leading and managing people is always values-driven.

Linking Leading and Managing People to the Organisation's Culture

The approach that is used in practice to lead and/or manage people in the workplace connects directly with its culture. Indeed, for most people within an organisation, it is the culture that plays a significant part in influencing the way they each develop and enact their individual approach to leading and managing and/or how they expect to be led and managed (Bennett, 2001, pp. 98–122). In the case of the overall leader, the situation is likely to be reversed in that the culture that predominates is usually attributable to that person as an expression of his or her personal values and philosophy of education. Therefore, in seeking to understand how and why people behave in educational organisations it is relevant to include a study of organisational culture.

Focusing on the culture of a school, Prosser (1999, p. xii) explains it, in its broadest sense, as a totality, as a way of constructing reality. He adds that it is 'a useful if intricate and elusive notion'. However, he suggests that, in practice, culture is usually defined as a system of related subsystems, for example, organisational communication, resource allocation and control systems, combined together with factors such as values and beliefs, norms of behaviour, roles and status, rituals and traditions. Fidler (1997, p. 37) also emphasises how 'hard it is to capture' and describes it as a 'sophisticated' concept. Adopting a different approach from Prosser, Fidler (1997, p. 40) identifies six dimensions to the minimum number of independent factors that are required to describe the essential assumptions that are the major influences on the life of a school. He lists aims of school and attitudes to innovation and parents as the external perspectives and adds examples of each assumption (academic, balanced, social; prospector, defender, reactor; customer, partner, mentee). Likewise, his internal factors and their descriptors are leadership style (autocratic, consultative, participative), working together (collaborative, co-operative, independent) and relationship with children (friendly, business-like, repressive) (ibid., pp. 40–41). Combining these linear and continuous scales, it is evident that there are a large number of cultural 'positions' for schools – or other educational organisations. Moreover, the links to leading and managing people in educational organisations are evident. The style of leadership and way in which people work together within an educational establishment are both factors that are pertinent to issues relating to HRM and emanate from the organisational culture.

On the basis that workplace culture is significant in understanding the way in which people lead and manage and are led and managed in educational organisations, Hall (1997, p. 154) considers whether culture can be managed. She bases her discussion on what she calls her eight 'Cs' of workplace culture – commitment, conditions of service, communication, consultation, creativity, collaboration, conflict, control – issues that she describes as forming 'a tight woven context for HRM practices' (ibid.). Consideration of each 'C' suggests there are ways in which these areas can be developed and culture changed over time. In particular, Hall (ibid., p. 158) points to communication, consultation, conflict and control and suggests that these provide 'some clues as to how . . . boundaries can be made more permeable and obstacles to achieving this'. Her point is that, although these processes provide opportunities to influence the culture of the organisation through choice, they are also demanding and can constrain. For example, consultation may enhance employee commitment but it is also time consuming and can also raise issues of conflict and control.

Leading, Managing and Performance

The performance of individuals and teams within the organisation is a key issue for both leaders and managers. Whatever their values, beliefs and ways of doing things, leaders and managers' *raison d'être* is to enhance the performance of the people within their organisation and make it more effective in whatever way effectiveness is judged. Thus, understanding performance and how it can be managed are important aspects of leading and managing people.

Performance – the way in which people carry out their work – is influenced by many factors and it may change over time, in both the short and long term. A starting point for performance is the individual's, or team's competency to carry out the work or task. If the appropriate knowledge, understanding or skills are not available, adequate performance is not possible. A lack of information, resources, authority or power can influence performance adversely. Situational variables such as organisational characteristics or leadership affect performance as can external, 'out of work' matters that may, or may not, be in the control of the individual. Other factors, like relationships between colleagues, can also be influential. Uncomfortable relationships can develop that result in anxiety and tensions. These can hinder effective performance because emotions are involved which can affect people's performance at work, both positively and negatively. Unlike other resources, people, as a human resource, have feelings about themselves and their role in the workplace and these influence their motivation to work.

Inevitably, if the purpose of leading and managing is to achieve success and that depends on effectiveness, objective information about actual performance is important for leaders and managers. However, Riches (1997, p. 17) points out that evaluation of performance is fraught with subjectivity. People are inconsistent in their performance or conditions in which performance takes place may vary (Cascio, 1991). Different methods of observing job performance may result in different conclusions about it and, although a variety of predictors can be used, in practice this does not happen and results tend to be unreliable (Ronan and Prien, 1971). Withstanding these reservations, management approaches include evaluation and operate in an attempt to effect performance. Two overall approaches are acknowledged here: those that are performance-centred and those that focus on people and factors such as motivation. Performance-centred approaches are distinguishable by their use of frameworks for 'measuring' performance, for example, management by objectives, management competences, inspection frameworks and value-added measures. It is important to acknowledge that performance-centred approaches differ in the extent to which the performance standards in each are internally generated, customised, developmentally orientated or confidential (Middlewood and Lumby, 1998, p. 18). Performance, then, can be managed in a variety of ways and there are obvious similarities with Storey's 'hard' and 'soft' management models.

Leading and Managing to Motivate

It goes without saying that a workforce with low morale and self-esteem, and few rewards, will lack motivation. Thus, the management of motivation is a key factor in the successful leadership and management of people within an organisation whether a people- or performance-centred approach is adopted. By understanding what motivates and managing to achieve it, leaders and managers can enhance the performance of the people and teams in the organisation. Various theories of motivation have been put forward although Maslow's (1943) hierarchy of needs is probably the best known. Maslow argues that motivation relates to meeting a hierarchy of needs represented within an isosceles triangle. Motivation is directly influenced by the satisfaction of a sequence of needs that move from survival at the lowest level through security, belonging, prestige to self-fulfilment at the apex of the triangle. Maslow's key finding is that people display no motivation to pursue higher-level needs until lower ones are satisfied. Other ideas on, and theories of, motivation abound; (for example, see McClelland, 1961; Adams, 1965; Herzberg, 1966; McGregor, 1970; Hofstede, 1980; Neider, 1980; Peters, 1989 Locke and Latham, 1990; Handy, 1993). Although they differ in their approach to understanding motivation, according to Riches (1994), they can be loosely classified as content and process theories. As the name suggests, the first group are based on the identification of specific things that motivate the individual while the second set are concerned with the dynamic relationships between the motivational variables. The latter include the expected impact of actions, the achievement of goals and people's perceptions of whether they are treated fairly or not (Riches, 1997, pp. 24–25). However, whichever theories appeal, general knowledge of human nature indicates that motivation is aligned with rewards, although the issue, then, is what counts as reward.

Like people, rewards come in various shapes and sizes and are, to a large extent, personal to the individual in as far as he or she values the reward and feels it is appropriate. Pay is the obvious reward although its role in this context is not only about the material welfare it provides. Thierry (1992) suggests that pay is meaningful to the employee because it conveys information about important aspects of employment other than its basic monetary value. In other words, pay is an indicator of the level of recognition for the work contributions made. It values behaviour and signifies the organisation's attitude to individual performance and achievement.

Individuals also seek and, hopefully, achieve rewards from their work in other ways, such as through a sense of 'fit', job satisfaction and self-fulfilment. These are intrinsic rewards and are influenced by a range of factors operating at various levels. They include people's individual attitudes, interests and specific needs, factors that relate to the nature of the job such as level of responsibility and control and, at the organisational level, variables like culture, relationships, leadership and systems-wide rewards (Vandevelde, 1988, p. 12). Some people have what has been described as a 'vocational calling' to a particular professional role while others thrive on responsibility and it is in these types of ways that the rewards of job satisfaction and self-fulfilment can be actualised.

Using a typology adapted from Steers and Porter (1991), Goss (1994, p. 87) categorises rewards using a two-dimensional model. Rewards are either extrinsic or intrinsic and are offered to individuals or to a group of people collectively. This model is adapted in Figure 1.1 to show types of reward that are relevant to teachers, lecturers, tutors and trainers. According to Goss, it is useful to think of the quadrants not as mutually exclusive categories but as aspects of a particular reward policy that may be present (in combination) to a greater or lesser extent.

In relation to educational organisations, particularly those in the public sector, there is often little scope for managers to affect extrinsic rewards. Indeed, rates of pay and the availability of other benefits are generally open and well known to people before they make the decision to work within the sector. Thus, it is argued that intrinsic approaches to motivation are of greater importance

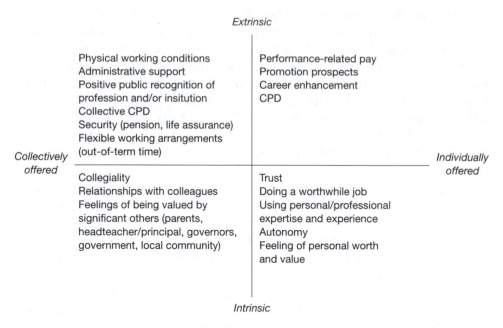

Extrinsic

Collectively offered	Physical working conditions Administrative support Positive public recognition of profession and/or insitution Collective CPD Security (pension, life assurance) Flexible working arrangements (out-of-term time)	Performance-related pay Promotion prospects Career enhancement CPD	Individually offered
	Collegiality Relationships with colleagues Feelings of being valued by significant others (parents, headteacher/principal, governors, government, local community)	Trust Doing a worthwhile job Using personal/professional expertise and experience Autonomy Feeling of personal worth and value	

Intrinsic

Figure 1.1 *Examples of types of reward used in education*
Source: Steers and Porter (1991)

here. Furthermore, the ways in which leaders and managers can enable these rewards to be attained link to the issues and themes of this chapter. Here, again, the organisational culture and style of leadership are significant as are the effective management of the functional aspects of HRM. In respect of the latter, investment in the induction process and knowledge of the individual alongside a strategic approach to staff development are examples of ways in which managers can address the motivation and, hence, the performance of their colleagues.

A Leadership Approach to Managing People

In setting the context for the book, this chapter has highlighted a number of themes and issue for leading and managing people and teams in education. Among them is the relationship between these two functions and its importance, at both a theoretical and practical level, in bringing about the improvement of educational organisations. Moreover, the focus on the first in recent times suggests that it is relevant for those people involved in a leadership capacity at any level within an educational organisation to understand the concept of a leadership approach, alongside the overall management of people within their organisation. This includes knowing about the people being led and managed, communicating values and priorities and modelling good practice. Effective leaders adopt a strategic approach and lead by example; the key point here being that leaders and managers are themselves subject to HRM practices and, therefore, they have a vested interest at a personal level as well as in terms of the effectiveness of their organisation. Perhaps, most importantly, they know that people are their key resources and, without them, there would be no organisation to lead and manage.

References

Adams, J.S. (1965) Inequality is social exchange. In L. Berkowitz (ed.) *Advances in Experimental Psychology*. Vol. 2. New York: Academic Press.

Bennett, N. (2001) Power, structure and culture: an organisational view of school effectiveness and school improvement. In A. Harris and N. Bennett (eds.) *School Effectiveness and School Improvement: Alternative Perspectives*. London: Continuum.

Bennett, N., Crawford, M. and Cartwright, M. (eds.) (2002) *Leadership and Effective Education*. London: Paul Chapman Publishing.

Bennis, W. and Nanus, B. (1985) *Leaders*. New York: Harper & Row.

Bryman, A. (1986) *Leadership and Organizations*. London: Routledge & Kogan Page.

Bottery, M. (1992) *The Ethics of Educational Management*. London: Cassell.

Bush, T. and Middlewood, D. (eds.) (1997) *Managing People in Education*. London: Paul Chapman Publishing.

Bush, T. and West-Burnham, J. (eds.) (1994) *The Principles of Educational Management*. Harlow: Longman.

Cascio, W. F. (1991) *Applied Psychology in Personnel Management* (4th edn). Englewood Cliffs, NJ: Prentice-Hall.

Craft, A. (1996) *Continuing Professional Development*. London: Routledge.

Crawford, M. (2002) Inventive management and wise leadership. In N. Bennett *et al.* (eds.) *Leadership and Effective Education*. London: Paul Chapman Publishing.

Davies, B. and Ellison, L. (1999) *Strategic Direction and Development of the School*. London: Routledge.

Everard, K. and Morris, G. (1990) *Effective School Management*. London: Paul Chapman Publishing.

Fidler, B. (1997) Addressing the tensions: culture and values. In B. Fidler *et al.* (eds.) *Choices for Self-Managing Schools*. London: Paul Chapman Publishing.

Foreman, K. (1998) Vision and mission. In D. Middlewood and J. Lumby (eds.) *Strategic Management in Schools and Colleges*. London: Paul Chapman Publishing.

Glover, D. and Law, S. (1996) *Managing Professional Development in Education*. London: Kogan Page.

Goss, D. (1994) *Principles of Human Resource Management*. London: Routledge.

Grace, G. (1995) *School Leadership: Beyond Educational Management*. London: Falmer Press.

Graham, H.T. and Bennett, R. (1995) *Human Resources Management* (8th edn). London: Pitman.

Gunter, H. (2001) *Leaders and Leadership in Education*. London: Paul Chapman Publishing.

Hall, V. (1997) Managing staff. In B. Fidler *et al.* (eds.) *Choices for Self-Managing Schools*. London: Paul Chapman Publishing.

Handy, C. (1993) *Understanding Organisations*. London: Penguin Books.

Herzberg, F. (1966) *Work and the Nature of Man*. Cleveland, OH: World Publishing.

Hodgson, P. (1987) Managers can be taught, but leaders have to learn. *ICT*, November/December.

Hofstede, G. (1980) *Culture's Consequences*. Beverley Hills, CA: Sage.

Hunt, J. (1986) *Managing People at Work*. Maidenhead: McGraw-Hill.

Law, S. and Glover, D. (2000) *Educational Leadership and Learning*. Buckingham: Open University Press.

Locke, E.A. and Latham, G.P. (1990) Work motivation: the high performance cycle. In U. Kleinbeck *et al.* (eds.) *Work Motivation*. Hillsdale, NJ: Lawrence Erlbaum Associates.

Maslow, A. (1943) A theory of human motivation. *Psychological Review* 50: 370–96.

McClelland, D. (1961) *The Achieving Society*. Princeton, NJ: Van Nostrand.

McGregor, D. (1970) *The Human Side of Enterprise*. Maidenhead: McGraw-Hill.

Megginson, D. and Clutterbuck, D. (1995) *Mentoring in action*. London: Kogan Page.

Middlewood, D. and Lumby, J. (eds.) (1998) *Strategic Management in Schools and Colleges*. London: Paul Chapman Publishing.

Neider, L. (1980) An experimental field investigation utilising an expectancy theory view of participation. *Organisational Behaviour and Human Performance* 26(3): 425–42.

O'Neill, J. (1994) Managing human resources. In T. Bush and J. West-Burnham (eds.) *The Principles of Educational Management*. Harlow: Longman.

O'Neill, J., Middlewood, D. and Glover, D. (1994) *Managing Human Resources in Schools and Colleges*. Harlow: Longman.

Paisey, A. (ed.) (1985) *Jobs in Schools*. London: Heinemann.

Peters, T. (1989) *Thriving on Chaos*. London: Pan/Macmillan.

Prosser, J. (ed.) (1999) *School Culture*. London: Paul Chapman Publishing.

Riches, C. (1994) Motivation. In T. Bush and J. West-Burhum (eds.) *The Principles of Educational Management*. Harlow: Longman.

Riches, C. (1997) Managing for people and performance. In T. Bush and D. Middlewood (eds.) *Managing People in Education*. London: Paul Chapman Publishing.

Riches, C. and Morgan, C. (eds.) (1989) *Human Resource Management in Schools*. Milton Keynes: Open University Press.

Riley, K. and Seashore Louis, K. (eds.) (2000) *Leadership: For Change and School Reform*. London: RoutledgeFalmer.

Ronan, W.W. and Prien, E.P. (1971) *Perspectives on the Measurement of Human Performance*. New York: Appleton-Century-Crofts.

Sammons, P., Hillman, J. and Mortimore, P. (1997) Key characteristics of effective schools: a review of school effectiveness research. In J. White and M. Barber (eds.) *Perspectives on School Effectiveness and School Improvement*. London: Institute of Education, University of London, Bedford Way Papers.

Seifert, R. (1996) *Human Resource Management in Schools*. London: Pitman.

Simkins, T. (1997) Autonomy and accountability. In B. Fidler *et al.* (eds.) *Choices for Self-Managing Schools*. London: Paul Chapman Publishing.

Smith, P. and West-Burnham, J. (1993) *Mentoring in the Effective School*. Harlow: Longman.

Southworth, G. (1990) *Staff Selection in the Primary School*. Oxford: Blackwell.

Steers, R. and Porter, L. (eds.) (1991) *Motivation and Work Behaviour*. New York: McGraw-Hill.

Storey, J. (1987) Developments in the management of human resources: an interim report. Warwick papers: In industrial Relations, 17. IRRU School of Industrial and Business Studies. University of Warwick.

Thierry, H. (1992) Pay and payment systems. In J. Hartley and G. Stephenson (eds.) *Employment Relations*. Oxford: Blackwell.

Thomson, R. and Mabey, C. (1994) *Developing Human Resources*. Oxford: Butterworth-Heinemann.

Tomlinson, H. (ed.) (1997) *Managing Continuing Professional Development in Schools*. London: Paul Chapman Publishing.

Vandevelde, B.R. (1988) *Implications of Motivation Theories and Work Motivation Studies for the Redeployment of Teachers*. Sheffield: Sheffield City Polytechnic for Educational Management and Administration.

West-Burnham, J. (1990) Human resource management in schools. In B. Davies *et al.* (eds.) *Education Management for the 1990s*. Harlow: Longman.

Whitaker, P. (1993) *Practical Communication in Schools*. Harlow: Longman.

Wilkin, M. (ed.) (1992) *Mentoring in Schools*. London: Kogan Page.

Part 2

Learning to Lead

2

Learning for Professional Development

Roger Harrison

Introduction

Debates about professional development are extensive and deeply embedded in other debates in education, training and the wider social formation. For example, contemporary discourses of economic competitiveness suggest the need for entrepreneurial capabilities among workers in the public, private and voluntary sectors and from all levels of staff. Learning and development are seen as essential if workers are to adapt to ever-accelerating change in their fields of practice and if they are to make positive contributions to driving up standards and increasing efficiency. Here 'development' is not only co-terminous with professionalism but is presented as never complete or conclusive, with no closure on the need for further learning. The possibility of achieving mastery in a given area of practice remains tantalisingly in the future; part of the ethos of professionalism, yet never fully accomplished. This provides a very different account of what it means to be professional and to act professionally from those which were in circulation only a few decades ago. Three sorts of distinctions can be drawn. First, initial training, delivered through classroom-based curricula with the aim of instilling a body of knowledge and skills appropriate for a lifetime of practice, is no longer seen as sufficient. The pace of social, economic and technological change is suggested as the reason why all of us must now become lifelong learners (DfEE, 1998), and why professionals must engage in continuous development. Secondly, learning for capable practice is now understood as occurring not just through participation in formal courses of study, but is just as likely to occur through informal work-based interactions with colleagues (Eraut *et al.*, 2002) or through personal research on the Internet. The proliferation of

Source: Commissioned.

29

opportunities for learning, driven by market competition among providers of education and training and intensified by developments in information technology, has challenged the power of traditional providers to determine what counts as professional knowledge. So the knowledge on which professionals base their actions has become less stable and secure, and the ways in which it is acquired have become more diverse. Finally, responsibility for ensuring the acquisition and maintenance of relevant professional expertise has been devolved to individual practitioners who are expected to be entrepreneurial and proactive in managing their own development (Rose, 1996; du Gay, 1996). Professionals now need to be able to assess their own capabilities and learning needs, choosing their own pathways to professional development rather than relying on standardised routes based on formal training.

The point I want to emphasise in this introduction is that there are no fixed definitions or understandings of what constitutes professional knowledge, or of how professionals learn in and through their practice. These understandings are controversial, contested and always contingent on the social, economic and political conditions in which they occur. In addition, whilst the stages of professional development have been described, notably in the Dreyfus brothers' model of skill acquisition (1986), the learning processes underlying this progression, and the way in which knowledge is used in the practice setting, has not been fully understood or articulated (Daley, 2001). What I want to explore in this chapter are some of the explanations of professional development which are currently available, examining in particular those assumptions about the place of knowledge and the role of the learner which are embedded in each of them.

Debates about the nature of professional development are doubly relevant to managers in education. First, managers are themselves professionals, responsible for their continuing development. Secondly, the role of managers means that they carry some responsibility for developing the 'human resources' of those they manage. Carrying out each of these responsibilities in a professional manner suggests the need for a critical understanding of the meanings and implications which underpin differing theories of learning and development, since it is our 'theories in use' (Argyris, 1982), whether or not these are explicitly acknowledged, which condition our actions. As Fenwick (2000, p. 245) has commented: 'However much we may resist, we educators are still and always attempting to configure ourselves in cognition's processes as active agents who ultimately manage processes we call learning from various positions: enhancing, directing, resisting, observing, or analysing'. Becoming more reflective and reflexive about these processes and their implications is itself a form of professional capability.

Knowing in Practice

The role of knowledge in skilled performance is a particular concern in most areas of professional practice. It is the way in which people use knowledge to solve the problems they encounter in practice settings which can be said to characterise professional activity. The traditional paradigm describes a simple linear process whereby a body of scientifically established knowledge – propositional knowledge – is applied to practice situations. The role of the practitioner is instrumental – applying existing theory appropriately but mechanistically to solve problems as they emerge in the field. The choices open to the practitioner are limited and essentially technical, dictated by the available scientific knowledge. The conceptual relationship between theory and practice lies in the application of the former to the latter. This is what Donald Schon (1983) has characterised, and criticised, as the 'technical-rationality model'. Within this model 'professional activity consists of instrumental problem solving made rigorous by the application of scientific theory and technique' (ibid, p. 24). Here we see a hierarchy in operation, one which ascribes high status to activity which generates theoretical knowledge, and low status to the application of that knowledge through practice: 'the concept of "application" leads to a view of professional knowledge as a hierarchy in which "general principles" occupy the highest level and "concrete problem solving" the lowest' (ibid.).

The existence of a body of generalised 'propositional knowledge', scientifically validated, transmitted through initial professional education and subsequently applied in practice, forms a central plank in any claim to the status and privilege attached to being a 'profession' (Eraut, 1994). Once this body of specialised knowledge is established, the authority of the professional as the person best placed to determine the real needs of clients, and to provide them with advice based on knowledge, is secure. The established professions of law, medicine or engineering set the pattern, having well defined bodies of knowledge to draw on, encoded in the curricula of higher education courses and the codes of practice of professional bodies. In recent years aspiring professions such as social work, nursing and teaching have acted to follow their example by stressing the role of theory in their work, by revising and often extending initial training, by restricting entry levels, and by developing research and scholarship relating to their work. The notion of technical rationality thus dovetails into and supports a definition of professional status to form a powerful ideology which still exerts a profound influence over our understandings of the nature and function of professional activity.

The process of development within this paradigm becomes one of acquiring propositional knowledge which has been produced outside the practice setting, storing this up against the time when it can be applied to best effect.

The metaphor which has been used in relation to this notion of learning is one of 'acquisition' (Sfard, 1998, p. 5): 'This approach . . . brings to mind the activity of accumulating material goods. The language of "knowledge acquisition" and "concept development" makes us think about the human mind as a container to be filled with certain materials and about the learner as becoming the owner of these materials'. Knowledge is understood as a stable commodity, something which can be moved about between the mind of a teacher and that of a learner, or between one practice setting and another, without changing its nature or meaning. Here we see how ideas about learning and development are closely tied in with ideas about pedagogy, identity and knowledge construction. The notion of learning as 'acquisition' suggests a positivist view of knowledge and a transmission model of learning, in which the learner's role is simply to annex the knowledge of others and the role of the teacher is to assemble it into manageable chunks which can be more easily digested. Whilst this image of knowledge as an entity which exists outside ourselves is deeply embedded in our habitual ways of thinking, it has not gone unchallenged.

Doubts about the status of scientifically produced knowledge as definitive and value free, particularly when dealing with situations where 'the facts' are open to dispute and interpretation, have produced scepticism about the authority of professionals. Doubts have emerged about the real purposes for which scientific and technical knowledge are being used: is it to promote the interests of researchers, teachers and professionals or those of clients? If science and reason are capable of producing explanations and solutions relevant to practice-based problems, why is there so much confusion and difference of opinion in establishing 'best practice'? Loss of faith in the foundations of professional expertise has been accompanied by movements which seek to empower the client, promoting 'lay epistemology' and 'client rights' as a counter to professional expertise (Williams, 1993). Central to this attempt to shift the balance of power is the move to privilege the knowledge held by the client over that held by the professional. Another movement has been towards valuing the experience and expertise of the practitioner, as against that of the academic producer of knowledge. This latter movement is characterised by the pre-eminent role of the 'reflective practitioner'.

Reflection on Practice

As positivist notions of knowledge and technical rational ideas of how this came to be translated into action have begun to lose their authority, different ideas about professional knowledge and expertise have emerged. Prominent among these is Schön's notion of 'reflection-in-action'. Here the process of reflection mirrors the individual learning cycle described by Kolb (1984) in which learning is presented as a dynamic and fluid process which incorporates both direct experience and theoretical knowledge. Learners reflect on their direct experience, producing generalised explanations and concepts which are then tested out in practice settings. The results of these experiments are then subject to further reflection and analysis as the cycle continues. No two revolutions of the learning cycle will be identical since reflection on experience will lead to new understandings, which will result in different approaches to subsequent practice situations. The process develops from the two-dimensional circle to a three-dimensional spiral as ideas are formed and reformed through experience (see Figure 2.1).

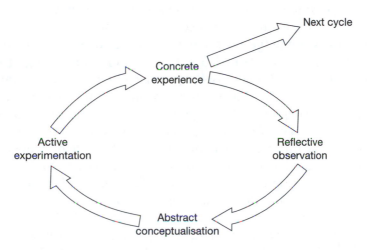

Figure 2.1 *The learning cycle*
Source: Adapted from Kolb (1984)

As a representation of the learning process, this has considerable significance for learners and those who organise the learning of others. Rather than being dependent on knowledge produced elsewhere it shows learners as actively constructing meanings for themselves, building on their previous learning, selecting some aspects of their experience and discarding others, using their own judgement and feelings as they interpret and evaluate experience. In other words, it is learners who have seized control of the learning process and become the producers of knowledge. The process of reflection is central to this shift and has been the focus of considerable attention within learning theory (Brookfield, 1987; Boud *et al.*, 1996; Boud and Walker, 1998). It is through reflection that learners are able to make informed decisions, taking into account not only the complexities of the context or the problem but also their own tacit knowledge, assumptions and values; the cumulative effect of their personal, social and cultural history which underpins their judgements.

The idea of reflection as central to learning is echoed by that of reflection as central to professional practice. Here the work of Donald Schon (1983; 1987) has been enormously influential. Schon's concern was to develop a theory of professional action which acknowledged the messiness and unpredictability of the practice setting. This led him to question the traditional paradigm of 'technical rationality' whereby scientifically established knowledge can be applied directly to deal with problems in the practice setting. In proposing the 'reflective practitioner' as better suited to the complexities and ambiguities of the practice setting, Schon placed practice and the practitioner in the centre of the frame. Here it is the contextualised rationality of the professional which counts: interrogating and interpreting the situation in hand, scanning a repertoire of existing experience and knowledge, and evaluating the efficacy of solutions in the immediate circumstances of the practice setting. Scientific knowledge becomes a resource to be drawn upon when required, rather than the starting point in the problem-solving process, and professional action is characterised by 'artistry' (Schon, 1987) rather than 'technical rationality'. The discourses of learning from experience and reflective practice each suggest a shift in power from the traditional producers of knowledge, such as higher education, to the contextualised experience of the individual. It is the individual who now takes on the role of generator of new knowledge – as 'experiential learner' or 'practitioner-researcher'.

The notion of the reflective practitioner has been widely adopted as the underpinning theory of professional formation, for instance in the professions of teaching (Clift *et al.*, 1990), nursing (Palmer *et al.*, 1994), physiotherapy (Clouder, 2000) and social work (Brodie *et al.*, 1995). It fits well with recent formulations of lifelong learning emphasising the importance of learning which occurs outside traditional institutional contexts – in workplaces, informal networks, from the Internet. It reinforces the idea that practitioners, and learners in general, need to be constantly adapting to changing circumstances and understandings of their roles, always taking responsibility for their own learning and development. It suggests learning as diverse and progressive, as different forms of knowledge, experiential, informal, formal, are sifted and integrated through processes of reflection. Finally it suggests that professional development is most effectively promoted through the facilitation of problem-solving where practitioners engage in processes of reflection and knowledge construction.

However, Schon's representation of the 'reflective practitioner' is not without its problems. Eraut (1995) has pointed out the limited evidence base provided by the professional contexts studied by Schon, and Usher *et al.* (1997) argue that in drawing general conclusions from his research Schon ignores the situatedness of practitioner experience. In other words, reflection-in-action may work as a description of these practitioners in these settings, but that doesn't mean it will work for others elsewhere. Others have suggested that the powerful and seductive image of the reflective practitioner is undermined by the current experience of many engaged in professional practice, where they discover diminishing opportunities for exercising their own judgement and autonomy. Changes taking place in the organisation and management of work, for instance through the introduction of quality standards and various forms of work-planning and outcome-auditing, together with continuing pressures to increase productivity, are tending to limit the scope for professional autonomy. If practitioners are increasingly subject to measurement against externally imposed standards of perform-ance, in what ways can they be said to be a profession and able to act on the basis of autonomous judgement? For some, therefore, professional autonomy is held to be diminishing and there is no need for, or time, or requirement to reflect on practice. In this situation competent performance may be suffi-cient, as the opportunities to reflect on and question experience are marginalised. Pragmatic forms of reflection come to displace ones that are more critical and professional practice becomes adaptive rather than chal-lenging. If the reflective practitioner model flatters the self-image of professionals but fails to match their experience, questions are raised about the role it plays at the forefront of contemporary professional discourses. There are two aspects of this role which I want to examine in more detail.

First, the emphasis placed by Schon on 'practice' as the source of knowl-edge sets up a polarisation against 'theory', constructed as remote from, or irrelevant to, the concerns of the practice setting. Yet in the absence of alter-native theoretical framings it is unclear how practitioners are expected to generate critical perspectives through which they can evaluate practice. Reflection in the absence of theory appears to offer a rather limited space for critical thinking:

> Reflective practice offers a space for critical thinking wider than competence, but the sense of critical thinking made available by reflective practice is still limited – reflective practice gives priority to practice: the critical frames that the professional uses to interrogate her professional experience are somehow generated by the practice itself (Barnett, 1997, p. 138).

Thus reflection-in-action has been seen by some as providing legitimation for the removal of theory from teacher education (Furlong, 1995), and the intro-duction of notions of vocational competence, for instance through the National Vocational Qualification system in England (Ecclestone, 1996). In the context of further education in the UK, ideal or 'designer teachers' have been described as those 'who demonstrate compliance to policy imperatives and perform at high levels of efficiency and effectiveness' (Sachs, 2001, p. 156). In this sense they become, not autonomous and reflective practitioners, but technicians who implement policy decisions taken elsewhere. The exclusion of theory from debates about practice can be seen as jeopardising the capacity of professionals to think critically, asking questions about the 'what' and 'why' of educational practices, rather than simply 'how?.'

The relationship between the notions of reflective practice and competence is worth noting since they often appear to co-exist within contemporary discourses of professional development. Whilst both can be seen to take a stance against the dominant position of academic knowledge, in other respects they could not be further apart. The notion of the reflective practitioner suggests an autonomous professional, making judgements based on an accumulation of practical and academic knowledge, synthesised through reflection and adapted to the specific context. The model of vocational competence current in the UK and in many other industrialised nations is a system of 'top-down' control aimed at standardisation, rather than providing spaces for the improvisatory practices and contextualised rationalities of the reflective practitioner. Within these frameworks reflection is often reduced to a limited and impoverished process in which the practitioner is offered only a narrow range of possibilities for thought and action. Here we see the contested and ambiguous role of the discourse of reflective practice, as it is taken up by, among others, those who wish to emphasise the importance of professional autonomy, and those who wish to promote a more standardised and instrumental construction of practice. As these issues play out, what constitutes professional development, what are taken to be the valued attributes of the developed professional, are themselves reshaped.

This discussion leads into my second point which relates to the ways in which discourses of professional development shape the contours of professional identities. Researchers looking at the context of education (for example, Ainley and Bailey, 1997; Avis, 1999), as well as those looking at wider contexts of employment (for example, Casey, 1996; du Gay, 1996; Farrell, 2000), have noted that the characteristics of the contemporary worker which are seen as appropriate to the flexible post-Fordist workplace are those of adaptability, self-reliance and enterprise. Whilst this appears to offer liberating and enabling possibilities for workers, Farrell (2000) has observed that the move towards autonomy in contemporary workplace discourses may not be as risky an enterprise as it first seems. What Casey (1996, p. 78) has described as 'the hidden curriculum of work that shapes and socialises adult workers' using a range of 'spoken and unspoken social and cultural messages, rules, codes and symbols . . .' ensures that workers understand the limits of their autonomy and the expectations of their managers. In the context of higher education Nicoll and Harrison (2001) point to the ways in which criteria for professional performance operate to normalise and shape what it means to be a 'good teacher' and what is meant by 'acting professionally'. Thus the significance of the discourse of the reflective practitioner might lie, not so much in the apparent offer of professional autonomy in decision-making as in the responsibility for self-management at a time of rapid and unpredictable change: 'Individuals are now held responsible for decisions with regard to their life courses that are largely beyond their influence' (Janson and van der Veen, 1997, p. 265). It is precisely at the time when traditional institutional arrangements and working practices, as well as notions of knowedge and professionalism, are breaking down that certain types of identity, such as the autonomous, self-reliant worker, become both attractive and necessary.

The discourse of the reflective learner and reflective practitioner produces a generalised account of what it means to be a learner and a practitioner, characterised by 'a disembodied and abstract individualism' (Edwards and Usher, 2000, p. 129) which can be used to support this self-regulating identity. Learning is understood in terms of cognitive processing, something which occurs in the mind of the learner; an individual construction which is achieved at a distance from those people who share in its production and those environmental features which make it possible. Understood in this way, responsibility for learning is then more easily devolved to the individual rather than society as a whole. Critiques of these understandings point to the ways in which discourses of the reflective learner and practitioner make claims to universal applicability, whilst they are grounded in particular disciplinary traditions and represent distinct cultural practices. In claiming a 'taken-for-granted' status they seek to erase the role of culture, power and language in making appear natural understandings about learning and the identity of learners which are not natural or neutral, but 'eminently political and contestable' (Usher *et al.*, 1997, p. 102).

The Social Dimension

Dominant notions of learning as an individualised process occurring in the mind of the learner, and of knowledge as an entity which exists outside ourselves, are deeply embedded in our habitual ways of thinking. However, they have been challenged by the suggestion that learning is not an individual but a social process, and that knowledge is not a commodity but is socially constructed, context dependent and not readily transferred between different settings. Anthropological studies carried out by Jean Lave (1996) sought to study the learning which was occurring in specific contexts, viewing cognition as embedded in the whole social and cultural environment in which it occurs. This presents a very different perspective, moving from one which sees learning as acquisition, occuring 'in the head' of the individual, to something which is a joint production between culture, co-participants and individual mind. Learners are seen as engaged in the social construction of knowledge through participation in a continuing dialectic between themselves, other people and the culture in which they operate.

In formulating a theoretical account of how learning is generated through activity, or 'learning by doing', Vygotsky's (1978) concept of a 'zone of proximal development' has been influential, particularly as a way of describing learning in the workplace where models based on apprenticeship are common. Vygotsky (ibid., p. 85) defined the 'zone of proximal development' as: 'The difference between the actual development level as determined by independent problem solving and the level of potential development as determined through problem solving under adult guidance or in collaboration with more able peers'.

This understanding of the learning process has spawned various pedagogic strategies to describe how development to more advanced levels of skill and understanding can be facilitated. For example, Brown *et al.* (1989, p. 39) describe a process of 'cognitive apprenticeship' in which '. . . the mentors (1) "model" by making their tacit knowledge explicit and revealing their problem-solving activities; (2) "coach" by supporting students' attempts to perform new tasks; and then (3) "fade" after having empowered the students to work independently'. Mentors or teachers provide a 'scaffold' for new learners, making available appropriate forms of guidance to enable learners to master the new skills and knowledge for themselves. The role of the teacher becomes one of facilitator of learning: tracking progress, building collaborative learning environments, encouraging reflection and continually assessing the intellectual growth of the individual and the community of learners. Here the content of the learning required for skilled performance is recognised as including an understanding of the 'rules of the game', whether this relates to the reading, writing and communication strategies appropriate to postgraduate study, or the codes of behaviour appropriate to a new work environment. It acknowledges that learning involves a combination of 'everyday' concepts, often picked up through informal interactions, and 'scientific' concepts usually acquired through textbooks or formal teaching.

The attraction of this model of learning is that it moves us away from individualist assumptions about the learner and transmission models of the learning process. Further development of this concept by Lave and Wenger (1991) and Lave (1996) has extended the zone of proximal development to focus attention on the social and cultural aspects of learning. Their account of participation in a range of communities of practice highlights the ways in which engagement in social, cultural, technological and linguistic practices provides individuals and groups with opportunities to learn. In doing so they draw attention to the collective nature of learning and also to its basis in active participation. As Rogoff (1990, p. 14) has argued, this represents a fundamental shift in which '. . . the basic unit of analysis is no longer the [properties of the] individual, but the [processes of] socio-cultural activity, involving participation in socially constituted practices'.

For Lave and Wenger (1991) the traditional functions of teaching, as in organising the content and outcomes of learning, become marginal or even counterproductive, since learning is dynamic and unpredictable, not easily contained by formal processes of curriculum and assessment. Our attention is drawn away from attempts to convey bodies of knowledge into the minds of individual learners towards the affordances for learning offered by the contexts in which they are operating; from the acquisition of commodified knowledge to participation in learning activities. Noting the shift away from descriptions of learning as the acquisition of 'knowledge', to ones which denote action and 'knowing', Sfard (1998, p. 6) writes: 'In the image of learning that emerges from this linguistic turn, the permanence of *having* gives way to the constant flux of *doing*.'

Here we see how ideas about learning and development are closely tied in with ideas about pedagogy, identity and knowledge construction. The notion of learning as 'acquisition' suggests a transmission model of learning in which the learner's role is simply to annex the knowledge of others and the role of the teacher is to assemble it into manageable chunks. Whilst in some ways representing a radical break from a transmission model of learning, reflection is still understood as a cognitive process, something which occurs in the mind of the learner, and knowledge remains an individual possession. In contrast, a notion of learning as 'participation' suggests the mind of the learner cannot be understood as a free-floating autonomous agent but as part of a process of constructing, and being constructed by, the social and cultural environment in which it operates. Knowledge is constructed within specific contexts and interactions, a socio-cultural phenomenon rather than a fixed commodity, making it less easily packaged for pedagogical or managerial purposes. Finally, learners become co-producers rather than owners of knowledge.

It is a view of learning which suggests quite different roles for teachers, trainers, mentors or human resource managers. A key implication of viewing learning as a social and situated phenomenon is a need to move from a focus on teaching to a focus on supporting learning. No longer the fountains of knowledge, the role of teachers becomes one of organising or promoting forms of participation which offer access to communities of practice. Rather than a fixed curriculum what is required is a more flexible approach which can accommodate fluctuations in the context of practice. Curriculum planning becomes a dynamic process which involves forming and reforming goals as they emerge and are modified in the learning context. There is no single or final aim but a series of 'aims-in-view'. The teacher becomes a facilitator of learning – tracking progress, building collaborative learning environments, encouraging reflection and continually assessing the intellectual growth of the individual and the community of learners.

Conclusion

In this chapter we have examined a number of theoretical perspectives on learning and development, drawing out some of the distinctions between them and the implications of adopting them for how we see learners and how we organise learning. This might suggest the possibility of clear delineation between them; of defining and positioning each in relation to the others so that similarities and differences can be seen. In practice the theories, and the pedagogies on which they are based, are characterised more by hybridity and fluidity than by purity or consistency. The boundaries between them are permeable, shifting and contentious, and the account given here should be treated as part of that discussion rather than a definitive version. Similarly, the arrangement of the theoretical descriptions suggests a linear or developmental trajectory, with each new theory positioned as a corrective to previous misconceptions. Such a progressive narrative would be misleading. It would, for example, imply some degree of consensus about the direction in which we might locate 'progress'. Instead theories of learning and development might best be seen as a series of understandings which bring into focus certain aspects and characteristics of the learning process whilst excluding others from the picture. Each approach might present itself as progressive, but with different values and purposes in view.

How we understand processes of learning and knowledge production has a profound effect on how we conceptualise, plan and support processes of professional development. The practices we use in promoting professional development within our own organisations are not neutral or innocent of theory but imbued with prior understandings, assumptions and value judgements. In this context the capability of the reflective and reflexive practitioner might be said to consist of knowledgeably locating his or her own position in relation to a range of theoretical and practical possibilities, aware of the potentialities, limitations and implications of whatever strategies for professional development might be selected.

References

Ainley, P. and Bailey, B. (1997) *The Business of Learning*. London: Cassell.

Argyris, C. (1982) *Reasoning, Learning and Action*. San Francisco, CA: Jossey-Bass.

Avis, J. (1998) The myth of post-Fordist society. In J. Avis *et al.* (eds.) *Knowledge and Nationhood: Education, Politics and Work*. London: Cassell.

Avis, J. (1999) Shifting identity: new conditions and the transformation of practice – teaching within post-compulsory education. *Journal of Vocational Education and Training* 51(2).

Barnett, R. (1997) *Higher Education: A Critical Business*. Buckingham: Open University Press.

Boud, D., Cohen, R. and Walker, D. (1996) Understanding learning from experience. In, Boud *et al.* (eds.) *Using Experience for Learning*. Buckingham: Open University Press.

Boud, D. and Walker, D. (1998) Promoting reflection in professional courses: the challenge of context. *Studies in Higher Education* 23(2): 191–206.

Brodie, I., Reeve, F. and Whittaker, R. (1995) Delivering the DEAL: implementation of a work-based learning programme at degree level. *The Vocational Aspect of Education* 47(4).

Brookfield, S. (1987) *Developing Critical Thinkers: Challenging Adults to Explore Alternative Ways of Thinking and Acting.* Milton Keynes: Open University Press.

Brown, J., Collins, A. and Duguid, P. (1989) Situated cognition and the culture of learning. *Educational Researcher* 18: 32–42.

Casey, C. (1996) *Work, Self and Society after Industrialisation.* London: Routledge.

Clift, R., Houston, R. and Pugach, M. (eds.) (1990) *Encouraging Reflective Practice in Education: An Analysis of Issues and Programmes.* New York: Teachers College Press.

Clouder, L. (2000) Reflective practice in physiotherapy education: a critical conversation. *Studies in Higher Education* 25: 211–23.

Daley, B.J. (2001) Learning and professional practice: a study of four professions. *Adult Education Quarterly* 52(1): pp. 39–54.

Department for Education and Employment (1998) *The Learning Age: A Renaissance for a New Britain.* London: HMSO.

Dreyfus, H.L. and Dreyfus, S.E. (1986) *Mind over Machine.* Oxford: Blackwell

Du Gay, P. (1996) *Consumption and Identity at Work.* London: Sage.

Ecclestone, K. (1996) The reflective practitioner: mantra or model for emancipation? *Studies in the Education of Adults* 28(2).

Edwards, R. and Usher, R. (2000) *Globalisation and Pedagogy: Space, Place and Identity.* London: Routledge.

Eraut, M. (1994) *Developing Professional Knowledge and Competence.* London: Falmer Press.

Eraut, M. (1995) Schon shock: a case for reframing reflection-in-action? *Teachers and Teaching: Theory and Practice* 1: 9–22.

Eraut, M., Alderton, J., Cole, G. and Senker, P. (2002) Learning from other people at work. In R. Harrison *et al.* (eds.) *Supporting Lifelong Learning. Vol. 1. Perspectives on Learning.* London: Routledge-Falmer.

Farrell, L. (2000) Ways of doing, ways of being: language, education and 'working' identities. *Language and Education* 14(1): 18–36.

Fenwick, T. (2000) Expanding conceptions of experiential learning: a review of the five contemporary perspectives on cognition. *Adult Education Quarterly* 50: 243–72.

Furlong, J. (1995) *Mentoring Student Teachers.* London: Routledge.

Guile, D. and Young, M. (2002) Beyond the institution of apprenticeship: towards a social theory of learning as the production of knowledge. In R. Harrison *et al.* (eds.) *Supporting Lifelong Learning. Vol. 1. Perspectives on Learning.* London: Routledge-Falmer.

Janson, T. and van der Veen, R. (1997) Individualisation, the new political spectrum and the functions of adult education. *International Journal of Lifelong Education* 16: 264–76.

Kolb, D. (1984) *Experiential Learning.* Englewood Cliffs, NJ: Prentice-Hall.

Lave, J. (1996) Teaching, as learning, in practice. *Mind, Culture and Activity* 3(3): 149–65.

Lave, J. and Wenger, E. (1991) *Situated Learning: Legitimate Peripheral Participation.* New York: Cambridge University Press.

Nicoll, K. and Harrison, R. (2001) Following the lodestone or lost at sea? Continuing professional development for reflective practice. In *Proceedings of the 31st Annual Conference of SCUTREA*, pp. 302–06.

Palmer, A., Burns, S. and Bulman, C. (eds.) (1994) *Reflective Practice in Nursing: The Growth of Professional Practitioner.* London: Blackwell Scientific.

Rogoff, B. (1990) *Apprenticeship in Thinking: Cognitive Development in Social Contexts.* New York: Oxford University Press.

Rose, N. (1996) *Inventing Ourselves: Psychology, Power, Personhood.* Cambridge: Cambridge University Press.

Sachs, J. (2001) Teacher professional identity: competing discourses, competing outcomes. *Journal of Educational Policy* 16(2): 149–61.

Schon, D. (1983) *The Reflective Practitioner*. London: Temple Smith.

Schon, D. (1987) *Educating the Reflective Practitioner*. San Francisco, CA: Jossey-Bass.

Sfard, A. (1998) On two metaphors of learning and the dangers of choosing just one. *Educational Researcher* 27(2): 4–13.

Usher, R., Bryant, I. and Johnson, R. (1997) *Adult Education and the Postmodern Challenge: Learning beyond the Limits*. London: Routledge.

Vygotsky, L. (1978) *Mind in Society: The Development of Higher Psychological Processes*. Cambridge, MA: Harvard University Press.

Williams, J. (1993) What is a profession? Experience versus expertise. In J. Walmsley *et al.* (eds.) *Health and Welfare Practices: Reflecting on Roles and Relationships*. London: Sage.

3

Leading Academics: Learning about their Professional Needs

Stephen J. Marshall, Moya J. Adams, Alison Cameron and Gavin Sullivan

Introduction

It is well recognized that universities internationally have changed profoundly over the last decade. These changes, stimulated by a variety of social, political, economic and technological forces, have manifested themselves in:

1 larger and more diverse student populations;
2 new teaching and research methods (including use of information technology to mediate/ facilitate instruction);
3 larger and more competitive arenas of operation (due to pressures to internationalize programmes and operations);
4 a broader range of undergraduate, postgraduate and continuing education programmes, including those specifically designed to meet a variety of social justice objectives; and
5 increased selectivity and concentration of research activity.

However, this period of change is far from over. Rapidly developing information and communications technologies, continuing government and community demands for greater accountability and economy of operations, and increasing expectations from academic and administrative staff for more self-determination and greater workplace flexibility will ensure that universities worldwide continue to face the issue of how to position themselves strategically for the future. The fundamental issues of 'Who are we as an organization?', 'What do we value?',

Source: International Journal for Academic Development, Vol. 5, no. 1, 2000, pp. 42–53. Edited version.

'What do/should we do?', 'How do/should we do it?', and 'Why are we important?' will become increasingly important as universities face the challenges of an increasingly competitive environment.

While vice-chancellors and university presidents must grapple with these strategic questions for organizations as a whole, deans, directors and heads must contemplate the same issues for their faculties, centres and departments, and mainstream academic and administrative staff must resolve them in relation to their own programmes, activities and services. Failure to address these issues at all levels can have catastrophic consequences, including the withdrawal of programmes and the closure or forced amalgamation of entire departments and/or institutions. Consequently, the task of defining the values, purposes and strategies of the universities of the twenty-first century (that is, exercising leadership in such institutions) cannot be left to those in formal positions of leadership or management responsibility alone, but must be shared by all staff.

The challenge for those in formal, senior, positions in universities will be to become 'leaders of leaders': to create environments and workplaces in which academic and administrative staff feel – and in fact *are* – capable of influencing the directions in which these institutions will go. Strategic leadership and management behaviour – that is, behaviour that is goal-driven, proactive, and where opportunities are recognized and seized and threats identified and overcome (Bryson, 1988) – must therefore be a defining feature of all university staff.

However, ongoing, visionary strategic planning has not traditionally been a widespread feature of higher education institutions or their staff. Planning has generally been restricted to what has been necessary to satisfy the conditions, or to realize the goals associated with particular short-term operations, projects or research grants. Rarely have planning processes in universities focused in any sustained, coordinated or systematic way on the review and revision of organizational goals, values and strategies in order to ensure that they are appropriate for the emerging contexts within which these organizations must operate.

Lack of progress in this area, however, does not necessarily reflect a lack of understanding, willingness, or support on the part of university executives for such programmes. As has been recognized in the adult learning literature for some time (for example, Brookfield, 1986; Knowles, 1973), participation rates for professional development/in-service activities are closely related to prospective participants' perceptions of the relevance of the activities to their needs. Lack of progress in establishing ongoing, successful, leadership and management development programmes for university staff may have more to do with a perception by academics and administrative staff that such programmes are irrelevant to their needs, than with a lack of willingness by university executives to establish such programmes.

The purpose of this study, then, was to conduct a preliminary examination of this proposition. Specifically, the research was designed to determine the extent to which staff in one particular higher education institution, in one particular country, believe that:

1 the development of knowledge and skill in leadership and management is important to their work; and that
2 they need to develop knowledge and skills in leadership and management.

Conceptual Framework

One of the principal problems associated with such a study is that of definition. What does 'leadership and management' mean in the context of a higher education institution? Preliminary discussions with a number of academic and administrative staff from within and beyond the institution that was to be the focus of the study revealed that many different definitions exist. On careful analysis, however, it is clear that these definitions recognize that leadership and management is practised at a number of *different levels* within higher education institutions. At the strategic apex are vice-chancellors and deputy or pro-vice-chancellors; at middle management level are deans and heads of schools, departments or centres; and at the operating core are the academic and administrative staff of the various departments. Leadership and management have both strategic and operational dimensions. The *strategic* dimensions are concerned with 'setting the organization's mission, strategy and policy to take full account of the organization's internal and external environment' (UCoSDA, 1994, p. 15). The *operational* dimensions are concerned with the management of change, the management of finance and physical resources, the management of information, the management of quality, and the management of human resources.

These characteristics of leadership and management are not unique to higher education institutions but what *do* characterize leadership and management in higher education institutions are the context within which they are exercized, and their focus on the academic issues of teaching, research and community service. With this in mind, Marshall (1997) suggested a framework for *leadership and management development* in higher education institutions that comprises seven key dimensions. Marshall contends that a truly effective leader and manager in a higher education institution develops knowledge and skills in each of these seven areas.

1 *Professional identity*. Leaders and managers in higher education institutions must have a good understanding of the context within which they work. They must understand the nature of the higher education sector generally, the higher education institution in which they work in particular, as well as the nature of their role as a leader and manager within this institution.

2 *Strategic leadership and management*. Leaders and managers must understand the important roles that they play in defining their organizational unit's *raison d' être*, its strategies and policies, and the unit's relationship to the larger environment – particularly the university of which it is a part. They must understand and be highly skilled in strategic planning, and in the definition and management of strategic issues.

3 *Operational leadership and management* (i.e. managing *change* and *quality*). Leaders and managers in higher education institutions need to be effective change agents. They must be able to plan, implement, monitor and evaluate change as well as assure the quality of organizational inputs, outputs and processes. To do so they must be cognizant of, and effective in, dealing with the structural, human, political and cultural aspects of managing change and quality.

4 *Financial and physical resources management*. Effective operational management requires leaders and managers to deal efficiently with finances and physical resources within the policy frameworks of the university of which their organizational unit is a part. Leaders and managers must be able to develop and manage budgets and accounting systems that reflect the core business of their organization. Further, they must be able to plan, develop, maintain and dispose of physical assets in sympathy with their unit's strategic priorities and initiatives.

5 *Human resources management*. People are the principal resource of any university. Leaders and managers in higher education institutions must have good knowledge of planning, recruiting, selecting, inducting, motivating, supervising, evaluating and rewarding staff. They must be familiar with equal opportunity and occupational health and safety legislation, and capable of designing and implementing management practices that meet the requirements of such legislation.

6 *Information management*. Planning and decision-making is a key role of any leader and manager. Appropriate, timely and accurate information is essential to effective planning and decision-making. Thus it is important for university leaders and managers to understand how to design, use, maintain and evaluate management information systems, how to access and use their university's systems; and how to design and implement such systems within their own organizational units.

7 *Academic leadership and management*. Developing and maintaining quality teaching, research and community outreach is central to the work of all leaders and managers in higher education institutions. Thus it is essential

that leaders and managers in higher education systems develop knowledge and skills in designing, developing, implementing and evaluating high quality teaching, research and community outreach as well as in the development of excellent teachers, researchers and community outreach workers.

Method

Using this conceptual framework as a basis for organization and analysis, written surveys and focus group discussions were used to determine staff perceptions of the importance of having knowledge and skills in each of these areas of leadership and management practice, and more particularly academics' perceptions regarding their need to develop such knowledge and skills.

Written questionnaires requiring respondents to indicate their perceptions of the *importance* of knowledge and skills in each of these areas, and their *need for development* in each, were distributed to a sample of 50 per cent (n = 404) of the academic staff of a relatively small (20,000 equivalent full time student enrolments), metropolitan, research-oriented and publicly funded Australian university. Responses were received from 42 per cent of the sample and respondents were representative of the total staff group of the university with respect to gender and academic rank. Analyses of these data were restricted to simple descriptive statistics (means, medians, modes and frequency distributions). Generalizability of the results was checked via telephone surveys of a group of randomly chosen academic staff from across the university who indicated that they had not completed the written questionnaire. The results indicated that non-respondents appeared to hold similar views to those of respondents.

Focus groups were conducted with:

■ members of the University Executive, both academic and administrative;
■ heads of academic units;
■ a group of academic staff selected to be representative in terms of gender, discipline and rank; and
■ a representative group of general staff.

A variety of professional development issues was explored with these groups using a semi-structured interview schedule to guide discussion. Comments made by participants were recorded by hand and later collated and checked with representatives from each group. The purpose of the groups was twofold: 1) to enable the researchers to explore some of the findings of the questionnaire survey in greater depth; and 2) to enable the researchers to compare the findings of the survey with the views expressed by particular stakeholder groups.

▌ Findings

Since Marshall's seven dimensions for leadership and management development in higher education institutions were used as an organizing framework for data collection, they will also be used here to report the findings.

Professional identity

One of the principal concerns of this research was to explore the question '*Do academics perceive themselves to be leaders and managers and, if so, how do they understand these roles?*'. More than 80 per cent of respondents to the written survey acknowledged that their academic work roles required them to *exercise leadership* (88 per cent) and plan, coordinate, monitor or control (i.e. *manage*) programmes, activities or resources (91 per cent). However, while respondents acknowledged these aspects of their roles, they markedly discriminated among the areas of leadership and management they perceived to be important. For example, across the range of items requiring respondents to indicate how important each area of leadership and management was to their role, response rates ranged from around 40 per cent for items concerning budgeting, finance, and human resource management to close to 90 per cent for items concerning the management of change and academic leadership.

These findings appear to be consistent with comments made by members of both the academic and general staff focus groups. For example, in relation to questions concerning financial management, an academic commented 'I am an academic not a manager. We've got staff in our school who do that for us', while a member of the general staff focus group observed 'there are certain times of the year when I seem to spend all my time helping [academic staff] to develop budgets for grants and projects – nothing else gets done.' In contrast, there seemed to be general agreement among members of both focus groups that the academic staff of the university assume responsibility for 'planning, managing and assuring the quality of their teaching and research'.

These perceptions of highly differentiated roles for leadership and management within the higher education sector reflect the traditional structural model for universities, where academic staff predominantly focus on the core business of teaching, research and community outreach, while large, dedicated, and expert support staffs attend to administrative and technical support matters associated with the effective running of the institution. While such perceptions might have been appropriate for universities of the early and middle twentieth century, their validity must be questioned in the current context where administrative support positions in most academic units are declining, and financial and human resource management responsibilities are being devolved further and further down the organizational hierarchy. Inevitably, academics at the school/department/discipline level will be required to assume much greater responsibility for these functions, and if quality processes and outcomes are to be maintained, academics will require appropriate knowledge and skills in these areas.

It is interesting, therefore, to note that survey responses to questions seeking respondents' perceptions of their need to develop knowledge and skills in these areas ranged between 26 per cent for items to do with human resource management and 36 per cent for items concerning financial management. The question must be asked as to whether academics are sufficiently aware of the implications for their academic work of these changing structural arrangements within universities. Perhaps a key area of focus for professional development in the future should be the evolving nature of academic work, with a special focus on the implications of efforts to downsize, restructure and devolve many traditional management and administrative functions to the local faculty, school, centre, discipline or department level.

Academic leadership

Eighty-eight per cent of survey respondents considered knowledge and skills in academic leadership to be important to their role. However, when this issue was teased out with the members of different focus groups to determine what they meant by academic leadership, two things became clear. First, mainstream academics' perceptions of their academic leadership roles were clearly focused on issues to do with the planning, development, implementation and evaluation of teaching, research, and community service. (By implementation here is meant delivery or production of academic products or services – teaching programmes, publishable articles, conference papers, and the like.) Issues of quality management, human resource management, and financial and physical resources management, while understood to be directly linked to effective and efficient academic work, were not generally perceived to be central to an academic leader's role.

Second, both academic and administrative members of the University Executive appeared to define academic leadership in broader terms than did mainstream academics, with both groups including quality management, human resource management, and financial and physical resources management in their definitions. As one member of the Executive remarked, 'The devolution of responsibility for budgets, personnel, and assets to the lower levels of the University means that Heads and Deans must now consider these matters more deliberately when deciding which courses to run and which research projects to undertake. It's now to them to decide how their staff and budgets will be utilized to support their academic goals'.

In a changing context for academic leadership, it is of concern to note that only 58 per cent of respondents to this survey believed that they needed to further develop their knowledge of, and skills in, academic leadership. While higher education institutions are rapidly evolving into very different organizational entities, requiring academic staff to assume responsibility for a greater range of management functions, members of the mainstream academy remain committed to a view of academic leadership that narrowly focuses on the design, development, implementation and evaluation of their teaching, research and community service functions. Left unexplored, this difference in perception of the role of academic leaders in modern universities has the potential to create major difficulties, and raises the question of how academic leadership should be conceptualized so that it reflects the changing nature of academic institutions and academic work. A key area of focus for professional development in higher education institutions in the future should be the nature of 'academic leadership': what is it? and how should it be practised?

Strategic leadership and management

Consistent with their belief that knowledge and skills in academic leadership and management were important to their work as academics, 88 per cent of respondents agreed that knowledge and skills in the strategic role of planning for innovation and/or change was important in their work. However, closer analysis of the data reveals that respondents' views about the importance of such knowledge and skills for different areas of their work varied widely. While over 74 per cent indicated that they felt academic leadership skills were important for all those items concerning the planning of innovation and change in teaching and research, less than 39 per cent indicated its importance for items concerning the financial, personnel and quality management aspects of their role. This same differentiation was found regarding perceived need for development in planning for innovation and change. In the case of items concerning teaching and research, over 68 per cent of respondents believed they had a need for development, but less than 28 per cent expressed a need for further development in relation to the planning of the financial, personnel and quality management aspects of their role.

These findings appear to further support the notion that academics maintain a relatively narrow view of their leadership and management roles and that an appropriate focus for professional development activities in the future might be the changing nature of academic leadership in a context of rapidly changing organizational structures and environments.

Operational leadership and management

Respondents strongly endorsed the importance to their work of understanding the operational dimensions of leadership and management. Ninety-one per cent suggested that knowledge and skills in the *management of change* were important, while 72 per cent agreed that knowledge and skills in the processes and procedures of *quality management* were important.

'Being an effective coordinator' was considered of prime importance to 91 per cent of respondents. Being able to coordinate the full range of complex and inter-related tasks and activities associated with change was considered to make the difference between 'success as an academic leader and failure', to cite the focus group comment from one of the academic unit heads. For this group of heads, and for the majority of survey respondents, being an effective coordinator of change meant having knowledge and skills in effectively planning (88 per cent), implementing (87 per cent) and evaluating (82 per cent) change.

However, despite the fact that the majority of survey respondents felt that knowledge and skills in these areas were important to their work, barely half (56 per cent, 54 per cent, and 48 per cent respectively) believed that they were in need of further development. This finding is of particular significance since there was considerable agreement among members of the academic and general staff focus groups that 'senior management' and 'heads of academic units' (each of which represent different groups of academic leaders) desperately needed development in these areas. It prompts the question of how the views of mainstream academics and general staff of their academic leaders' needs for development as 'leaders and managers of change' might be effectively utilized to recruit academics into leadership and management development programmes.

More than 72 per cent of respondents believed that knowledge and skills in the processes and procedures of quality management were important to academics in their work. Specifically, 75 per cent believed that knowledge of the general principles of quality assurance was important, while 73 per cent also believed that it was important for academics to have the knowledge and skills required to implement these principles into practice in the workplace. Once again, however, despite the perceived importance of knowledge and skills in quality management, less than 45 per cent of respondents believed that they required further development in this area. Given the strategic importance of developing and maintaining the quality of our academic programmes and services, a further challenge to staff developers in higher education institutions is to raise staff awareness of the need to develop knowledge and skills in this area.

Information management

Access to appropriate, high quality information is central to effective planning and decision-making, so it is of little surprise that the 'management of information' was recognized by the majority of respondents (81 per cent) as being an important area of knowledge and skill for an academic leader/manager. However, well planned and managed information systems and strategies are difficult to design, and even more difficult to implement (Adriaans, 1993). Consequently, it is of concern to find that less than half of those who responded to this survey (46 per cent) believed that they have developmental needs in this area. Does this mean that they already have the relevant skills, or rather, that they underestimate the difficulties associated with designing and managing such systems? If the latter, how should staff development units respond to this challenge?

Financial and physical resources management

One of the clearest findings of the focus group discussion with members of the University Executive was that, with continued devolution of responsibility for financial management to lower levels, academic staff generally will need to assume much greater responsibility for budgeting and accounting processes in the future than they have in the past. This position was reflected in the comments of one member of the Executive who remarked that 'knowing how to prepare and manage a budget is going to become a required skill of all staff'.

However, despite almost unanimous support for this position among the University's senior management, barely half (53 per cent) of all respondents from the ranks of mainstream academics perceived knowledge and skills in financial management to be important to the effective performance of their job. Moreover, less than one third of respondents believed that they needed to further develop their knowledge and skills in this area (33 per cent indicated that they needed further development in budgeting and 31 per cent in accounting). A key question for academic professional developers, therefore, concerns what staff development units can do to assist academic leaders to better appreciate the importance of their expanding financial management roles.

A similar issue seems to arise in relation to the management of physical resources. While 74 per cent of respondent's perceived knowledge and skills in this area was important to university leaders and managers, only 33 per cent believed that they personally needed to develop their knowledge and skills further. This is not a surprising result, given that management of physical resources has not tended to be of central concern to most academics. However, given the strategic significance of physical resources (they facilitate the realization of organizational goals), it is important that this aspect of leadership and management development, particularly its relationship to strategic planning and the management of change, not be overlooked.

Human resource management

While between 50 and 70 per cent of survey respondents indicated they perceived knowledge and skills in various aspects of human resource management to be important, considerably less than half of those who responded expressed a perception that they themselves needed further development in these areas.

A university's human resources are probably its most valuable asset, both in terms of their contribution and their cost. And there is a growing trend in higher education institutions that responsibility for human resource management be devolved to the lower levels of the organization: for example, supervision and performance management of staff, job design, staff recruitment and selection, staff development. It is of concern that such a small proportion of academic staff believe that they have need for development in these areas. Lack of knowledge and skills in leading and managing people can not only lead to disharmony and conflict in the workplace, but may also result in unfair and unsafe practices that leave universities exposed to expensive legal challenges in the courts. An important priority for staff development units, therefore, is to assist academics to understand the implications of poor practice and the importance, for individuals and institutions, of keeping abreast of developing policies and practices in this area.

Discussion

The findings of this research show that academics place relatively little value on some aspects of their roles as leaders and managers. They also demonstrate that academics discriminate among different types of leadership and management roles in terms of their perceived importance for work effectiveness. Those aspects that specifically focus on defining, planning, coordinating, implementing and evaluating teaching, research and community service were afforded much greater importance than other dimensions that relate to information, financial, physical, and human resources management. Further, the results of this research highlight a gap between respondents' perceptions of the importance of key dimensions of leadership and management and their own need for development in these areas.

Leadership and management development: a possible way ahead

The seven dimensions of leadership and management analysed and discussed in this chapter have generally been acknowledged as fundamental to 'best practice' in the management literature (e.g. Fombrun, 1992; Stace and Dunphy, 1996), in government papers and reports (Dawkins, 1988; Industry Task Force on Leadership and Management Skills, 1995), and in reports on higher education management (Committee of Inquiry into Higher Education Management, 1995; Commonwealth Tertiary Education Commission, 1986). The research described in this chapter has reinforced the importance of these dimensions for the day-to-day work of university management and staff.

Three major challenges exist for university staff development units to focus attention on the acquisition of appropriate leadership skills. These are:

1 to help academics develop more broadly based understandings of the nature of academic work – understandings that acknowledge the growing emphasis on leadership and management roles;

2 to assist universities to develop policy frameworks and infrastructures that reflect this broader conceptualization of academic leadership and work; and

3 to design, develop, and implement professional development strategies that support all academic staff in acquiring knowledge and skills in each of the seven key dimensions.

It is the view of the authors that any efforts to address these challenges are doomed to fail without a committed, coherent programme of interventions at the institutional, departmental and individual levels. Any institutional change is difficult, but changing long-standing, deeply held views about the nature of academic work and leadership is probably one of the most demanding things that an institution or staff developer will ever undertake. The values and beliefs embodied in traditional views of academic work and leadership have, over the years, been enshrined in a variety of powerful symbols: institutional structures and strategies, institutional policies and procedures, and institutional work roles (Bolman and Deal, 1991), and their appropriateness is taken for granted. If these views are to be effectively challenged or changed, we believe that the impetus will need to come from within the institution itself. If staff believe that the need to question current conceptions of academic work and leadership arises from internal institutional initiatives, not as a result of external imposition, they may feel greater ownership of the process. Further, if the process of intervention used is consistent with the daily work practices of staff, then they may also feel greater involvement and be more willing to engage in the debate. How does an institution stimulate such a debate among its staff? Louis and Miles (1990) have suggested that in order to initiate change a combination of 'pressure' and 'support' is required. Pressure is needed to overcome the inertia associated with individuals' and institutions' work practices. Change is effortful, particularly that which challenges basic values and beliefs, and requires individuals and organizations to commit energy, time and resources to areas other than their immediate core business. Pressure is required to ensure this commitment.

However, pressure alone has been proven to be unsatisfactory in effecting change (Louis and Miles, 1990). Change processes are rarely effective unless appropriate support mechanisms are put in place to ensure that those involved in the change have the capacity to engage safely and effectively. There is no point in pressuring individuals and institutions to effect change if they do not have the capacity (i.e. knowledge, skills, resources) to act. To this end, those attempting to bring about change must ensure that appropriate support is provided to individuals, groups and institutions when it is required. And for this reason, we believe that a successful programme of activities to support academic leadership development should include interventions at a variety of levels.

Conclusions

The findings of this research clearly demonstrate that perceptions of academic leadership and management vary enormously between different stakeholder groups. Mainstream academics from the sample surveyed tended to limit their conceptualizations to those aspects of leadership and management associated with the planning, implementation and evaluation of teaching, research and community service. On the other hand, university administrators and other staff from the same institution appear to define academic leadership more broadly and include the management of change, quality, information, finances, and physical and human resources. Academics responding to this survey generally did not place as much importance on these aspects of management, nor did they consider themselves in need of further development in these areas.

This creates a major challenge for university staff development units; one that requires careful intervention at all levels to:

1 assist academics to develop more broadly based understandings of the nature of academic work and leadership;
2 assist universities to develop policy frameworks and infrastructures that reflect this broader conceptualization of academic leadership and work; and
3 design, develop, and implement professional development strategies that support all academic staff to acquire knowledge and skills in each of the seven key dimensions of leadership and management relevant to higher education institutions, namely, professional identity, academic leadership and management, strategic leadership and management, operational leadership and management, information management, financial and physical resources management, and human resources management.

References

Adriaans, W. (1993). Winning support for your information strategy. *Long Range Planning*. 26 (1), 45–53.

Bolman, L., and Deal, T. (1991) *Reframing organizations: artistry, choice and leadership*. San Francisco, CA: Jossey-Bass.

Brookfield, S.D. (1986) *Understanding and facilitating adult learning: a comprehensive analysis of principles and effective practices*. San Francisco, CA: Jossey-Bass.

Bryson, J. (1988),. *Strategic planning for public and nonprofit organizations: a guide to strengthening and sustaining organizational achievement*. San Francisco, CA: Jossey-Bass.

Committee of Inquiry into Higher Education Management. (1995). *Higher education management review: Report of the committee of inquiry*. Canberra: Australian Government Publishing Service.

Commonwealth Tertiary Education Commission. (1986), *Review of efficiency and effectiveness in higher education*. Canberra: Australian Government Publishing Service.

Dawkins, J. (1988),. *Higher education: a policy statement*, Canberra: Australian Government Publishing Service.

Fombrun, C.J. (1992) *Turning points: creating strategic change in corporations*. New York: McGraw-Hill.

Industry Task Force on Leadership and Management Skills. (1995). *Enterprising nation: renewing Australia's managers to meet the challenges of the Asia-Pacific century*. Canberra: Australian Government Publishing Service.

Knowles, M.S. (1973) *The adult learner: a neglected species* (4th edn). Houston, TX: Gulf Publishing.

Louis, K.S., and Miles, M.B. (1990) *Improving the urban high school: what works and why*. New York: Teachers College Press.

Marshall, S.J. (1997) *A framework for leadership and management development in higher education institutions*. Macquarie University, Centre for Professional Development Working Paper.

Middlehurst, R. (1991) *The changing roles of university leaders and managers*. Sheffield, England: Committee of Vice-Chancellors and Principals.

Middlehurst, R. (1993) *Leading academics*. Buckingham, England: Society for Research into Higher Education and Open University Press.

National Committee of Inquiry into Higher Education (Dearing Committee). (1997). *Higher education in the learning society*. London: Her Majesty's Stationery Office.

Stace, D., and Dunphy, D. (1996) *Beyond the boundaries: heading and creating the successful enterprise*. Sydney: McGraw-Hill.

'Universities and Colleges' Staff Development Agency (UCoSDA). (1994). Higher education management and leadership: Towards a national framework for preparation and development. Sheffield, England: UCoSDA.

4

Social Processes, Work-based Learning and the Scottish Qualification for Headship

Jenny Reeves, Christine Forde, Brian Morris and Eileen Turner

Introduction

The original design of the Scottish Qualification for Headship (SQH) programme was based on the notion that professionals develop their practice most effectively by maximising their experiential learning through engaging in reflective processes (Schon, 1983; Kolb, 1984). The model we used was essentially cognitive and one that is very familiar to educators. It is based on the premise that the actions of individuals are driven by their perceptions and understanding of the context for action. Therefore, the effectiveness of any learning experience lies in its influence on the formation or modification of concepts that guide the individual's basis for action. Using and applying new insights that alter practice will also usually involve the development of new skills and aptitudes. The answer to this problem of transfer and application is commonly seen to be the extension of learning opportunities into the workplace. Through the provision of coaching and mentoring, an environment can be provided where appropriate skills and practices can be developed, refined and incorporated into daily routines (Joyce and Showers, 1988; Joyce *et al.*, 1999).

The SQH was constructed on the assumption that candidates would learn through taking action and reflecting on their experience. In order to enable them to do this the Standard for Headship in Scotland (SOEID, 1998) was to serve as their most important tool. The SQH programme requires candidates to consider the three elements of the standard: their professional values, their performance of the functions of school management, and the abilities they need to carry out the functions effectively at a number of stages in the learning process:

Source: Commissioned.

■ At the point of entry to the programme when they are asked to evaluate themselves against the Standard during a four-day taught programme (Unit 1).

■ In developing a rationale for the planning and implementation of a whole-school development project in school and their own learning programme (Units 1 and 2).

■ In making claims for competence and evaluating their work on the project and their learning in the reflective commentary they are required to submit for assessment (Unit 2).

The latter two stages are then repeated, focusing on different management functions, during a second school-based project (Unit 3).

Undertaking action in school was central to the learning process and this was deliberately constructed so that candidates took on a piece of work requiring them to experience the responsibility of seeing through a substantive management project from beginning to end. We did this both to help them develop a holistic overview of management processes and also so that candidates would experience the inevitable ups and downs of seeing through developments in real-life settings.

In planning the SQH we also identified certain social processes as essential to developing candidates' understanding, but we defined these very much within the limitations of a 'course' concept in that the benefits were seen to arise from candidates engaging in professional discussion with:

■ peers on the taught parts of the course and at network meetings held locally during the work-based Units;

■ experienced managers, normally the candidates' headteachers, acting as mentors; and

■ tutors during the tutorials provided for Units 2 and 3.

The SQH therefore offers candidates a variety of opportunities to learn through:

1 ongoing self-evaluation and reflection on practice using the Standard and their reading, etc.;

2 accessing a body of knowledge about school leadership and management through reading, oral input from speakers, tutorials and discussions;

3 undertaking leadership and management projects in school designed to allow them to develop and demonstrate practical competence;

4 discussing their practice with their mentors, peers and tutors; and

5 preparing portfolios of evidence and reflective commentaries on their work which meet the terms for competence as defined in the Standard.

One strand of the research is to compare the contents of the reflective commentary written at the end of Unit 2 with that written at the end of Unit 3 almost a year later. The assumption is that candidates who showed the most positive developments in their conceptualisation of the role would also show the greatest change in their practice and therefore have a more positive impact on the work of others.

Our focus in this chapter is to advance a rather different interpretation of the learning process from the rational cognitive model, which is one that seems to be indicated by our analysis of the data relating to candidates' accounts of their experiences of the course and the material in the Unit 2 commentaries.

Our sample consists of 40 candidates drawn from across Scotland, who have been selected as being broadly representative of the 164 candidates who enrolled on the course in 1999 in terms of sector, gender, size of school and location. The sources of data from our sample comprise their portfolios and commentaries together with evaluations at the end of Unit 2 (first year of the programme) and notes taken during semi-structured interviews with 20 of the sample about their experience of the course.

The Foundations of an Alternative Interpretation

The initial results of our exploration of the nature of the candidates' experience of the course and their observations on their own learning and professional development indicate that changing practice is bound up in a network of socio-political processes, within and in some cases beyond the boundaries of the school. In exploring some of the evidence which suggests that a reinterpretation of our current approach to continuing professional development (CPD) might well be fruitful, we address the following issues:

■ access to learning opportunities in the workplace;
■ learning in public;
■ the Standard as an authority; and
■ self-evaluation, identity and power.

Access to learning opportunities

There is evidence from our research that the introduction of the SQH and the use of the Standard are serving to legitimate new practices at quite a basic level in a number of schools and thereby opening up opportunities for learning. The evaluation returns showed that 39 per cent of the primary respondents identified the opportunity to lead and manage school projects as the major benefit of the course whereas secondary candidates were more likely to remark on the benefits of reading, coursework and discussion. This theme of being given the opportunity to lead and manage because of participation on the SQH was also a theme in the interviews. Whilst some SQH candidates are class teachers (in small schools) the vast bulk of the candidates already occupy posts which supposedly carry with them responsibility for whole-school management. It is therefore surprising to find so many attesting to the novelty of being allowed to take full responsibility for a management project.

The sectoral difference may well reflect the rather different level of opportunities for gaining management experience that prevail between the two sectors. In secondary schools in Scotland teachers generally serve quite lengthy apprenticeships in a number of promoted posts which carry defined management responsibilities. In primary there are fewer rungs on the ladder and the apparently dominant role of headteachers (Southworth, 1995) may mean that even deputy heads have little direct experience of whole-school management. The SQH, as one candidate typically explains, offered up new areas of experience and learning:

> The one aspect that I have got most out of was the fact that I had to take on
> sole responsibility for the development of one aspect of the school's
> development plan over the session. I would have been heavily involved in that
> as a matter of course but the fact that I was in 'full charge' gave me a lot of
> opportunities that maybe I would not have got otherwise to develop myself and
> my own beliefs and views further (Unit 2 commentary).

The course had a similar impact in introducing candidates to new experiences in some secondary schools, particularly in relation to certain aspects of management relevant to adopting a strategic approach to development.

> I wasn't involved with previously, had no experience of finance and I have
> managed to get myself sucked into that through this project (interview).

However, more typically, the impact of the SQH in several of the secondary accounts was to be found in the reordering of work because a more strategic and holistic view of an initiative had been developed as a result of someone being on the course:

> More than for most developments I have undertaken, a good deal of time was spent
> on planning this project. This was partly because of the innovative nature of the
> approach within the school. A more well-worn approach to these tasks would have
> been to divide them up among the various members of the senior management
> team. In order to create some coherence of approach, it was important to ensure
> there was a coherent vision of what was to be attempted (Unit 2 commentary).

What seems to be the case in a significant number of instances is that the course and the Standard legitimate access to certain types of management activities which a number of participants feel they probably would not otherwise have experienced. It is also providing access to a public role within these schools of 'being responsible for' and 'being in charge of'.

Learning in public

The vividness of the experience of learning in the workplace was apparent from our interviews. The SQH may lead to an individual award but the activities it requires are school based and therefore collective in nature. This public characteristic of SQH perhaps makes it inevitable that the experience, and the learning involved tends to express itself through the professional relationships already established in the school.

The Standard requires that candidates work closely with a group of their colleagues on a priority from the school's development plan. Since the candidates will be using evidence derived from the work of their groups they must make it clear to their colleagues that they are assisting them to undertake a project for the SQH. Enrolment on the course is thus inevitably a matter for public knowledge within the school. Candidates and their colleagues in school could be seen as engaging in an initiation process whereby the former enter a new role as 'aspiring headteachers'. Usually colleagues are seen as sympathetic and committed to trying to achieve a positive outcome, as one interviewee described:

> It has its drawbacks sometimes, when I did put out things like questionnaires . . .
> The children were wonderful at it but the staff – I had to do it again because a lot
> of them ticked the boxes because they thought it would help me in my course. I
> had to get the message across to them that they were not helping anyone if they
> were not honest.

However, the public nature of their learning means that candidates face a very real risk of loss of professional credibility in the eyes of their colleagues if they fail to gain the award. Their level of commitment to the course is likely to be substantially increased because they have voluntarily made a public and 'irrevocable' choice to join the course and accept the role. In order to maintain face there is a lot of pressure on them to succeed (Weick, 1995). One of the features of the SQH is an unusually high retention and completion rate for a work-based scheme (85 per cent on average for each cohort).

Even where the group in school is less supportive the pressure to succeed remains very high. The fact that candidates are essentially pursuing their own career development can be used against them.

This apparent tension between individual and institutional benefit may explain why securing positive outcomes for the school is so important to candidates. As one explained in interview:

> It definitely did [have an outcome] – the maths results went up. They [the
> children] felt much more confident too because they were doing bigger things
> mentally and they were more confident in written work. It raised their confidence
> and that raised their ability.

The relationship between candidates and their headteachers can also be said to be an important element in the experience and the learning of candidates. In turn, the relationship itself can itself be affected. Headteachers generally act both as course sponsors as well as supporters/mentors to the candidates. Evidence in this regard can be drawn from the survey undertaken by Simpson *et al.* (2000, p. 14) who found that just over 70 per cent of candidates regarded the role of the supporter as necessary. Those who valued the role felt that the most important functions supporters served were:

1 As a sponsor:
   encouraged me to join the programme (71 per cent);
   makes it possible for me to carry out the necessary practical projects
   (70 per cent).
2 As a professional counsellor:
   is always ready to listen to my problems (82 per cent);
   acts as a sounding board for my ideas (77 per cent);
   acts as a critical friend (71 per cent).

Candidates preferred an internal supporter to someone coming into the school from outside. Certainly the sponsoring role would appear to be more effectively managed by a powerful insider who has the advantage of contextual knowledge when it comes to acting as a professional counsellor. The influence of the supporter role could also be evident even when advice was not being offered.

However helpful, the existence of an internal supporter would appear to add appreciably to the level of scrutiny candidates feel in undertaking the course. An element in headteacher support is perhaps an accompanying pressure (motivation?) on the headteacher supporters to ensure that 'their' candidate's project is a success. Indeed according to Simpson *et al.* (2000), 77 per cent of headteacher supporters felt their candidates' involvement on the course had led to beneficial changes in school.

Nevertheless, the relationship between candidate and headteacher could present challenges, particularly where the work undertaken by candidates resulted in an implied criticism of, or challenge to, existing practice in teaching and learning and in management. This tended to focus on two areas central to the SQH. These were participation and evaluation. Perhaps surprisingly given the history of advice to schools in these areas (see HMI, 1988; 1991) a large number of respondents claim that their schools still use rather superficial consultative procedures. The course can therefore open up areas of tension within the school. Typically one candidate wrote about the difficulties in adopting a participative approach that ran counter to normal management practice in the school:

> In some respects I felt I was trying to work in two directions. I wanted the staff
> to see that I was sympathetic to their problems in developing writing. I also
> wanted to show the headteacher that I could take the staff with me and get
> positive results and feedback by the way I interacted with the staff.

The public nature of SQH is further extended by the nature of the assessment process into the local authority. As part of the process of assessing the work-based assignments a field assessor, usually a serving headteacher from the same local authority as the candidate, will visit the school. In addition to interviewing the candidate about what has been achieved he or she will also interview both the head and one of the candidate's colleagues in order to verify the contents of the portfolio and the outcomes of the project. In more traditional methods of assessment, external involvement can be limited to a university tutor. However, in this case, members of the school and the local authority are involved in the assessment process. Although confidentiality is maintained by those involved this does nevertheless introduce another element of the 'public' to the assessment process.

What emerges from this discussion is that, in many ways, social processes serve both as sources of support and pressure, often at one and the same time:

> The importance of sponsorship and being given appropriate opportunities to learn and the obligation this places on the learner.
> The risk and pressure involved in being publicly assigned important responsibilities and being seen as introducing new ways of working.
> The involvement and engagement of others in the project and hence their 'complicity' in the candidate's actions and learning.

The Standard as a source of authority

The favourable responses to work-based learning and assertions of the efficacy of the Standard sit alongside what seems, on the face of it, a puzzling observation on the part of a significant number of the interviewees. The experience of 'doing' the course is described in almost coercive terms. This impression comes from the interviews where expressions such as 'it forces you', 'it makes you' or 'the SQH pushes you' were used by 12 of the interviewees in discussing the effects of the course. Candidates seem to be identifying that working towards the Standard constrains them to act in certain ways and that this is significant in their learning.

It may be that two requirements embedded in the assessment process are responsible for this kind of reaction:

■ to provide evidence that the project brought about improvement and was carried out in accordance with the standard; and
■ to justify actions.

However, things are probably not that simple. As we have already pointed out the implementation of the standard does seem to be requiring general changes in management practice in a significant number of schools in addition to the particular changes in the behaviour of the candidates themselves. Given the risks attached to such changes, being able to displace responsibility to 'the SQH' is probably less dangerous than taking individual responsibility:

> I certainly did things differently in the past and the SQH made me think about
> things differently and it made me really examine what I did and not just how to
> do them but why I was doing them. I had never thought why I did it that way.
> It gave ways of looking and improving things and it certainly made a difference
> to the way I thought and the way I managed. The SQH allowed me to do things
> very differently because my headteacher allowed me to do the project my way.
> Sometimes in the past you managed things and they were very much
> influenced by the person above you (interview).

The use of the Standard as a source of authority leads to its further reification
so that it almost becomes 'an actor' in the change process at the level of both
the individual and the school. At an individual level the 'makes you' comments are more than matched by references to the cognitive effects that
candidates claim for working with the Standard. The phrases most frequently
used to describe the experience are:

> It has given me a structure/a framework for analysing/checking out what I
> want to do. I used to be instinctive, now I stop before I make decisions/I
> choose from options. I look at management in a different way. It has helped
> me firm up my ideas, make my philosophy clearer, I can now justify my
> actions (extracts from interviews).

There is an interesting link made here by candidates between internal mental
processes and action centred round the work-based learning project. Some
possible reasons for the power of the standard in this process are hinted at in
the following quotation:

> I have found the information in 'The Standard for Headship in Scotland' text to
> be of great help. It has helped focus my thoughts on the work I was doing and
> has helped to justify to myself that it was right to do some of the things in a
> particular way. I think it would be fair to say that a lot of information in the
> booklet reflects what most people who are head teachers or aspire to be head
> teachers believe in. The difference is that it's written down in black and white
> and in a concise format that you can refer to (Unit 2 commentary).

There are three important themes here:

1 the accessibility, specificity and concreteness of the Standard;
2 the Standard as affirmation of practice; and
3 the aspirational aspect of the Standard.

The first theme is significant because it allows learners to clarify expectations
and provides clear guidance on action. In this sense it operates very much in

line with the goal theory used as the underpinning logic for managerial approaches to performance management where providing feedback and agreeing clear and challenging goals with employees are seen as a primary means of enhancing performance (Armstrong and Baron, 1998). The theme of achievement and gaining greater control over the quality of one's work is important. In a sense the SQH provides many participants with powerful and detailed feedback on their performance both through the conduct of the school-based projects and through the formal assessment procedures. Given the relatively low level of implementation of personal review processes in Scottish schools at the time this could also partly explain why this has been such an important developmental experience for a number of candidates.

However, there is a noticeable variation as to which element of the Standard strikes a particular candidate as significant. For those who are new to management or who have not constructed what they do in a managerial framework the functions often have the most impact. For others it is exploring values or looking more closely at their professional abilities that they find most interesting.

The significance of the second theme is the need for affirmation that emerges strongly for both primary and secondary candidates. The Standard allows them to make judgements about their performance and is seen as providing legitimacy for their actions which boosts their self-confidence. More practically it serves as an external authority which provides them with a basis for making claims for opportunities, resources and permission to innovate within the school. In this sense it has three functions:

1 Personal validation and hence positive emotional impact on the candidate.
2 Political support in that it legitimates the candidate's position and actions.
3 Resource procurement.

The third theme indicates the importance for candidates of the inclusion of a strong statement about professionalism in the key purpose and the professional values section of the Standard. This significantly adds to the authority of a standard if it is seen as having, or can be claimed to have, a moral authority within the profession and to embody for the candidates and their colleagues a 'respectable' vision of what they might want to become.

At an apparently more pragmatic level, another major advantage of the Standard, which also emerged in an earlier study of the use of management competences in Strathclyde Region (Reeves and Forde, 1994), is that it enables candidates to acquire a 'language' for describing, discussing and justifying their management practice:

> It's given me a language to raise things, greater confidence, I articulate things much better, you can explain to yourself, recognising what I was trying to do, recognising what had gone wrong. I am more conscious, more aware, I can explain and articulate my ideas (interviews).

This quotation contains an important element of aspiration embedded in the notion of entry into the 'discourse' of leadership and management and the sense of being empowered by this. In some ways this acquisition of the language is more profound, or less innocent, than simply developing the capacity to understand the jargon. One major reason for emphasising the importance of training for head-teachers on the part of policymakers is to support the drive to modernise the public services through the adoption of a managerialist discourse and practice. Our evidence would seem to indicate that the Standard does help to achieve this.

However, the SQH does not always elicit significant change in candidates. A few students, for one reason or another, are driven by the need simply to 'play the game' without learning much as a result:

> I suppose I do. I document everything and keep all the paper. I wasn't very good at keeping evidence. I'd do it for my class, evidence of the children but not for management things I tended not to write enough down (interview).

Indeed in response to the question, 'Is there anything new that you do?' the candidate replied, 'I don't think so'. Another asserts that all this is nothing new:

> I think that a lot of the decisions I made were made in the light of my experience as an assistant headteacher prior to starting the SQH. That's maybe not what you want to hear but it's what I think. My own experience tells me that if I had started SQH as an assistant headteacher with less experience in post it would probably have helped me get to answers quicker and made me broaden how I looked at things. But because of the experience I have had as a manager in a school and the breadth of over 10 years before I started SQH – I mean I do reflect on my own practice, that's part and parcel of what I have always done (interview).

Looking at the minority of candidates who claim to have gained little from their participation in the course the theme of already having the necessary experience and expertise comes across most frequently. Clearly it is not motivating if the standard is perceived as merely a summary of what the candidate has already learned. This lack of perceived novelty could possibly be even more prevalent as an issue when looking at standards for teaching as developmental tools. Certainly our evidence indicates that the standard appears to be having more impact at primary level where the experience of, and identification with, being a school manager is more likely to be novel to candidates.

Self-evaluation, identity and power

The centrality of the role of reflection within the SQH has been recognised by candidates right from the beginning of the piloting (Morris and Reeves, 2000). For current candidates the process continues to be important and showed that 90 per cent of candidates said they were more reflective as a result of their involvement in the course (Malcolm and Wilson, 2000). In this regard the requirement to justify your actions creates an added and often novel pressure. As part of the reflective process on the SQH candidates are asked to express and describe their professional selves and articulate what they think, believe and want to achieve. This is often both difficult and 'embarrassing' for candidates:

> The most uncomfortable aspect of this course so far has been holding up for scrutiny my present practices and processes and the values that underpin them (Unit 1 assignment).

An essential issue in such public reflection is how candidates situate themselves in this process. However, many candidates do recognise that initial unease is something that is worth overcoming:

> Values have tended however, to be implicit in projects and actions. Very real benefits arise through making these positions explicit from the outset. In future I would seek opportunities to articulate my values (Unit 1 assignment).

There is also strong evidence of the importance of a change in the understanding of self and the perception of self-efficacy. A significant number of candidates from the primary sector highlighted issues of professional identity. Even people who had been in a senior post for some time, including those who are already headteachers, found composing the portfolio and commentary quite a powerful experience. Entry into the language, the discourse associated with the Standard, seems to function as a means of realigning and/or affirming a professional identity about which the person has perhaps been unsure (Knowles, 1993) or even composing a new identity. It is almost for some candidates as though they are redefining themselves through the process and affirming their professional role as a school leader and manager.

As we have already noted, what also comes through in the interviews is the link between a successful experience of the project and feelings associated with increased self-confidence and self-esteem. A candidate made the following observations:

> I also get the feeling from some of the heads round about that they are a wee bit scared of me now. A wee bit of insecurity about what we who have done the SQH have done that they haven't. I am a bit ahead of some of the others in things like evaluation.

The analysis of the interviews indicates that there is an intermingling of two sets of responses: first, the adoption, or confirmation, of an identity as a school leader and manager and, secondly, the power that this identity and the knowledge on which it is based confers on the candidate. A triangular relationship is inferred between knowledge, power and identity and, for a number of candidates where these links are perceived as positive, this has reportedly had a dramatic effect on their capability and taste for action.

Last, it is important to consider certain key features of the accounting process in order to underline how completely situated in context and experience developing practice is for most of the candidates. In order to illustrate this, it is useful to look at one of the common themes in the Unit 2 commentaries, which is the difficulty many candidates have with delegation, something that they must successfully demonstrate in their portfolio. Below are two extracts where candidates explain why they feel they are now able to delegate effectively:

> However this year I have reflected much more on the amount of work that I perform within the group. The tension between teaching staff volunteering and requiring tasks to be completed by definite times has caused me to take on more than is realistic. This project has made me analyse people's motivation for being involved. I have realised that by developing a system of motivation through personal and professional development that groups can progress themselves. Leading by example is important but I realise in leading if you want to be trusted you must trust others (Unit 2 commentary).

> In general, I feel that sometimes I sacrifice my sense of humour, when I feel under pressure to get certain work done, and I need to give attention to this. However, I feel I have more confidence about trusting that a team will take forward tasks and policy developments. They have developed their vision and their evaluative systems so that my direct and detailed role is much less (Unit 2 commentary).

These extracts illustrate how individual and personal the process of changing practice is. Delegation is not an abstract idea for these people; it is woven into personal perception through a unique mixture of associations bound up in a particular context at a particular time. Each of these candidates claims to have arrived at the same insight about the value of delegation and some commonality about the means to achieve it, but by their own individual route.

These accounts do not reflect the rather technical-rational and abstract descriptions that are often given of the practice of critical reflection but point to a rather more visceral process where the personal and the professional are very closely intertwined. They also indicate the crucial role of the social arena in which change occurs and the importance of the micro-political dimensions of changing practice.

Conclusions

Theoretically these initial outcomes from the research project raise a number of very interesting issues which warrant further exploration. First, if people are to change their professional practice substantively, does this inevitably entail that they must also establish a change in their work identity? Secondly, as an insider to a particular community of practice, is it possible for you to change your own practice unless others are prepared to be complicit in the changes and alter their own behaviours to accommodate your new behaviour? Thirdly, what is the relationship between altering practice and changing your account of yourself by composing your actions on to a new template, in this case a Standard (Burroughs, 2001)? Is the result 'real' or simply the adoption of another version of self as part of social practice? There is also an issue here about the role of discourse, in the case of the SQH that of 'managerialism'. Does command of a new discourse give you access to a new activity system – a new stage and persona on and in which to act?

These questions have important implications for the design and delivery of CPD. They suggest that our current concentration on the 'learning' of the individual may be mistaken and that perhaps we should instead be thinking in socio-cultural terms about effecting activity systems (Engestrom, 2001) or communities of practice (Lave and Wenger, 1991). Such post-Vygotskian models currently lack any clear basis for accounting for change and development. The role of the SQH might indicate that there could be ways of effectively introducing external 'viruses' into a given community through the medium of work-based CPD (Figure 4.1) while at the same time providing an insight as to why promoting change through the medium of CPD has often proved rather ineffective in the past.

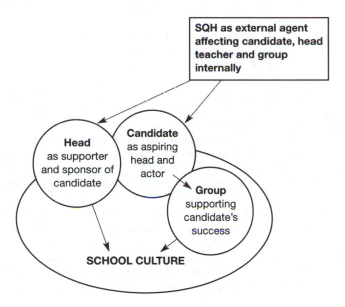

Figure 4.1 *The entry of the SQH into the activity systems of the school*

Perhaps we should be thinking of CPD provision in terms of the permissions and spaces it opens up for interactive change between the target individuals and others and supporting socio-political processes for growth and change rather than concentrating on content and learning outcomes.

References

Armstrong, M. and Baron, A. (1998) *Performance Management: The New Realities*. London: CIPD.

Burroughs, R. (2001) Composing Standards and Composing Teachers: The problem of National Board Certification. *Journal of Teacher Education* Vol. 52 May/June 2000, pp. 223–32

Engestrom, Y., (2001) Expansive learning at work: toward an activity theoretical reconceptualisation. *Journal of Education and Work* 14 (1): 133–56.

Engestrom, Y., Miettinen, R. and Punamaki, R–L. (eds.) (1999) *Perspectives on Activity Theory*. New York: Cambridge University Press.

Eraut, M. (1994) *Developing Professional Knowledge and Competence*. London: Falmer Press.

HMI Scottish Office Education Department (1988) Effective Secondary Schools. Edinburgh: HMSO.

HMI Scottish Office Education Department (1991) MER5 The Role of Development Plans in Managing School Effectiveness. Edinburgh: Scottish Office Education Department Audit Unit.

Joyce, B., Calhoun, E. and Hopkins, D. (1999) *The New Structure of School Improvement*. Buckingham: The Open University Press.

Joyce, B. and Showers, J. (1988) *Student Achievement through Staff Development*. London: Longman.

Knowles, J.G. (1993) Life history accounts as mirrors: a practical avenue for the conceptualisation of reflection. In J. Calderhead and P. Gates, (eds.) *Conceptualising Reflection in Teacher Development*. London: Falmer Press.

Kolb, D.A. (1984) *Experiential Learning: Experience as a Source of Learning and Development*. Englewood Cliffs, NJ: Prentice-Hall.

Lave, J. and Wenger, E. (1991) *Situated Learning: Legitimate Peripheral Participation*. Cambridge: Cambridge University Press.

Malcolm, H. and Wilson, V. (2000) The Price of Quality: An evaluation of the costs of the SQH programme. Edinburgh: Scottish Council for Research in Education.

Morris, B. and Reeves, J. (2000) Implementing a National Qualification for Headship in Scotland: (a) critical reflection. *Journal of In-Service Education* 26 (3): 517–31.

Reeves, J. and Forde, C. (1994) Can management competences support the development of a learning organisation? In procedures of the Scottish Education Research Association. September, Dundee University of Dundee.

Reeves, J., Morris, B., Turner, E. and Forde, C. (2001) Exploring the impact of continuing professional development in the context of the Scottish Qualification for Headship. *Journal of In-Service Education* 27 (2): 203–33.

Schön, D.A. (1983) *The Reflective Practitioner: How Professionals Think in Action*. London: Temple Books.

Simpson, M., Gooday, M. and Payne, F. (2000) *SQH Programme Evaluation: The Role of the Supporter and the Effects on School*. Edinburgh: University of Edinburgh and Northern College.

SOEID (1998) *The Standard for Headship in Scotland*. Glasgow: SQH Development Unit.

Weick, K. (1995) *Sense-Making in Organisations*. Thousand Oaks, CA: Sage.

Southworth, G. (1995) Talking heads: Voices of Experience: An investigation into primary headship in the 1990s. Cambridge: Cambridge Institute of Education.

5

Mentoring and the Tolerance of Complexity

Bob Garvey and Geof Alred

Introduction

This chapter explores mentoring in the light of complexity theory and the premium placed upon knowledge in organisational viability. A key question is 'what is the role of mentoring, as a developmental and knowledge creating process, in a complex environment'? There are two parts to the discussion. First, we explore complexity at work, and what it means for the individual. We link the central ideas of complexity theory with the notion of a 'corporate curriculum, an inclusive concept intended to capture the complex nature of learning at work in all its variants. Secondly, we speculate on the contribution mentoring can make in complex organisations where employees are part of a knowledge economy by virtue of being knowledge producers and being engaged in learning at work. The environments in which we work are becoming more complex and mentoring is also complex. There is a synergy here. For people living in complexity where there are few rules, no right answers and no predictable outcomes, we suggest that mentoring can play a distinctive role in helping people to 'tolerate' complexity and remain effective.

Kessels (1996) argues that 'organisations have a direct stake in the personal enrichment of employees because excellence on the job requires employees who are comfortable with their work and who have strong and stable personalities. Personal enrichment is thus less an employee privilege than a condition for good performance'. His may be a challenging statement for people working within a capitalist society as it suggests that economic progress is strongly associated with social conditions, learning and a sense of morality.

Source: Futures, Vol. 33, no. 6, 2002, pp. 519–30. Edited version.

Mentoring is becoming increasingly employed in a range of occupational settings (Garvey, 1999). We speculate that this is because mentoring activity encourages and facilitates informal or 'open' leaning. More traditional formal or 'closed' approaches to learning are increasingly being criticised for not delivering enhanced capability and performance to organisations (Broad and Newstrom, 1992). Against this background it becomes inevitable that alternatives to the 'formal' are investigated by organisations.

In the context of workplace learning concepts such as 'situated learning' (Lave and Wenger, 1991) and the 'zone of proximal development' (Vygotsky, 1978) take on particular significance for there can be little doubt that the message in these theories is very clear that learning is a social activity.

Workplace mentoring, because it is social, situated in the 'zone of proximal development' (Vygostsky, 1981) and involves both the cognitive and the meta-cognitive, is all-engaging and is therefore learning of a higher mental order. Gladstone (1998) cites Bolles as stating that 'a mentor is the highest level educator'. And, Vygotsky (1981) would agree:

> Any higher mental function necessarily goes through an external stage in its development because it is initially a social function. . . Any higher mental function was external because it was social at some point before becoming an internal, truly mental function. (p. 162)

Mentoring is related to and associated with reconceptualisations of organisations, such as the 'knowledge-creating company' (Nonaka, 1996).

Changing Organisations

Organisations tend to be motivated by ideas which may help them achieve competitive advantage, survival or progress in their activities. But, the world is changing. For instance, the business world in the late 20th century saw 'the quality boom'. This was primarily driven by organisations seeking competitive advantage through the superior quality of their products or services. This, combined with a drive to cut costs, resulted in great developments in technology and changes in working practices. Manufacturing industries saw the introduction of sophisticated automation and consequently the increased demand for a technically skilled workforce able to be flexible and adaptable. Ironically, some skilled workers started to become de-skilled as a result of introducing new technology (Garvey, 1995b).

The public sector in the UK has also seen many changes. In the main, these were driven by a political desire to reduce public expenditure but at the same time there was an attempt to improve the quality of service. Many public sector organisations become subject to 'market principals' with compulsory competitive tendering and 'commercialisation' of its activities.

High quality products and service at reduced cost became the entry point at which organisations could do business (Hamel and Prahalad, 1989; 1991). As competitive advantage based on quality alone became more difficult to sustain businesses started to develop new customer led strategies. This meant the need to focus on people and relationships and slogans began to appear in organisational documents such as 'people mean business', 'people are our most important asset'.

Some organisations are now attempting to develop into 'learning companies' (Pedler *et al.*, 1991) in order to achieve competitive edge. This requires paying attention to people's need for support, encouragement, challenge and learning through and from situated experience. This challenges managers stuck in the old paradigms of management control and command and the Taylorist concept of economic organisation.

The human landscape of working and living in this new century is evolving and perhaps involves an increasingly more complex set of demands. The complexity of working and living within a capitalist community seems likely to accelerate. This is due in part to technology becoming more sophisticated, communications faster and competition keener. In such a climate, the demands on people increase as their working lives change rapidly. As Jarvis (1992) puts it '. . . change, then, is one of the conditions of the modern world'.

■ The Aim of the Chapter

This chapter explores mentoring in the light of complexity and the premium placed upon knowledge in organisational viability. It draws on current discourses about future organisational viability in the operating conditions of early 21st century industrialised society. These discourses draw on complexity theory and the broad range of theories pertaining to being and learning at work. Against the above backdrop it becomes necessary to ask – what can mentoring contribute and what is its role in a complex environment?

Our discussion is in two parts. First, we attempt to give an impression of complexity at work, and what it means for the individual. We link the central ideas of complexity theory with the notion of a corporate curriculum (Kessel, 1996), an inclusive concept intended to capture the complex nature of learning at work, in all its variants. These include an instrumental view of learning but goes further to embrace learning that is informal, experiential, reflective and the outcome of collaboration. This broader concept of learning is encouraged and supported by mentoring relationships.

Secondly, we speculate on the contribution mentoring can make in complex organisations where employees are part of a knowledge economy by virtue of producing knowledge and being engaged in learning at work.

■ Mentoring and the Organisation

Mentoring is versatile and complex. It is used for a variety of purposes in organisations and often where transitions are necessary. We propose that inherent in mentoring is the capacity that one person has to help another (Carden, 1990; Gladstone, 1988) and that this capacity needs to survive and thrive in a complex environment. However, there are challenges. Despite the acknowledged benefits, mentoring activity is not always recognised and is not always valued sufficiently within the work environment.

Research (Collin, 1979; Clawson, 1996; Clutterbuck, 1998, Garvey, 1994) shows that the authority which comes with a direct line-management position is not appropriate in a mentoring partnership. Mentoring is concerned with learning and development within a trusting relationship. Therefore, the mentor is best situated between the organisation and the mentee, knowledgeable about both and responsive to both. As Collin (1979) puts it, the mentor 'acts as the leading edge in the process of socialisation in which the individual adapts to the needs and *ambience* of the company, whilst retaining his own individuality and, thereby, achieves his own style of managerial development' and, the mentor 'personifies the company's *psychostructure* and acts as midwife in the process of socialisation' (original italics).

Organisational factors that influence mentoring forms include the perceived purpose of mentoring; organisational culture and management style; and the 'dominant logic' (Garvey, 1995a) and organisational environment. In relation to purpose, there is evidence of an association between an instrumental form of mentoring and a perception of mentoring as a 'management tool' to fast track employees seen as having exceptional talent (Garvey, 1994; 1995a; 1999). This encourages mentor control, an emphasis on giving advice, and, in some cases, manipulation.

There are other examples of the form mentoring takes. Here the focus is the holistic development of the mentee. Where the development of the mentee and organisational goals coincide, it is appropriate to talk of a 'mentoring organisation' where employees use a number of people to assist in different ways to enhance their learning at work (Caruso, 1996). In contrast, there are organisations where mentoring works against the grain of organisational culture. Antal (1996), for instance, has observed that 'unfortunately, many companies foster highly competitive behaviour and stress bottom-line results in a way that discourages supportive behaviour between members of the organisation'. She speculates, from her experience of mentoring schemes for women, that mentoring 'is more sensitive than other training activities to the corporate culture in which the individuals work'. One reason for this is that much of the learning at work, and much of the nature of organisational culture, stems from informal rather than formal activities. An effective mentor knows this and is effective by virtue of understanding how the organisation works and how to get on in it. The mentor is in a key position standing 'off-line' between the organisation, its values, culture and practices, and the developing employee.

More generally, the informal learning that takes place in mentoring is affected by what has been referred to as 'organisational mindset', an outlook that reflects organisational culture. Senge (1992) describes it as a 'mental mode' comprising 'deeply ingrained assumptions, generalisations, or even pictures or images that influence how we understand the world and how we take action'. Similarly, Bettis and Prahalad (1995) use the phrase 'the dominant logic' to emphasise that the influence of the organisation on individual thinking can be subtle and indirect. Both Senge and Bettis and Prahalad argue that organisational mindset influences both behaviour and thinking, and has the potential to inhibit or enhance learning capabilities.

In sum, the form mentoring takes is influenced by the 'mindset' management style and culture of the organisation. Paradoxically, it can both be constructive and destructive, helpful and manipulative, confirm cultures and change them. Mentoring is about learning and learning is complex, paradoxical (Jarvis, 1992) and associated with change. Mentoring also involves iterative learning, reflexive and reflective learning. These are essential learning processes in a complex environment.

Complex Systems and Mentoring

Stacey's (1995) application of complexity theory to organisations recognises three types of system: stable; unstable; and complex. All are non-linear feedback systems, where there are many outcomes to any action, group behaviour is more than the sum of individual behaviours, and small changes can escalate into major outcomes.

Mentoring in a stable organisation takes place against a background of relatively clear paths, both short and long, that the mentee will tread in the organisation. Here there is an emphasis on means rather than ends, such that mentoring may involve largely instrumental teaching and learning. We suggest that stability within an organisation at the beginning of the 21st century is likely to be a short-lived reality. Consequently. mentoring activity may be based on faulty assumptions. These assumptions, based on a concept of stability, may include a clear and recognisable career path and a continuity and stability of employment within the same organisation. People with such assumptions may see mentoring as a way to maintain the existing system and thus become disappointed when mentoring does not match their expectations (Garvey, 1995b).

Mentoring is an activity that addresses a combination of short, medium and long term goals, and concerns primarily 'ends' as well as 'means'. Hence, mentoring is severely challenged in an unstable environment. It may become focused exclusively on short term goals, disappear or be displaced by friendship between people sharing a common difficult fate (Rigsby *et al.*, 1998). Mentoring may slip into the 'shadow-side' (Egan, 1993) where it has the potential to be both destructive or add value. The outcome of it falling into the shadows depends on the prevailing management style and culture.

A complex system is both stable and unstable. It is a dynamic system at the edge of instability characterised by short-term predictability and long-term unpredictability. Instability is ever present, and a complex system is described as being in a state of 'bounded instability' (Stacey, 1995): there are limits but they do not operate in a deterministic fashion; and there are rules, but these are local and other rules are found in other parts of the system. Hence, following rules does not ensure predictable outcomes, and is not always intelligent behaviour. The effects of actions of one part – an individual, a team, a department – arise in complex interactions with the actions of other parts. The best course of action is difficult to discern because the final outcome emerges in an unpredictable way from a multiplicity of actions by others. Hence, decisions need to be coupled with a capacity and a readiness to deal positively with whatever ensues from the complex interactions of the whole. This includes the ability to compromise, to be resilient and accept that there may not be a 'right' answer.

Mentoring is partly in the shadows, by its very nature (mentor discussions happen in private and are bound by confidentiality) and partly in the light, when valued and resourced by an organisation through logistical and personnel support. This places mentoring in a state of 'bounded instability'.

An example of complexity, such as the performance of music, is perhaps more intuitively analogous to learning at work. The nature of a particular performance is complex: there are rules set by the score, performance notes, the instruments and limits of the performers, hence the instability is bounded; but the music collectively played is unique to that performance, to that occasion. The good conductor is one who knows she cannot control everything that happens but rather will allow the fullest participation of each player within the vision and spirit of the music. The classical recording industry thrives on the variety of performance that arises from the complexity of performing groups of musicians. What is new in a performance, the emergent innovation, is heard most explicitly when musicians improvise and it is striking that Druker (1992) and Barrett (1998) have used the improving jazz band as a metaphor for learning at work. The point made by these writers reminds us again of the importance of informal learning, of learning that departs from the rules, away from overt training and instruction, and within the daily flow and flux of experience at work. This is the province of mentoring.

Mentoring deals with people's experience and behaviour, and certainly, at an individual level, human behaviour is complex, as is human experience. At times of change, when mentoring is most valuable and developmental, the mentee is likely to experience themselves and their situation as complex. For people experiencing complexity, attempting to reduce the situation to simple terms ignores their reality and creates personal tensions and conflicts. It is also dishonest. An organisation in a state of bounded instability is complex and is better understood as such.

Taking a complexity perspective allows us to go beyond instrumental mentoring and the view of the mentor's socialising role in the mentee's adaptation to the 'needs and ambience' of the organisation. Mentoring, as a powerful means of learning informally, has a significant role in knowledge productive organisations, namely to help the mentee function productively in a complex environment. In a complex system, networks become more important and an individual will have and need multiple connections. Some of these connections will be mentoring relationships. We assert that the role for mentoring can only increase as more organisations seek to operate as knowledge productive organisations.

The Knowledge Economy and a Corporate Curriculum

The concept of a complex system serves as an analogy for people working and learning in organisations. We believe that the analogy is particularly useful in understanding organisations that succeed by virtue of being knowledge productive. Hence, we turn now to one characterisation of a knowledge productive organisation (Kessels, 1996) and assert that this exemplifies a complex system. We attempt to substantiate our assertion by illustration rather than formally.

Knowledge management is currently a much discussed imperative in organisations. To manage knowledge is an understandable aim, but it is unlikely to be attained using traditional approaches, as knowledge, in contrast to information, 'cannot be managed by purposeful planning, systematic arrangement, and control' (ibid.). The fluid, emergent quality of learning in a complex organisation and the importance of informal learning require an organisational dynamic that allows the organisation to 'operate at the edge where long-term outcomes are unknowable' (Stacey, 1995) and probably unmanageable in the traditional sense.

The notion of a corporate curriculum provides a useful way of describing and discussing the workplace as a complex learning environment. Kessels (1996) regards the corporate curriculum as an inclusive concept of learning at work. He describes it as a 'rich landscape' of learning. In broad terms, curricula may be closed or open (Bernstein, 1971). If the curriculum is closed, the 'teacher' tightly controls the content of the learning and the outcome is socialisation by boundaries of certainty. The closed curriculum, in assuming a rationality and orderliness in human activity tends to develop orderly, logical thinkers who assume that human activity is rational.

If the curriculum is open, the content of the learning is more integrated and boundary free. The outcome of this approach is socialisation and understanding through active engagement and participation. The open curriculum, in assuming a less orderly and holistic base to learning, tends to develop a tolerance and understanding of uncertainty, change and paradox. It helps to develop creativity, lateral thinking and flexibility (Bernstein, 1971). We believe that this concept has relevance to adult learning in a complex environment.

The features of Kessel's corporate curriculum are as follows:

acquiring subject matter expertise and skill directly related to the scope of the target competencies;
learning to solve problems by using this domain specific expertise;
developing reflective skills and metacognitions conducive to locating paths leading to new knowledge and means for acquiring and applying this asset;
securing communication skills that provide access to the knowledge network of others and enrich the learning climate within the workplace;
acquiring skills that regulate motivation and the emotional dimension of learning;
promoting peace and stability to enable specialisation, cohesion, and integration;
causing creative turmoil to instigate improvement and innovation.

Learning in this rich landscape goes far beyond formal training. By combining both the closed and open curricula and by paying attention to these 'landscape' features, an organisation may be able to develop its own rich landscape where learning occurs through active engagement and participation. This will not only develop specific skills and knowledge but also create flexibility, adaptability, creativity and innovative thinking – the generally accepted attributes of 'knowledge workers' (Drucker, 1992; Senge, 1992). We suggest 'that mentoring activity is one way to help and support people as they become 'knowledge workers'.

The following section aims to illustrate how mentoring, a complex activity itself, can assist people to tolerate complexity.

■ Learning and Tolerating Complexity

There are two senses of the word 'tolerate'. First, and one commonly used, is the sense of 'putting up with'. Tolerance in this sense implies that a person views situations as simplistically tolerable or intolerable so that the very perception of a situation becomes part of what makes it more or less tolerable.

This, we believe, chips away at the personal qualities and abilities that determine optimal performance. Complexity here is experienced as 'complication', a source of frustration, discomfort and a drain on energy.

A second sense of 'tolerate', and one closer to its etymological root, is 'to sustain' to keep going and remain effective in prevailing conditions. This is a more positive connotation. If a mentee works in a complex environment, they will prosper and contribute if they can remain effective in a state of bounded instability. This requires perception of the situation for what it is. If the situation is a 'rich landscape of learning' then the successful mentee will have an appreciation of themselves in respect of all seven elements of their learning and performance at work.

Any one issue, which might be examined in mentoring, may involve all or several of the elements of the corporate curriculum. These elements interact in complex ways. For example, problem solving may involve both detailed discussions with others and effective team work. If skills in these areas are undeveloped, problem solving may suffer. Improving the necessary communication skills may in turn depend upon how an individual responds emotionally when working in a team. Deciding on appropriate action is not straightforward – attending a course on communication skills may or may not help. A situated approach, such as working towards a degree of 'peace and stability' at work may be more beneficial. Individual efforts in this direction are likely to be subject to organisational constraints and 'mindset' but mentoring may offer one opportunity. So, instead of talking about communication skills per se, mentor and mentee will discuss the value of reflection, of drawing breath, of standing back and viewing a situation afresh (Mezirow, 1994). Hence a difficulty with problem solving may be ameliorated by exploration of some other part of the rich landscape that initially seems far removed. In this way, understanding of oneself as a learner, and work as a place to learn, is deepened; or, in other words, a complexity-informed perspective is recognised, assimilated and acted upon. In this way complexity is tolerated, lived with and accepted as normal.

When complexity cannot be tolerated, an employee's learning in the corporate curriculum and mental health suffers. Then the employee may resort to any of three sorts of response. First, they may 'run faster' in the belief that doing more of what appears to work will resolve the situation. Garvey (1995a) decribes this as the 'time pressure culture' Here a person works long hours, becomes task oriented and often becomes stressed and ineffective. In such an environment mentoring has difficulty in surviving because neither mentor nor mentee feel that they have the time to participate in anything other than the immediate work in hand (Garvey, 1995a). Secondly, they may deflect from their own responsibility and attempt to get what they want from others through manipulation and playing political games. Thirdly, they may retreat from complexity in a major way and become cynical, alienated, tired, stressed, burnt out or ill.

■ Complexity in the Mentoring Role

The mentor's role, itself, is complex. Clutterbuck (1998) identifies the various ways in which mentors help mentees. These are organised along two dimensions to distinguish the mentor role as the coach, the counsellor, the networker, facilitator or the guardian (Figure 5.1). We have altered this framework by suggesting that rather than roles, a different perspective could be gained by examining the skills employed in mentoring activity. The first dimension in Clutterbuck's framework refers to the extent to which the mentor is directive or non-directive. We have adapted the second dimension to distinguish between work related or the personal needs of the mentor.

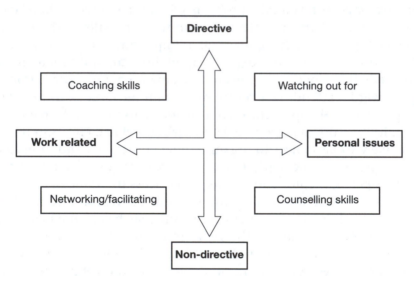

Figure 5.1 *The role of mentor*
Source: After Clutterbuck (1998)

This typology is useful in clarifying the various ways in which mentoring is understood. The four mentoring approaches, as broad descriptions, exist in complex organisations and contribute to mentor development. In the spirit of this discussion, we would like to extend Clutterbuck's framework by adding a third dimension, orthogonal to the first two – the dimension of complexity.

Then, each of the four approaches may be more or less complex, depending upon the psychological make-up of the mentee and mentor, the nature of their relationship and on the complexity of the organisation.

Each role then has the potential to be in a state of bounded instability. When the framework is extended in this way, three aspects of mentoring in a complex organisation can be identified. First, helping another person tolerate complexity requires certain personal qualities. It is important, for instance, for the mentor to be tolerant, patient and generous towards the mentee. As discussed above, traditionally mentoring has been seen as an activity in which 'ends' are more important than 'means'. In a complex organisation, the emphasis on 'ends' remains but deciding on the 'means' is itself far from straightforward. If a mentee doggedly persists with a 'run faster' strategy when it is clearly becoming counterproductive, the mentor's contribution to changing this will depend upon his or her ability to help the mentee hold on to all the elements and aspects of the situation – organisational, interpersonal and intrapersonal – before greater understanding can lead to a new approach. This is when mentoring requires persistence and resilience.

Secondly, the content of mentoring sessions will allow for the mentee to appreciate the complexity of their situation. There will be value in looking in detail at specific incidents or events and exploring the mentee's experience of these. The seven elements of the corporate curriculum provide a useful framework for an employee to examine their experience of being a learner at work.

Learning lessons from experiences of being knowledge productive is itself complex. Nonaka (1996) has observed that the creation of new knowledge 'depends on tapping the tacit and often highly subjective insights, intuitions, and hunches of individual employees and making those insights available for testing and use by the company as a whole' (p. 19). The mentor is in advantageous position, part in the shadow, part in the light, to link individual achievements and organisational goals.

Thirdly, mentoring in complex organisations is likely to amplify the diversity of mentoring. This is generally recognised in Clutterbuck's typology but with less emphasis on the mentee's experience and the diversity of mentoring any one mentee may seek. In complex organisations, the mentee will value the mentor who helps them tolerate the complexity. This will include, for both parties, a high degree of self understanding and a recognition of the importance of restoring oneself, so that tolerating as 'sustaining' does not give way to tolerating as merely 'putting up with'. To be restored is to achieve a measure of the necessary stability in one's position at work (despite the complexity all around), to appreciate those talents and qualities that are exchanged for employment, and to renew one's personal commitment and 'sense of identity with the enterprise and its mission' (Nonaka, 1996). In this sense, the mentoring relationship is a core relationship for the mentee in the organisation.

Conclusion

We have highlighted that rather than the mentor helping the mentee do the job in hand, the role is to help the mentee ask – what is the job in a complex environment? – a central question in a developing knowledge productive organisation. However, if the role were only that, the mentee would sooner or later not have a job to do! The task is also to discover what the mentee needs to do a job that is ever changing and subject to multiple influences in unpredictable ways. It is to explore the mentee's need to be true to themselves and to thrive in a state of bounded instability – a state, we have argued, in which organisations will increasingly find themselves in the future.

There is a challenge here for all people in the work place. Mentoring, located within a rich landscape of a corporate curriculum, has the potential to help people tolerate the increasing complexity of their lives. However, mentoring, being complex, is not always readily accepted or understood. It is often simplified (Garvey, 1995b) and thus its potential remains untapped. Therefore we suspect that were a connoisseur of wine to discuss 'mentoring and the appreciation of complex wine', their argument would have parallels with what we have sketched above. The connoisseur of wine may prefer the term 'fine', rather than 'complex', and they may describe the challenge of mentoring as the avoidance of yet one more coarsened and oversimplified palate.

References

Antal, A. (1996) Odysseus legacy to management development: mentoring. *European Management Journal* 114: 448–54.

Barrett, F.J. (1998) Managing and improvising: lessons from jazz. *Career Development International* 3 (7): 283–86.

Bernstein, B. (1971) On the classification and framing of educational knowledge. In M.D.F Young (ed.) *Knowledge and Control: New Directions for the Sociology of Education*. London: Open University/Collier-Macmillan.

Bettis, R.A. and Prahalad, C.K. (1995) The dominant logic: retrospective and extension. *Strategic Management Journal* 16: 5–14.

Bolles, R.N. (1988) What colour is your parachute? In M.S. Gladstone (ed.) *Mentoring: A Strategy for Learning in a Rapidly Changing Society*. Quebec: Research Document CEGEP, John Abbott College.

Broad, M.L. and Newstrom, J.W. (1992) *Transfer of Training. Action-Packed Strategies to Ensure High Pay Off from Training Investments*. Reading, MA: Addison-Wesley.

Carden, A.D. (1990) Mentoring and adult career development: the evolution of a theory. *Counselling Psychologist* 18: 275–99.

Caruso, R.E. (1996) Who does mentoring? Paper presented at the 3rd European Mentoring Conference, London.

Clawson, J.G. (1996) Mentoring in the information age. *Leadership and Organisation Development Journal* 173: 6–15.

Clutterbuck, D. (1998) *Learning Alliances: Tapping into Talent*. London: Institute of Personnel Development.

Collin, A.D. (1979) Notes on some typologies of managerial development and the role of mentor in the process of adaptation of the individual to the organisation. *Personnel Review* 84: 10–12.

Drucker, P.F. (1992) *Managing in a Time of Great Change*. Oxford: Butterworth-Heinemann.

Egan, G. (1993) The shadow side. *Management Today Se*ptember: 33–38.

Garvey, B. (1994) Mentoring, the heart of the vision. In *Opleiders in Organisaties, Capita Selecta, Mentoring en coaching*. Amstelveen, the Netherlands: Kluwer Bedrijfswetenschapen.

Garvey, B. (1995a) Healthy signs for mentoring. *Education and Training* 375: 12–19.

Garvey, B. (1995b) Let the actions match the words. In D. Clutterbuck and D. Megginson (eds.) *Mentoring in Action*. London: Kogan Page.

Garvey, B. (1999) Mentoring and the changing paradigm. *Journal of Mentoring and Tutoring* 7(1): 41–54.

Gladstone, M.S. (1988) *Mentoring: A Strategy for Learning in a Rapidly Changing Society*. Quebec: Research Document CEGEP, John Abbott College.

Hamel, G. and Prahalad, C.K. (1989) Strategic intent. *Harvard Business Review* May/July: 1–14.

Hamel, G. and Prahalad, C.K. (1991) Corporate imagination and expeditionary marketing. *Harvard Business Review* July/August.

Jarvis, P. (1992) Paradoxes of Learning – on Becoming an Individual in Society. *Higher Education Series*. San Francisco, CA: Jossey-Bass.

Kessels, J.W.M. (1996) Knowledge productivity and the corporate curriculum. In *Knowledge Management: Organization, Competence and Methodology*, proceedings of the Fourth International ISMICK symposium, 21–22 October, Rotterdam.

Lave, J. and Wenger, E. (1991) *Situated Learning: Legitimate, Peripheral Participation*. Cambridge: Cambridge University Press.

Mezirow, J. (1994) Understanding transformation theory. *Adult Education Theory* 444: 222–31.

Nonaka, I. (1996) The knowledge-creating company. In K. Starke (ed.) *How Organisations Learn*. London: International Thompson Business Press.

Pedler, M., Burgoyne, J. and Boydel, T. (1991) *The Learning Company. A Strategy for Sustainable Development*. London: McGraw-Hill.

Rigsby, J.T., Siegal, P.H. and Spiceland, J.D. (1998) Mentoring among management advisory services professionals: an adaptive mechanism to cope with rapid corporate change. *Managerial Auditing Journal* 132: 107–16.

Senge, P.M. (1992) *The Fifth Discipline*. Chatham: Century Business.

Stacey, R.D. (1995) The science of complexity: an alternative perspective for strategic change processes. *Strategic Management Journal* 16: 477–95.

Vygotsky, L.S. (1978) In M. Cole *et al.* (eds.) *Mind in Society: The Development of Higher Psychological Processes*. Cambridge, MA: Harvard University Press.

Vygotsky, L.S. (1981) The genesis of higher mental functions. In J. Wertsch (ed.) *The Concept of Activity in Soviet Psychology*. New York: Armonk.

Waldrop, M.M. (1992) *Complexity: The Emerging Science at the Edge of Order and Chaos*. London: Viking.

6

Principals and Headteachers as Chief Executives

Hugh Busher

The book in which this chapter was originally published had its origins in work under-taken for the 1995 National Conference of the British Educational Management and Administration Society (BEMAS – now BELMAS: The British Educational Leadership, Management and Administration Society). The theme of the conference in that year was Leaders and Leadership and, in preparation for the event, nine individual conversations on leaders and leadership took place between the heads of a variety of different kinds of educational institutions and a researcher from higher education. These conversations were used as the basis for papers, innovative sessions during the conference and for the book. This chapter draws on data generated during the nine conversations.

For completion, the names of the headteachers and principals, together with the type of institution they were leading at the time, are listed here:

Roy Blatchford	*secondary*
Keith Bovair	*special*
Mick Brown	*further education*
Bernard Clarke	*secondary*
Kenneth Edwards	*higher education*
Mary Gray	*primary*
Helen Hyde	*secondary*
Mary Marsh	*secondary*
Rosemary Whinn-Sladden	*primary*

Source: Ribbins, P. (ed.) (1997) *Leaders and Leadership in the School, the College and the University*. London: Cassell. Edited version.

Introduction

Hughes (1973) first suggested that headteachers' (principals') roles could be conceptualized as both leading professional and chief executive. The latter role was given greater prominence by changes in society and by legislation in the 1980s in the UK. The role of leading professional was conceptualized collegially, mainly concerned with curriculum matters and pastoral care, although also responsible for providing an effective administrative framework within which teachers could work with considerable autonomy in the classroom. The role of chief executive is seen more in administrative terms, being concerned with managing a school as an organization, directing, planning and co-ordinating its resources and activities in a coherent manner.

The moves to local autonomy for schools which occurred in the UK and elsewhere during the 1980s and 1990s have, perhaps, enhanced this shift in the principal's role, putting greater emphasis on the chief executive aspects than formerly. Some of the educational leaders interviewed for this project describe themselves as chief executives (Kenneth Edwards) or managing directors (Mary Gray). Similarly, Keith Bovair saw himself as a 'co-ordinator of other people's work'. Similar statements can be found in other texts. Valerie Bragg, for example, in Ribbins and Marland (1994), characterizes herself as 'chief executive'. Evetts (1994), in her study of headteachers in the Midlands in the UK, commented on the extent to which secondary school principals had become corporate managers. Alongside the greater autonomy given to schools since 1988 has been imposed the greater accountability of headteachers since 1986 in England and Wales to restructured and greatly empowered school governing bodies (Ribbins, 1989). This accountability has been tightened by regular OFSTED inspections since 1992.

The emergence of the school principal as a chief executive raises questions about the extent to which they remain school leaders, whether leading professionals or corporate bosses. The distinction between the functions of leading and managing is an important one conceptually even if, as Bryman (1992) points out, it is difficult to sustain the distinction in practice when observing people at work. Leaders have an important function in influencing events (Hunt, 1991), whether using their authority of office or the informal micro-political processes (Blase and Blase, 1995) that are embedded in the interpersonal dynamics of organizations. Bolman and Deal (1994) suggest that this influence occurs through the creation of shared meaning for the people with whom a leader works. Manipulating the symbols of an organization to create a coherent vision of purpose for a school, then, may be central to the work of leaders. How they manipulate these symbols gives rise to the styles of leadership people use, of which there have been numerous attempted categorizations (e.g. Kakabadse and Parker, 1984; Handy, 1985; Heller, 1985), some of which offer illuminating descriptions rather than critical analytical frameworks.

There have also been attempts to dichotomize the approaches to leadership which place central emphasis on vision and symbols from those which focus on leaders directing and gaining compliance from their followers, one form being categorized as transformational leadership, the other as transactional leadership (e.g. Bass, 1985; Bryman, 1992). Gronn (1995) amongst others doubts the substantive quality of this distinction, pointing out that it mirrors the more global differences between leadership (creating visions) and management. The latter can be described as a succession of transactional relationships with other people to direct, plan, co-ordinate, and evaluate their activities. In this framework, administration is the co-ordinating function of management. In practice, too, it is hard to find examples of the distinctions which such casuistry invents. Whether defined as leading professionals or chief executives, school principals have to manipulate symbols to help give schools an identity and coherence, and have to engage in managerial/administrative activity to co-ordinate a school's functioning. What tends most obviously to distinguish the one role from the other are the symbols manipulated and, in particular, the language which is used to help people frame meanings for their actions. Within this language are embedded values which convey messages about the purposes of an organization, how actions within in it are to be construed and how people are to be perceived.

In focusing on leaders and leadership, as Gronn (1995) points out, the role of followers is revealed. Leaders manipulate organizational symbols not only to give meaning to their own work but also to help the other people, with whom they work, to give meaning to their engagements with an organization. In the context of a school these other people include teaching and non-teaching staff, pupils (students), parents, and perhaps school governors, too, although the last group could be conceived of as the intended vision givers in the context of locally managed schools with powerful governing bodies. However, followers have to give willing credence to the activities of a leader if a leader's functioning is not to decline into mere headship. Gibb (1974) perceives the latter as holding titular office without either having the power to act effectively or knowing how to use the power available to act effectively.

A micro-political perspective provides an antidote to the charismatic view of leadership that agency is all important. It helps to avoid the unbalanced perception that somehow followers' roles are of less value than those of leaders in the effective functioning of a school, showing how a leader's influence is institutionaly located, rather than inherent in their personality, and dependent on their interpersonal skills in bargaining and negotiation with other people over resources. Not surprisingly, then, Huckman and Hill (1994) found that their headteachers chose to work within staff preference for the distribution of salary increments rather than implement performance related pay, the latter being perceived as undermining teacher professionality and collegiality, whatever its claimed merits as a mechanism for distributing scarce resources to more effective practitioners.

A micro-political perspective also disabuses the managerial view of leadership that implementing structures which are said to be effective will necessarily create effective institutions. On the other hand it does not negate the need for schools to create effective organizational structures which allow the creative interplay of personalities, interests and beliefs. It is these last which Gronn (1986) suggested lay at the heart of leading and managing schools. However, it does suggest that processes of school improvement involve more than simply imposing on schools a blueprint derived from factors known to be associated with effective schools. Leaders have a key role in building coalitions of staff who can help to take the work of a school forward. To do this leaders not only have to negotiate transactionally but also to create a vision inspirationally that will help to define the quality and purposes of interpersonal relationships within a school.

This intertwining of transactional and inspirational leader processes to influence individuals and groups of people in organizations suggests that the leadership and management given by school principals should be considered as two inter-related functions. As chief executives, principals not only have to co-ordinate the work of teachers and others for whom they are accountable but they also have to play a facilitating role in inspiring a school's personnel, whether staff or pupils, to meet the demands which they face from the external environment.

The core qualities and abilities of principals as school leaders are variously defined in the literature. Charismatic explanations emphasize the importance of vision and values. For example, Bolman and Deal (1991) thought that although leaders needed to have flexible strategies to cope with changing environments, they also had to develop and sustain core values and beliefs which, Bennis and Nannus (1985) argued, then needed to be translated, through effective communications, into clear meanings for followers. These meanings, they suggested, came from manipulating symbols, that is, managing the culture of an organization (Bolman and Deal, 1994; Gronn, 1995) to help it meet the challenges of its environment.

Managing symbols in a consistent manner creates trust in leaders amongst their followers. However, if leaders try to change the culture of a school by using symbols from a different culture, even when that culture is the dominant socio-political perspective, such as the attempted imposition of a market culture on schools in the UK in the late 1980s and 1990s, they are likely to arouse suspicion and hostility amongst followers who hold different sets of values. Locke (1992) and Busher and Saran (1995) perceived trust as the key to effective leadership and management in schools, arguing that leaders and followers had to develop mutual trust through working together collegially. Leaders develop and indicate their trust of colleagues through consulting with them and delegating responsibility to them whenever possible. The sustaining of a vision helps a team to believe it has a firm sense of purpose. It is this approach to leadership which some writers have called transformational leadership.

Consistency of managing symbols and beliefs, however, may not be sufficient to ensure effective leadership. Indeed it may lead to rigidity in meeting
the challenges of the environment and in taking account of the social needs
of leaders' colleagues, an important facet of leadership according to Hoyle
(1986) when negotiating the micro-political process in organizations.
Bolman and Deal (1991) circumvent this problem by arguing the need for
leaders to be flexible in developing strategies to meet the challenges of their
tasks while sustaining core beliefs. In a rational – technical model this distinction would appear as that between aims, the core beliefs and objectives.
Such flexibility allows leaders to take account of other people's interests and
concerns when meeting the changes in the environment so encouraging
those people to feel part of a team.

A bureaucratic view of the key qualities of the effective principal may well
look somewhat different. Hodgkinson (1991), for example, claimed principals needed to have knowledge of the task facing them, knowledge of the
situation in which a task was being undertaken, knowledge of the people
who were or might be engaged in particular tasks and situations, and knowledge of themselves. The last included the capacity to evaluate critically their
own actions. There is not enough space here to debate the quality of that
knowledge or whether it includes knowledge through experience as well as
knowledge through study and reflection.

A more detailed version of this bureaucratic paradigm emerged in the UK
in 1995 when central government, through various quangos, specified the
skills and abilities which heads (principals) needed to acquire. To embed this
definition within the education system, the Teacher Training Agency (TTA)
used it as the basis on which to decide whether or not to license some people
and institutions to be providers of training for newly appointed headteachers. Where a provider became so registered, headteachers attending relevant
training courses with it had their costs reimbursed by the TTA up to £2,500.
Headteachers on at least one such training course found that the list of skills
and abilities created a useful and all embracing structural framework within
which to consider their practices as school leaders and managers.

The rest of this chapter pursues the bureaucratic paradigm, exploring the
views of nine leaders of educational institutions on their roles as chief executives. Of the leaders, four were female and five were male; four came from
secondary schools, two from primary schools, and one each from special
schools, higher education, and further education. Seven of the nine institutions represented come from an area south of the river Trent and east of the
river Severn. With such an eclectic sample, it would be foolish to attempt
even to develop grounded theory, let alone derive generalizations. It will be
sufficient to report participants' views grouped according to the following
four questions:

1 What are their educational and leadership values?
2 What is their leadership style?
3 How do they manage people and resources?
4 How do they understand their accountability?

What are their Educational and Leadership Values?

Many of the principals interviewed thought that values were at the heart of their leadership. As Blatchford puts it 'The importance of values permeate everything you do as senior managers'. If these values were not in place then a school would lack a sense of purpose and people in it would not know what they were trying to achieve. As Mary Marsh explained: 'I kept realizing that until we'd had this debate about the aims and values of the school we really were in a vacuum.'

However, having a mission was not just parroting fine-sounding statements but enacting those values through the work undertaken in schools and colleges. In this way principals were able to make effective and visible their vision for their institution. Thus, for Keith Bovair 'Enacting the headteacher's vision through projects helps the students and staff begin to share that vision'.

The nine principals interviewed showed some degree of commonality over what that vision might be, surprisingly, given the diversity of their institutions. Several considered it important to have high expectations of their students and to expect the students to have high expectations for themselves: 'I certainly have a vision for raising children's self-expectations – my core vision if you like' (Blatchford). Others stressed the need to help students have such expectations and, in doing so, principals emphasized the importance of 'Creating a climate in which young people and adults can do their best' (Clarke). In this context, Mary Gray talked about 'creating the best working atmosphere I can for the children and offering them values where they will appreciate other people [and] recognize the contributions they can make both within the school . . . [and] within the community'.

Part of that vision was raising teachers' expectations of what children could achieve, according to Roy Blatchford: 'a teacher should be about widening those horizons for young people . . . clearly any vision for a school is about raising achievement.' This focus on student achievement manifested itself in the commitment to students which leaders claimed for themselves and for their staff. 'I have been impressed with the commitment of so many of the teaching staff, despite the pressures, to doing a good job for their students' (Edwards).

This commitment seemed to be based more on moral grounds of responsibility than on the commercial concerns of attracting large numbers of students, though the latter was not absent. Ken Edwards pointed out that without students he and his colleagues would be out of business. However, his main concern was for his accountability to students. He felt that 'They deserve the best that we can give them' and recalled, by way of a probable explanation for why he now held this view, how much value he had been given as a student.

Part of this commitment was to students' personal development as well as to their academic performance. Not surprisingly this showed up most clearly in the special school:

> [It is] important to have a depth of understanding of the dynamics of
> individuals when dealing with children with emotional difficulties because you
> need to handle the situation, the other people around the child, as well as the
> students themselves. (Bovair)

Facilitating such development involved creating an appropriate climate in a school, returning once again to the theme of what principals held as their core values. Rosemary Whinn-Sladden thought 'fairness is a key value to students and staff. I don't like having children picked on by teachers. If a child is having problems, teachers need to solve the problem not go on scolding the child.' While Bernard Clarke thought 'schools should be full of second chances for people because students don't usually get it right first time'.

The concern which principals showed for students as individuals found an echo in their attitudes to staff, where they emphasized the importance of caring for individuals, accepting differences of opinion but respecting views. In this person-centred culture of leadership, that strongly resembles the descriptions of transformational leadership considered earlier, several principals commented on their enjoyment at seeing others develop. As Mary Gray puts it: 'Personally I enjoy seeing people blossom. The headteacher is a facilitator of opportunities for both staff and students'.

Within this paradigm, staff development was seen to be for all staff, and went beyond a crude instrumentality of human resources management of just trying to fit staff to the purposes of an institution:

> the importance of Investors in People as a means of promoting staff
> development – it helps all staff, teaching and non-teaching . . . Staff
> development must not only emphasize promotion because this can be crushing
> on those staff who stay in the classroom. (Whinn-Sladden)

The means of fostering this support for staff lay in the development of groups of people working in teams and sharing purposes and values. Such teams had a tough dynamic rather than a woolly cosiness in private. As Roy Blatchford explained 'a team is more than a group of people: team members are publicly loyal to each other, however much they argue in private'. The development of such teams was of considerable importance to many of the nine principals interviewed, since as Bernard Clarke noted: 'It seems to me as a headteacher you can't do much, you can only achieve with the people you have around you, working with you.' Mary Gray also felt it necessary to 'promote collegiality among staff – giving people confidence by praise, by asking them to share ideas with other people' as a means of helping staff to improve their performances. Improving the quality of staff performance was seen as a crucial means of improving the quality of the teaching and learning experiences offered to students.

For some of the principals, delegation of responsibility was one of the key processes for promoting this improvement. As such 'It is important to be hands-off and to trust people. People are paid salaries for their responsibilities. People respond well to delegation' (Blatchford). To achieve this, however, principals needed to become adept in the micro-political processes of schools, 'as a headteacher you've got to be out there wheeling and dealing, making people feel that what they're involved with is worthwhile and is of value' (Bovair). This entailed being skilled in listening as well as talking, according to Helen Hyde, and adroit at diplomacy, 'learning to walk on cracked eggs', as Rosemary Whinn-Sladden put it.

Several principals expressed joy in the work they did. They liked working with other people to make things happen, although this was not an easy row to hoe. Several principals commented on the need for determination if they were to succeed in bringing about change: 'headteachers need to be brave to carry through what they believe to be worthwhile' (Whinn-Sladden). Bennis and Nannus (1985) also noted the need for leaders to be self-confident if they were to be successful. The enthusiasm which several principals claimed for their approach to their job was, perhaps, infectious to other staff. Mary Gray thought it important to act as you would like others to act. Roy Blatchford emphasized 'the importance of a leader leading by example by getting involved with a wide range of school activities'.

What is their Leadership Style?

The preceding section raises questions on the style of leadership interviewees espouse. There is no evidence available of what styles they actually used in different situations since members of their role sets were not interviewed. This is a key question for the culture and management of institutions since the impact of leaders on their institutions is well known. The influence of a leader entails 'a significant effect on an individual or group's well-being, interests, policies or behaviour and . . . is usually thought of as legitimate by those subjected to it' (Gronn, 1995, p. 3). As Mary Gray explained 'the headteacher is head of everything, not just the teachers . . . and sets the right atmosphere'.

The style of leadership which all the principals interviewed claimed to espouse was what might be described loosely as consultative or facilitative leadership, broadly meeting the definitions of transformational leadership discussed earlier in this chapter. Such a style was far removed from an abdication of leadership. 'Basically I am a managing director and the curriculum leader who identifies [a problem/opportunity] and delegates [responsibility for it]' (Gray). As Clarke explained, 'It is important to involve people in decision-making but part of your judgement as leader is knowing who to involve on which occasions. Not everybody wants to be involved in all decisions – they haven't time.'

Mary Gray perceived her style as benevolent and assertive. It involved putting strategies in place to achieve collegiality, e.g. staff meetings. Keith Bovair offered a similar view of being a supportive but ultimately directive co-ordinator of other people's work in which 'I don't try to manipulate or coerce staff, but I try to give them experiences which will carry them along'. To such principals, the hallmark of their styles was to 'Delegate responsibility . . . Give [staff] autonomy, with departments controlling their own budgets and curriculum decisions within the framework of the philosophy of the school' (Hyde). But it was the principals who retained the key levers of power and developed the framework of philosophy and the structures of organizational practice in collaboration with their senior management teams (Hyde). Ken Edwards described this as 'creating a managerial network in a series of layers all of which can pick up information and ideas and spread ideas and produce feedback'.

The collegiality these principals established was, at best, bounded ('partial collegiality', as Helen Hyde described it). They developed it by trying to motivate and support people, staff as well as students (Blatchford; Hyde), as well as by delegating responsibility. Mary Gray said an important aspect of this process was 'giving people confidence by praise, by asking them to share ideas with other people'. Finally, Keith Bovair pointed to 'the importance of teamwork, collaboration by staff on projects, but also between staff and students in business enterprize, such as running a market stall'.

Another important aspect was trying to ensure both that people were fairly treated and that they felt themselves to be so. This means, for Clarke, that 'The school's code of conduct for students and staff is reviewed each year. It sets out people's rights and responsibilities. . . Teachers need to treat each other and students with respect.' And for Marsh: 'Openness and trust are key managerial values, but they need working at each day, because people only need to feel badly handled once, or insufficiently consulted, for the headteacher to lose their trust.' A similar view led Helen Hyde, among others, to suggest that principals needed to be good listeners as well as enthusiastic and tenacious implementers of actions.

The workload of many of these principals was phenomenal (Whinn-Sladden), not only because of the amount of teaching which a few of them continued to do, but because of what was involved in managing a school. One principal talked about the necessity of breakfast meetings with her caretakers, this being the only time during the day when she and they could meet. Such hours of work are not uncommon according to the School Teachers' Review Body Report (1995). It is not known how their staffs perceived such examples of dedicated professionalism, nor the extent to which hardworking principals expected the same level of dedication from their staff and what impact this had on the cultures of the institutions.

Despite the emphasis on collegial styles of working, democracy did not seem to be even on the agenda, except as a rhetoric for indicating that people with interests in situations would be consulted. This was most clearly expressed by Bernard Clarke who said

> I want to say I'm all the nice words like democrat, benign and so on. I suppose I would aim towards those characteristics . . . [because] as a headteacher you can't do much, you can only achieve with the people you have around you . . . but people don't want to be involved in every decision. They haven't got time . . . and they may not be particularly interested.

Helen Hyde thought that there were some decisions which if she as principal did not make them would never be made. She claimed one of her junior staff had described her as a benevolent dictator, not an epithet of which she was particularly proud.

Whatever might be their appreciation of the merits of collegial styles of managing institutions, the nature of the principals' institutional structures ensured that they could never be completely democratic. Apart from the legal requirements on them to be accountable for the performances of the people in their institutions, as Ken Edwards, principal of the largest institution included in the interviews, pointed out 'with a responsibility for an organization which has £100 million turnover and 2500 employees . . . you can't really regard yourself as anything but a chief executive'.

The appeal, then, for leaders to be democratic in hierarchical organizations, such as that made by Davies (1995), perhaps has to be seen in terms not of its actual implementation but in terms of the manipulation of a powerful symbol from Western societies which associates involvement in decision-making, at least through consultation, with part ownership of the process and empowerment of those consulted. Consultation does not, however, even guarantee the influence of those consulted over the outcomes of decision-making, although there is evidence that where headteachers persistently use consultation in an insincere manner teachers quickly become aware of the sham (Busher and Saran, 1992). It may be this disjunction between the rhetoric and practice of consultation that in part leads to the suggestion of Sinclair (1995) that participative approaches to management can lead to lower employee satisfaction and consequently the need for teams to have leaders to be effective. Hargreaves (1990) describes such insincere uses of consultation as contrived collegiality.

■ How do they Manage People and Resources?

In their interviews principals acknowledged the administrative and financial loads which they carried, particularly since the 1988 Education Reform Act. As Sue Benton, quoted in a related study, has acknowledged, she had found this aspect of her work 'quite difficult at first' (Ribbins and Marland, 1994). As she explained: 'I did not come into headship expecting to carry out the detailed financial, staffing, marketing and other administrative responsibilities I am now expected to exercise'. Rosemary Whinn-Sladden thought the range of managerial responsibilities she had to undertake took her away from the curriculum, to the detriment of education. Similarly, Brian Sherratt, at the time head of the largest school in the UK, suggests that some headteachers preferred to retreat into their administrative work because achieving a worthwhile curriculum was very difficult in the UK in the mid-1990s, but he thought this to be the road to isolation for headteachers from their staff (quoted in Ribbins and Marland, 1994).

In talking about their management of educational institutions, principals gave much greater emphasis to and detailed comments on the management of people than on the management of physical and financial resources. This reflects, perhaps, the recognition in education service industries of the centrality of people and their relationship to the effective provision of those services. It is reflected in the balance of material in this section.

In reflecting on the management of people, many principals made reference to how this grew from and was informed by the culture of a school, an aspect discussed earlier in this chapter under the educational and managerial values of leaders. Several principals commented on the need to manage themselves as one of those people. Discussion of this aspect has been included in the section on principals' leadership styles since style in part includes how people manage themselves in relation to other people and to the tasks which they face.

Several principals suggested or implied that there were or ought to be commonalties between the way in which staff were managed and the way in which other people – students and parents, not least – were managed. Such common aspects would be reflected in how people were treated as individuals as an enactment of a school's culture; how the interactions of gender and status were handled; how conflict was handled; how decisions were taken and implemented; how staff development was fostered; effective networking with parents, governors and the local community. These were set in the context of how principals managed the changes in the socio-political environment of education and the delegation of funding to their institutions.

Gender, status and respect for individuals

Principals tended to be concerned to encourage people 'to develop themselves as fully as possible, to learn for life and to be different' (Hyde). This required principals 'to trust staff and to encourage people to take risks and challenges' (Marsh). To 'promote that sense of challenge several principals talked about trying to delegate decision-making to staff whenever possible or explaining decisions openly' (Marsh). It led Rosemary Whinn-Sladden to consider 'fairness . . . a key value to managing staff and children and the non-teaching staff'.

Principals claimed that they demonstrated respect for people through 'a deep commitment to equal opportunities . . . that we are all in this together' (Clarke) which meant that 'Non-teaching staff must be considered equal with other staff, e.g. all staff come to staff meetings and all are listened to if they wish to contribute' (Whinn-Sladden). It also meant that 'equal opportunities should permeate everything you do, even if there is no explicit policy' (Blatchford) and this should be revealed through the curriculum, too. For example, there should be 'a concern to give girls equal opportunities especially in sciences' (Hyde).

How conflict was handled

Many of the principals interviewed claimed to want to diffuse tension whenever possible, although this did not inhibit them from taking tough action when necessary.

> The changes in the Arts Faculty in the end were forced through. The staff didn't want to do any of this but I said 'look you either come up with some ideas and we discuss them or I make the decision, but the status quo is not an option'. (Edwards)

Changes in funding meant that the numbers of staff had to be reduced and the faculty restructured into a more effective shape.

Mary Gray felt good relations amongst staff were maintained by sustaining the self-esteem of staff, praising them when they did good work, encouraging them to take as much responsibility as they could (Hyde), and supporting staff when they faced problems (Whinn-Sladden). In addition the maintenance of agreed institutional values (Marsh), policies and practices (Whinn-Sladden; Marsh) were perceived as ways of preventing a build-up of tension, as was taking action quickly, if quietly, when things went wrong (Clarke; Gray). Finding out what people wanted from situations (Hyde) also helped, as did reducing people's anxiety (Hyde) about what might happen, sometimes by helping people to face situations which were inevitable (Clarke; Edwards).

This approach required principals to listen to what staff were saying to them: 'being aware of what is going on in every classroom and making time to talk with the teachers about it' (Whinn-Sladden). This could happen through formal processes of appraisal, through asking questions when there seemed to be a sense of unease amongst staff (Marsh), as well as through listening to grumbles. Keith Bovair thought that staff needed 'to sound-off occasionally, to have the opportunity to complain and grumble in a staff meeting. Then they are happy that the headteacher has listened.' Several principals emphasized that the way to handle conflict when it occurred was to be open with the protagonists but to see them quietly, away from a public arena: 'speaking with staff who are in conflict with you quietly and directly, explain that you can understand them but for the good of the school things have to be otherwise' (Gray). They also thought it important to reduce collateral damage from conflicts by being open about decisions. This reduced the degree of speculation amongst staff about what had been decided and the reasons for a decision. In turn this reduced the tendency for coalitions to form to support one or both camps in a conflict (Gray).

In routine cases of conflict, staff under-performance, for example, it was thought to be more effective to work through existing staff structures, within the framework of existing policy, than for a principal to intervene directly (Clarke; Edwards).

How decisions were taken and implemented

Although several principals perceived themselves as chief executives who had to take decisions and make judgements (Bovair), they also acknowledged that they had to have 'a well-oiled machine for running a school' (Blatchford). Ken Edwards thought it necessary to use 'a managerial network in a series of layers all of which can pick up information and ideas and spread ideas and produce feedback'. He believed the culture of universities precluded authoritarian leadership, a view which was echoed for schools by Brian Sherratt (Ribbins and Marland, 1994).

Several of the nine principals emphasized the importance of a collaborative approach to decision-making, pointing out that consultation (Clarke; Bovair; Hyde) and working alongside other people (Whinn-Sladden) were key means of developing teams of people who could take decisions in particular aspects of an institution's management: 'As a headteacher you can't do much on your own. You can only achieve things with people working around you' (Clarke). On the other hand 'delegating responsibility is difficult because you have to accept that staff will do the best they can although that may not be how you would have done it' (Gray), and there was a risk that action would not be taken or not be taken in time. To lessen the risks Mary Gray set clear datelines for tasks and offered support to those people who were struggling with them.

How staff development was fostered

Helen Hyde, among other principals, thought her most important job was to look after staff. Keith Bovair thought his school should apply its philosophy of empowering people consistently, equally to staff and to students. But other principals acknowledged the importance of appointing the right people in the first place (Blatchford; Whinn-Sladden) and then keeping in touch with their development (Edwards; Blatchford).

Effective staff development required principals to help people make the best use of the strengths they had at whatever point in their careers they found themselves (Bovair), although this sometimes meant helping them to face up to unpalatable choices (Edwards). Where staff development focused on preparing people for promotion, principals suggested a range of possibilities: 'work shadowing, working alongside more senior staff' (Hyde); 'being involved in conversations about decision-making particularly when there is conflict' (Clarke).

Delegation was also an important means of helping competent staff to develop because it gave them a chance to meet a school's needs creatively (Clarke). For senior staff it gave them a real opportunity to work with and support other staff. For heads of department and non-promoted teachers it gave them the opportunity to focus on particular tasks and take decisions in particular areas which were their delegated responsibilities (Hyde).

To promote staff development Roy Blatchford emphasized the importance of giving staff time when they needed it and of providing them with institutional support, though often that support would be to help them meet the school's needs (Whinn-Sladden) rather than, necessarily, their own idiosyncratic interests. Several principals thought training should be available for all staff, although there are problems in financing it for non-teaching staff in schools.

Effective networking with parents, governors and the local community

Principals placed considerable emphasis on the importance of helping parents and governors to share the values espoused by the schools. Helen Hyde described this as the need to talk excellence to parents. Rosemary Whinn-Sladden and Mary Gray stressed the importance of welcoming parents into schools and encouraging them to make a contribution to the pupils' education either by helping with the pedagogy or with the administration. She saw her school as part of a greater community and gave an example of parents helping the children plant trees to improve the environment. To recognize the help the parents gave, the school bought each a small plant. The importance of parental involvement to student educational development, particularly for younger pupils, is well attested. In turn this required principals to listen to what parents had to say about education (Bovair) and to allow them to influence the core values of a school (Hyde) developed by senior staff and governors (Bovair; Blatchford).

The benefits of collaboration with the civic community were seen to accrue to the students (Gray) who profited from good publicity. She also suggested that it reduced the level of vandalism to a school and the level of stress experienced by a headteacher. Schools gained positively from having greater access to resources to support the curriculum (Bovair) either from parents or from the local business community. Whinn-Sladden comments that 'We have a thriving education–business partnership which brings support and resources into the school. We are hoping to persuade the TEC to fund our use of GNVQs to develop non-teaching staff training.'

Roy Blatchford, amongst others, pointed out the value of a school having good professional links with other educational institutions to resolve problems and offer opportunities to students and also, perhaps, to staff. Rosemary Whinn-Sladden was rather less complimentary about her local professional networks of headteachers! Helen Hyde said that these networks offered her school considerable support, a view borne out by all the headteachers in a recent study of school networks by Busher and Hodgkinson (1996) in the midlands of the UK.

Managing resources in the changed socio-political environment of education

How senior staff managed the other people involved with their organizations was circumscribed by their administrative and financial responsibilities. These have been greatly increased in the UK in schools since the passing of the Education Reform Act (1988). Several principals commented on the long hours they worked, as was discussed earlier in this chapter, and that they worked most if not every evening of the week. Keith Bovair talked about needing to have help with the budget from two deputy heads, as well as making a great deal of use of computers in administration. Helen Hyde noted that despite the involvement of a deputy head and a bursar to help her she still had to have some meetings at 8 a.m. (with the site supervisor) to avoid interrupting people's work. Mortimore and Mortimore with Thomas (1994) noted the emergence of bursars as commonplace in maintained schools since 1990, and the School Teachers' Review Body (1995) noted a 30 per cent increase in non-teaching staff between 1989 and 1994 at a time when the employment of full-time teaching staff increased at a rate less than that of pupils in schools (2 per cent). Qualitative data from the east midlands of the UK suggests that much of this increase has been focused on clerical duties and posts to cope with the management of finance and personnel now undertaken by schools but previously carried out in maintained schools by LEAs. This suggests that the delegation of funding to school organizations has taken resources away from the core purposes of schools, students and the curriculum, into administration, of necessity to meet schools' new and increased administrative and financial responsibilities.

Although the delegation of funding 'had increased teachers' workloads, especially the amount of paperwork. The latter prevents headteachers being involved with teaching and learning' (Whinn-Sladden), several principals saw an advantage in the management of staff in the delegation of funding to schools. Mary Gray thought that in sharing school budget implications with staff it helped them to realize the problems the school faced in ensuring there were adequate resources available to meet the needs of pupils (Bovair). Helen Hyde and Roy Blatchford perceived it as a vehicle for giving staff increased autonomy within a whole-school framework, a view echoed by Ken Edwards in a university. On the other hand 'cut-backs in resources provided by the LEA have made it difficult to put in place ideas which will maximize existing resources. No sooner have you developed these than they are overtaken by another round of cuts' (Bovair).

How do they Understand their Accountability?

Simkins (1992) offers four main models of accountability for teachers and schools, first a professional model in which a licensed person is granted autonomy to act within a socially legitimated code, and then three other forms which represent various types of control by some people over the actions of others. These are a managerial model in which control is exercized through bureaucratic structures and power derives from the authority of office of the most senior person in an organization; a political model in which power derives from election to office; and a market model in which power is derived from consumer choice.

It is useful for purposes of analysis to recognize that teachers are called to account in a variety of ways, but more useful if those categories can be clearly distinguished. The East Sussex Accountability Project (1979) produced a threefold typology of responsiveness by teachers to their environment which offers such clarity. They suggested that one form of accountability was genuine, i.e. people could be called to account for their actions within an hierarchical process. If a person failed to carry out their prescribed duties they could be coerced and, ultimately, deprived of office. As power is hierarchically located in this model, it does not matter whether power derives from political election/acclamation or from the authority vested in a senior position in a bureaucracy. In this view political and managerial accountability are two closely related versions of the same model. Examples of such accountability by some of the principals who were interviewed are discussed below.

A second form, answerability, poses rather more problems since the location of power is not bureaucratically connected to the actor. Therefore the means of exercising that power are indirect. Indeed, power could be said to have become transmuted to influence, i.e. actors are open to various sorts of pressure, but not to legitimate coercion. It might be said, for example, that teachers are answerable to parents. In this case principals can feel they are obliged to respond to parental views about a school, as Mary Marsh indicated she felt she did. Were a principal not to respond, the parents would have to acquire political power through, say, joining the school governing body or influencing people already on that body, before they would have the right to coerce the principal into doing what they wanted. In doing so, of course, parents would move into an hierarchical relationship with the principal, activating the genuine or bureaucratic model of accountability.

Without recourse to a model of genuine (bureaucratic) accountability, were the parents so minded, they could exert influence over the principal in various ways, for example, by threatening or actually withdrawing their children from the school. The notion of answerability, then, fits comfortably with Simkins' (1992) notion of market accountability but has the advantage of keeping the term 'accountability' for one particular (bureaucratic) model of relationship between a professional worker and the stakeholders in an organization.

This leaves the model of professional 'accountability', which can, perhaps best be described as responsibility. In this, people may be said to be answerable for what they do, or morally accountable for their actions, though it is difficult to see how any pressure can be brought to bear through this model on a person for the quality of their work, apart from through the moral suasion of colleagues and others and the internalized values of the actor. It is in this sense, perhaps, that both Rosemary Whinn-Sladden and Ken Edwards acknowledge their accountability to their students and the *people who are devoting their lives to this institution* (Edwards). Such professional responsibility easily encompasses Helen Hyde's view that she set herself high standards of performance because *'staff have to be able to trust and rely on me as a real leader to represent and to guide and look after them [and] . . . I must be the best role model I can for the [students]'.* This sense of professional responsibility includes a professional ethic of how a person ought to behave. In other professions such ethics have been enshrined – the word is used deliberately – in professional codes of practice. These allow a bureaucratic accountability ultimately to be imposed on those practitioners who fail to implement sufficiently rigorously the work values which they are supposed to have internalized during their induction into a profession.

Within this framework of three types of responsiveness by principals to the stakeholders in their educational institutions, Rosemary Whinn-Sladden suggests there is a bureaucratic relationship of accountability between principals and their governors: 'They have got to be involved in those [school] decisions and not just ratify something that I say . . . They have been known to give me a hard time over things, but that is fair because I give them a hard time over things and we work together.' Being accountable, as this suggests, also implies that the people with the greater power have responsibilities to those with the lesser. We begin to close on Salisbury's notions of the ideal relationship between the classes in mid-nineteenth-century England, where although the rich had privileges, they also had responsibilities to the poor, not least to ensure social chaos did not develop. In this vein some principals, such as Keith Bovair, recognized their accountability to the LEA, acknowledging that they still had to keep its officers informed. In return they looked for what support they could from the more slimly proportioned LEAs of the 1990s.

The emergence of parent charters and student charters (Edwards) can be viewed as an attempt to give answerability an edge of bureaucracy, i.e. to begin to move the relationship between students, parents and principals into a mode of accountability rather than answerability. In this context it is curious that Roy Blatchford does not perceive himself as accountable to, or at least through, the school inspectors who work for OFSTED, although he acknowledges they are an important part of the system. They clearly seem to be agents through which schools are held accountable to the state, i.e. bring about a genuine (bureaucratic) accountability of schools to some of those who wield power in the education system – central government. The current inspectoral system with its central state control shows, perhaps, the extent to which the power of the Secretary of State reaches out to the periphery of the education system despite the rhetoric and the reality of the devolution of power to educational institutions and their governing bodies.

At any one time principals of educational institutions are likely to feel themselves engaged in all three types of responsiveness to different groups of stakeholders in their institutions. In the busy press of organizational life the principals in this study drew a crude distinction between formal accountability (genuine accountability and answerability) and their sense of professional responsibility for the quality of what they did. This is, perhaps, sufficient rational typology for processes which are essentially flows of power with particular strengths or valencies depending on the sources from which they emanate. More important in the future, perhaps, than further sophisticated casuistry in the naming of accountable parts is to understand the dynamics of how principals handle the ebb and flow of political, micro-political and moral influences in their relationships with those who have a stake in their institutions.

References

Bass, B. (1985) *Leadership and Performance Beyond Expectations*, New York: Free Press.

Bennis, W. and Nannus, B. (1985) *Leaders: The Strategies for Taking Charge*, London: Harper.

Blase, J. and Blase, J. (1995) 'The micropolitical orientation of facilitative school principals and it effects on teachers' sense of empowerment', paper given at the American Educational Research Association (AERA) Conference, San Francisco: April.

Bolman, L. and Deal, T. (1991) *Reframing Organisations*, Oxford: Jossey Bass.

Bolman, L. and Deal, T. (1994) 'Looking for leadership: another search party's report' *Educational Administrative Quarterly* 30 (1) 77–96.

Bryman, A. (1992) *Charisma and Leadership in Organisations*, London: Sage.

Busher, H. and Hodgkinson, K. (1996) 'Co-operation and tension between autonomous schools: a study of inter-school networking' *Educational Review* 48 (1) 55–64.

Busher, H. and Saran, R. (1992) *Teachers and their Conditions of Employment*, Bedford Way series, London: Kogan Page in association with the London Institute of Education.

Busher, H. and Saran, R. (1995) 'Managing staff professionally' in Busher, H. and Saran, R. (eds.) (1995) *Managing Teachers as Professionals in Schools*, London: Kogan Page.

Davies, L. (1995) *Who needs Headteachers?* Keynote paper given at the BEMAS Annual Conference 1995, 23–25 September, Oxford, UK.

East Sussex Accountability Project (1979) 'Accountability in the middle years of schooling', University of Sussex mimeo in McCormick, R. (ed.) (1982) *Calling Education to Account*, London: Heinemann Educational.

Evetts, J. (1994) 'The new headteacher: the changing work culture of secondary headship' *School Organization*, 14 (1) 37–47.

Gibb, C. (1974) 'The principles and traits of leadership' in Gibb, C. (ed.) *Leadership*, Harmondsworth: Penguin.

Gronn, P. (1986) 'Politics, power and the management of schools' in Hoyle, E. and McMahon, A. (eds.) *The Management of Schools*, London: Kogan Page.

Gronn, P. (1996) 'From transactions to transformations: a new world order in the study of leadership' *Educational Management and Administration*, 24 (1) (Keynote paper given at the BEMAS Annual Conference 1995, 23–25 September, Oxford, UK).

Handy, C. (1991) *Gods of Management*, London: Business Books.

Hargreaves, A. (1990) 'Contrived collegiality: the micro-politics of teacher collaboration' in Blase, J. (ed.) *The Politics of School Life*, New York: Sage.

Heller, H. (1985) *Helping Schools Change: A Handbook for Leaders in Education*, York: Centre for the Study of Comprehensive Schools.

Hodgkinson, C. (1991) *Educational Leadership: the Moral Art*, New York: SUNY Press.

Hoyle, E. (1986) *The Politics of School Management*, London: Hodder & Stoughton.

Huckman, L. and Hill, T. (1994) 'Local management of schools: rationality and decision-making in the employment of teachers' *Oxford Review of Education* 20 (2) 185–197.

Hughes, M. (1973) 'The professional-as-administrator: the case of the secondary school head' *Educational Administration Bulletin*, 2 (1) 11–23.

Hunt, J. (1991) *Leadership: A New Synthesis*, Newbury Park: Sage.

Locke, M. (1992) 'The application of trust in the management of institutions' paper given at the BEMAS Annual Conference, 12–13 September, Bristol.

Mortimore, P. and Mortimore, J. with Thomas, H. (1994) *Managing Associate Staff: Innovation in Primary and Secondary Schools*, London: Chapman.

Ribbins, P. and Marland, M. (1994) *Headship Matters: Conversations with Seven Secondary Headteachers*, London: Longman.

Ribbins, P. (1989) 'Managing secondary schools after the Act: participation and partnership?' in Lowe, R. (ed.) *The Changing Secondary School*, Lewes: Falmer.

School Teachers' Review Body (1995) *Fourth Report* CM 2765, London: HMSO.

Simkins, T. (1992) 'Policy, accountability and management perspectives on the implementation of reform' in Simkins, T., Ellison, L. and Garrett, V. (1992) *Implementing Educational Reform: The Early Lessons*, Harlow: Longman in association with BEMAS.

Sinclair, A. (1995) 'The seduction of the self-managed team and the reinvention of the team as a group' *Leading and Managing* 1 (1) 44–63.

7

The Female Secondary Headteacher: Leadership and Management Styles

Marianne Coleman

Introduction

The study of women in leadership and management in education is relatively rare. Hall (1996), when researching female headteachers, makes the point that:

> I found it difficult at first to avoid using men's behaviour as educational leaders as a yardstick for describing women in similar positions . . . Putting the picture straight by changing the subject from men to women does not involve saying women are different or better. My purpose is rather to explain how they are in this role [headship], in this context [schools] in this period of time [1990s]. (p. 3)

Theories of leadership and management have often been based on assumptions derived from the male discourse (Shakeshaft, 1989; Blackmore, 1989), but in relatively recent years the female manager in education has been studied in her own right (Adler *et al.*, 1993; Ouston, 1993; Ozga, 1993). The disproportionate number of female secondary headteachers, only 24 per cent in 1996 (DfEE, 1997), also raises issues of equity. Evetts (1994) studied twenty secondary heads of whom ten are male and ten female, making gender an important variable in her study and Grace (1995) included a chapter on women in educational leadership. Studies of individual headteachers have included a balance of male and female heads (Ribbins and Marland, 1994; Hustler and Brighouse, 1995; Ribbins, 1997). The author has conducted interviews with five women headteachers (Coleman, 1996) and, most notably, Hall (1996) has undertaken an in-depth study of six female headteachers of whom three are secondary and three primary. Elsewhere, Hall and Southworth (1997) point to the fact that research into headship is the weaker for largely ignoring the variable of gender:

Source: Educational Research, Vol. 42, no. 1, pp. 13–27. Edited version.

> Using a gender perspective creates new possibilities for exploring the lives of men and women who teach, manage and lead in education. As researchers into headship we have both concluded that educational leadership is firmly rooted in professional identity. Gender, in turn, is a crucial component of that identity. Future research into headship that fails to take this and the gendered nature of schools and colleges into account is likely to be incomplete. (p. 167)

However, research on the management and leadership of women in education has tended to be qualitative in nature.

Survey of Female Headteachers in England and Wales

In the summer of 1996, the author undertook a survey of all the 670 female secondary headteachers in England and Wales covering their leadership and management styles and their career progress to headship. The response rate of 70 per cent, well above normal response rates, gives an objective measure of the interest that the headteachers had in the area. Comments included on the returned questionnaires and accompanying letters showed the measure of this interest and indicated the relative isolation that was felt by many of the respondents. Female headteachers have not previously been surveyed separately as a group, although gender as a variable was included in the research of Weindling and Earley (1987), Jones (1987) and Jirasinghe and Lyons (1996).

The survey data reported here are those relating to the management and leadership styles of the headteachers including the values that they were promoting in schools. In addition, this chapter covers aspects of their experience of management and leadership, including the ways in which they relate to their staff and their professional development. Finally, data relating to the perceived difficulties and the advantages of being a woman headteacher are reported.

Approximately half of the headteachers were between 40 and 49 and half between 50 and 59, with very few under 40 or 60 or over. More than two thirds of the headteachers were married, with marriage more popular among the under than the over 50s. Just over half of the heads had a child or children, but childlessness was more common amongst those under 50. Just over two thirds of those responding were heads of co-educational schools, the remainder were heads of single sex schools. Of these only three individuals were heads of boys' schools.

The Management and Leadership Styles of Female Headteachers in England and Wales

In analysing management and leadership styles, there are certain qualities that are identified with a 'feminine' or a 'masculine' style of management. Both of these styles may be adopted by men or by women, although the expectation is that men might adopt a style that is predominantly masculine and women one that is predominantly feminine. The lists of qualities identified by Bem (1974) and by Gray (1989, 1993) are both attempts to identify such a paradigm or ideal type. In the survey, the headteachers were presented with the masculine and feminine qualities identified by Gray (1993), and were asked to indicate which of the qualities they felt applied to them. These qualities are derived from work associated with the training of headteachers, and are not based on empirical research. Their use in this questionnaire was intended to provide a possible re-definition of the paradigms. The qualities were not identified in any way as 'male' or 'female' in the questionnaire.

Six of the adjectives and descriptions that are included in the feminine paradigm (see Table 7.1) were identified by 59 per cent or more of the headteachers. More than three-quarters of them judged themselves to be 'aware of individual differences', 'caring' and 'intuitive'. However, there were also four adjectives in the masculine paradigim which were identified by over half of the headteachers as applicable to them. Although the characteristics identified most often were from the feminine paradigm, those chosen by more than 50 per cent ranged across both paradigms (see Table 7.2). The qualities listed in Table 7.2 present an empirically based alternative to the feminine paradigm identified by Gray (1993).

Table.7.1 *Qualities identified by the headteachers from the masculine and feminine paradigms of Gray (1993)*

Feminine paradigm	%	Masculine paradigm	%
Aware of individual differences	86.0	Evaluative	61.1
Caring	79.4	Disciplined	60.4
Intuitive	76.2	Competitive	50.6
Tolerant	68.7	Objective	50.6
Creative	63.0	Formal	14.9
Informal	59.4	Highly regulated	13.2
Non-competitive	21.5	Conformist	10.9
Subjective	13.8	Normative	4.0

(% indicating they felt they had the quality)

Table 7.2 *Qualities identified by 50% or more of the headteachers*

Quality	Sex	%
Aware of individual differences	(f)	86.0
Caring	(f)	79.4
Intuitive	(f)	76.2
Tolerant	(f)	68.7
Creative	(f)	63.0
Evaluative	(m)	61.1
Disciplined	(m)	60.4
Informal	(f)	59.4
Competitive	(m)	50.6
Objective	(m)	50.6

(f) = feminine; (m) = masculine in Gray's (1993) paradigm.

Overall, it would appear that there is a strong identification with most of the feminine traits on the part of the headteachers, and a weak identification with most of the masculine traits. However, there are a number of masculine traits, specifically 'evaluative', 'disciplined', 'competitive' and 'objective', which are identified by 50 per cent or more of the respondents, and which therefore temper the picture of a pure feminine paradigm of management style amongst the female secondary headteachers of England and Wales and indicate a more androgynous style of management.

Key Words to Describe the Headteachers' Style of Management

Open-ended questions included in the survey were intended to allow the headteachers to express their own perceptions of their style and of the values that they are trying to promote in the school. The headteachers were given the opportunity to list three separate words that describe their style of management. This question appeared in the survey before the question involving the list of masculine and feminine paradigms, so it is unlikely that these adjectives had any influence on the free choice of the three words. No guidance whatsoever was given, to allow them to provide unprompted responses. This led to there being a large range of adjectives offered. However, it was possible to group them, and establish some idea of the prevalent styles of management that the female headteachers considered that they adopted. The themes that were identified are listed below with the percentage of the total number of adjectives in each group:

1   A collaborative style of management, e.g. consultative, open (38.5 per cent).
2   A people-oriented style of management, e.g. team-related, supportive (23.8 per cent).
3   An autocratic/directive style of management, e.g. decisive, firm, (14.9 per cent).
4   An efficient style of management, e.g. focused, planned (11.7 per cent).
5   A values style of management, e.g. visionary, fair (11. 1 per cent).

There is clear indication that the single most popular style of management was that termed 'collaborative'. However, it is notable that most of the headteachers use terms like 'consultative', 'open', 'collaborative' and 'participative' rather than 'collegial' or 'democratic'. It appears that the majority of the headteachers adopting this style of management reserve the right to make the final decision. The potentially overlapping 'people-orientated' style of management was also strongly indicated by the choice of adjectives that were grouped within that theme. The range of adjectives chosen is very wide, but the styles of management that are indicated in the majority of responses are consistent with the adjectives that were most often chosen from the female paradigm; i.e. 'aware of individual differences', 'caring', 'intuitive' and 'tolerent'.

   Certainly, the identification of the collaborative and people-oriented style of management with the way that women manage is in accord with a range of earlier findings. Research on female headteachers and principals in the USA, the UK, Australia, New Zealand and Canada appears to indicate that female managers are likely to work in a co-operative style, empowering their colleagues and characteristically making use of team work (Blackmore, 1994; Adler, 1994; Hall, 1996; Jirasinghe and Lyons, 1996). This generalisation is borne out by research findings from outside education (Ferrario, 1994).

   The author's survey of all female secondary headteachers in England and Wales thus largely endorses earlier research, but, although it is clear that the preferred management style of female headteachers is collaborative, there appear to be a minority of the heads for whom this is not true. Although the collaborative and people-oriented styles were endorsed by a majority, there were a considerable number of adjectives offered that were grouped as either 'autocratic/directive' or 'efficient'. This represents a proportion of headteachers who, through their choice of adjectives, identified their style of management as probably more akin to the masculine paradigm than the feminine. This style of management might be identified with some of the 'male' adjectives, such as 'disciplined', 'evaluative', 'formal' and 'competitive'.

In the above analysis, the adjectives were considered singly. When considering the adjectives in their groups of three, it was rare for all three to be grouped within the same theme. For example 'efficient' adjectives might be combined with either 'people-oriented' or 'autocratic' adjectives. However, a dominant style was considered to be where at least two of the three adjectives came from either collaborative and people orientated or from the autocratic/directive and efficient categories.

For those headteachers aged 49 or under, about 10 per cent chose at least two of their three words from the automatic/directive style of management combined with the efficient style of management, but the proportion of those 50 or over doing so was just over 20 per cent. The tendency to be more collaborative may be linked with 'youth', this appeared to be the case in earlier research with headteachers (Weindling and Earley, 1987). Alternatively a difference in style of the younger heads may be linked to a change in the expectations of what was required in headteachers in the last years of the twentieth century. Several of the heads interviewed by Hustler *et al.* (1995) indicated that their management style had moved towards being one of collaboration in keeping with: 'a reformulated idea of the leading professional' (Thompson in Hustler *et al.*, p. 90). Hall (1996) comments on the need for a different style of headteacher to cope with the demands of the post 1988 reforms and identifies that all six of the women heads she studied are different from their predecessors whether male or female. In addition, a more collegial style of management is now generally considered to be normatively superior to other styles (Wallace, 1989; Bush, 1995), at least in Western cultures.

The final group of adjectives, termed 'values driven' represents a strand of thinking that is probably not separate from the others, but identifies the values that may well underpin the management style of many headteachers. The most common category of adjectives within this group referred to being 'visionary', the second to being 'fair' or 'honest'.

Overall, there appears to be a range of management styles indicated by the lists of adjectives provided, with one side of the spectrum occupied by the majority of the headteachers who adopt a 'collaborative' and 'people-orientated' style of management and the other side of the spectrum occupied by a minority of the headteachers operating an autocratic/directive style of management often linked to choice of the more 'efficient' adjectives. The 'values driven' style may well underpin any or all of the other styles (see Figure 7.1).

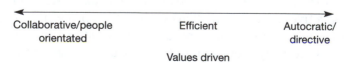

Figure 7.1 *Spectrum of styles of management*

Key Values Promoted in the School

The headteachers were also given an opportunity to indicate a free choice of the key values that they are trying to promote in the school. The respondents tended to indicate phrases, rather than individual words. The sentiments that are included in the value statements can be divided into four areas.

1 Academic excellence and educational achievement. Many of the value statements mentioned academic achievement sometimes in association with caring values: 'academic achievement in a caring community which develops all pupils for their own potential'; 'The pupils' learning is central.'
2 The importance of every individual achieving their potential. These statements are often linked to the importance of hard work: 'everyone committed to the success of each student'; 'everyone has the potential to achieve, but you must work hard to succeed.'
3 Respect for self. There was awareness of the need to promote: 'high self esteem for all'; 'The importance of self-worth, and valuing others.'
4 Respect and caring for others: 'respect for individual differences; valuing others (pupils and staff)'; 'students should aim high with compassion for those around them.'

The achievement of academic excellence could be considered an objective that is innate to the purpose of almost any school. This value is very much in accord with the key quality of strategic direction and development of the school outlined in the National Standards for Headteachers (TTA, 1998) in terms of the creation of an ethos and vision which will secure achievement by pupils. However, the remaining values identified are related to the qualities of caring and respect for individuals that the headteachers have already identified within the Gray (1993) paradigms, where the four most popular qualities, 'aware of individual differences, caring, intuitive and tolerant' were all drawn from the feminine paradigm.

The words in Table 7.3 are those that were mentioned most in all the statements about values from the headteachers. These words indicate the importance of both achievement and respect as key values; achievement, sometimes but not always, specifying learning, and respect including respect for self and for others including individuals and the community.

Table 7.3 *Words mentioned most often in statements relating to key values promoted in the school*

Word	Times used
achievement	126
respect	123
self	95
all	94
high/higher/highest	84
care/caring	80
value(s)/valued/valuing	80
others	69
learning	65
individual/s	56
pupil/s	52
community	47

Aspects of educational leadership can be seen very clearly in the key values that the headteachers, in the survey, were trying to promote in their schools and these aspects also endorse the idea that women are particularly concerned with the teaching and learning aspects of their role in comparison with administrative or other responsibilities. There is no doubt that the two key value words used most frequently: achievement and respect, are in keeping with the concept of educational leadership and very much in line with existing research on the ways in which women in educational management operate (Gross and Trask, 1977; Shakeshaft, 1989, 1995; Hill and Ragland, 1995; Riehl and Lee, 1996; Grogan, 1996; Gold, 1996; Kruger, 1996). This research was concerned only with female secondary headteachers, and it may be that a survey of male colleagues would reveal that men too are moving towards a 'feminine' style of management and share many of the key values.

Management in Action

The headteachers were asked a limited range of questions relating to the practicalities of their style of management. In particular, they were asked about their availability to staff, and the amount of time that they spent out of the office when in school. They were also asked about the ways in which they encouraged all teachers to develop their careers, and if there was any special way in which they tried to encourage the careers of female teachers.

The majority of headteachers seem to make themselves available to their staff whenever possible (see Table 7.4).

Table 7.4 *Opportunites for staff to talk to the head*

Opportunity	%
Any time if not in meeting	84.3
Any time within specified limits	8.9
By appointment	6.8

The headteachers also appear to be visible in the school for quite a large proportion of their time (see Table 7.5). In answer to the question 'while you are in school, what proportion of your time do you spend out of your office?' approximately 80 per cent claimed that they spent between 10 per cent and 50 per cent of their time in the school, but out of their office.

Table 7.5 *Time spent out of office*

Time	%
Under 10%	3.5
10–25%	32.0
26–50%	47.9
51–75%	16.6

Most of the headteachers report that they spend a considerable proportion of their time out of their office. They were not asked how this time was spent, but presumably some of it would be in teaching, and some would involve 'management by walking about'. When coupled with the information about the availability of the majority to talk to teachers, there would appear to be some evidence to support the dominant management style indicated by the majority of the headteachers. It seems that a large proportion of the headteachers consider that they operate in an open way and that they are highly involved with their staff and the operation of the school.

Encouragement of all the Teachers to Develop their Careers

Headteachers sought various ways to encourage teachers to develop their careers. Courses, appraisal and mentoring were the most often cited means, but 'other' ways were written in by 52.9 per cent of the respondents (see Table 7.6).

Of those that indicated 'other', most stated that they were encouraging one to one meetings for all members of staff to discuss career planning. The

Table 7.6 *Means of encouraging teachers to develop careers*

Means	%
Courses	87.2
Appraisal	69.6
Mentoring	65.7
Role play	3.0
Other	52.9

meetings either took place with themselves as headteacher, with another member of the senior staff, the INSET co-ordinator, a consultant or an unspecified person. The general feeling was that it is:

very important to find time to have one to one conversations about individual strengths and needs.

Other possibilities mentioned were career development opportunities inside and outside the school and other, generally practical, means of encouragement such as practice interviews. The development opportunities included specific interventions:

departmental monitoring, work shadowing, teacher placement.

There was some indication of encouragement of development through means other than promotion:

Involvement in teams to develop projects.
Opportunity for role rotation, being given support to lead initiatives (curriculum and pastoral).

One headteacher specified the development opportunity that was available in a largely female school:

> Taking on 'acting' responsibilities during our frequent maternity absences.

Since a minority of headteachers in England and Wales are women, they present important role models for other female teachers. The heads were asked if they particularly encouraged women teachers in their career progress. The largest single group responding to this question indicated that they did not treat women differently from men (see Table 7.7).

Table 7.7 *How do you encourage female teachers in their career progress?*

Means	%
No special ways	46.6
Women only courses	21.3
Mentoring	19.6
Other	37.2

Some of the headteachers indicated more than one way in which they encouraged female teachers. The large proportion indicating 'No special ways' is actually greater than 46.6 per cent, since some of those commenting in the 'other' category re-iterated that all staff were treated equally in their school (18.6 per cent) or that staff were all treated according to the equal opportunities policy (4.2 per cent). A further 6.7 per cent stated that they pursued the same policies that they had indicated for the staff as a whole.

In addition, some of the headteachers of all girls' schools commented in the 'other' comments that the question of treating female staff differently does not really arise for them, since the majority of their staff are women. Such comments accounted for about 10 per cent of those in the 'other' comments.

It is therefore likely that the majority of headteachers do not have any special policies with regard to the encouragement of female teachers. However, over 20 per cent do state that they encourage women through women only courses and a similar proportion through mentoring. In addition, the largest proportion of comments written in as 'other' referred to specific encouragement of women. This encouragement often included the headteacher's own importance as a role model, and in some cases referred to the doubts and lack of confidence evidenced by their women staff.

Personal conversation. I always encouraged competent women, from being a scale I teacher onwards, making sure they see themselves as possible runners, and boosting their confidence.

Individual discussion, also with male staff, but I find many women, although very good, do not have confidence to put themselves forward for promotion. Three examples in my school spring to mind.

The encouragement of women through being a role model was seen to be important, particularly in the context of the domestic role of women:

I talk to them about the issues, making it clear I have children etc. – i.e. trying to be a role model.

There was also awareness of the need to overcome stereotyping:

There is a high percentage of female role models – SMT, heads of science and maths etc.

Finally some of the encouragement specifically addressed to women was associated with issues such as the handling of maternity leave, and more radical suggestions to help women, such as job sharing.

Being flexible about moves between part-time and full-time. Job shares (though not yet at present school).

Finding opportunites for responsibility in a variety of ways – particularly important for returners. Enhancing the role of positive women in whole-school issues.

Flexible return to work after maternity leave.

Whilst there is a commitment to staff development as a whole, it would appear that a substantial minority of the headteachers are aware of a need to separately foster the career progress of women. However, it is only a small minority of the headteachers who have moved beyond courses and mentoring to actively encourage female staff in practical ways such as job sharing and flexible work practices.

Male Resentment of Female Leadership

Over half of the surveyed heads reported experiencing sexist attitudes from their male colleagues. This experience was reported more by those under 50, and those who were married and had children, in comparison with those who were single and childless. Similarly, the heads of girls' schools were less likely to report sexism from their peers than the heads of co-ed and boys' schools (see Table 7.8). These differences are statistically significant. It would appear that women who are married and who have children, particularly those working in co-educational schools may be identified more strongly with a domestic stereotype and implicitly considered less able to lead and manage.

Table 7.8 *Percentage of heads stating that they had experienced sexism from peers*

	%		%
Over 50	52.4	Children	57.7
Under 50	56.9	No children	51.1
Heads of girls schools	47.7	Married	55.7
Heads of other schools	57.7	Single	47.1
		Separated	35.7
		Divorced	66.7

Once established as headteachers they were strongly aware of the fact that men found difficulty in dealing with female leaders. Being patronised and feeling isolated were two common features of the experience of headship. The female heads also reported examples of stereotyping linked to their sex. Many comments express: 'difficulties with the concept of woman as a boss.' Some were more specific:

> I inherited a school with a good number of staff who didn't want a female head. The secretary and caretaker threatened to resign, some male teachers made it clear they didn't want a woman telling them what to do.

Occasionally the resentment is linked to disapproval of management style that is not seen as 'traditional':

> Some staff wanted as head a 'big man who shouted' – I'm the opposite.

There was also expectation that females would manage in a certain way:

> The assumption was that you will be a female stereotype – keep changing one's mind, can't handle difficult male pupils etc.

Whilst the stereotype of the woman as a 'soft' manager predominates, there is evidence of a different range of stereotypes associated with women:

the suggestion that career women are cold, hard and single minded.

more a question of little bits of prejudice against single woman role. Rumours seemed to vary: I'm assumed to be either a promiscuous heterosexual or a latent homosexual.

The majority of the headteachers (62.7 per cent) stated that as a woman they had felt the need to 'prove their worth' in a management position. There was little difference in the proportion of women who felt this amongst those of differing age groups, but some differences between those of different marital status, and those who headed girls only schools compared with the rest. The need to 'prove your worth' is felt more strongly by those with children, and less strongly by the single and heads of girls' schools. This difference may well be linked with the tendency to stereotype married women who are mothers with the domestic role which was particularly evident in responses relating to discrimination linked to promotion. The largest category of responses to the question of the need to 'prove your worth' related to combating the range of stereotypes that are held about women in management.

Despite the range of stereotypes relating to female leadership, much of the resentment was linked to the softer, more participatory style of management of the female heads on the part of subordinate males who were used to a more decisive autocratic style. The present research appears to replicate the findings from qualitative research in this country (Hall, 1996) and quantitative work in the USA (Riehl and Lee, 1995) and Israel (Goldring and Chen, 1994) that there are considerable difficulties for some men in adjusting both to working for a woman and adapting to the preferred management style of most women.

The Advantages in Being a Woman Headteacher

The majority of the group surveyed have been successful in terms of a traditionally male career path, and some have adopted the norms associated with a career that takes little account of family life. Only 10 per cent identified 'being a woman' as a reason for success. By far the most frequent reason for success quoted was 'hard work', with support from others being the second most important reason. Both of these tend to indicate the difficulties that a woman may face in reaching a position of leadership, particularly when the leader is stereotypically expected to be a man. However, there are benefits in being a woman once headship has been achieved. Nearly two thirds of the headteachers reported that they had found it an advantage to be a woman headteacher (see Table 7.9).

Table 7.9 *Advantages in being a woman headteacher*

Advantages	% of total examples given
Able to diffuse 'macho' behaviour	35.6
Being noticed	15.1
Not constrained by male stereotype	14.7
Approachable to women and girls	10.9
Using 'feminine guiles'	7.7
Empathy and use of emotion	7.1
None	3.2
Head of a girls school	2.9
Other	2.9

The advantage most mentioned was in terms of being able to defuse macho behaviour on the part of males; students, teachers and parents. In this case, the fact that men feel the need to be aggressive with other men, and that aggression is not associated with females, acts to their advantage. A number of the headteachers quite consciously acted up to the stereotype of femininity and played on the susceptibilities of males such as governors or local authority personnel who were likely to perceive them first and foremost as women.

Another advantage quoted by the headteachers was 'being noticed'. Since they were a relative rarity as a female, they tended to be offered opportunities, particularly by the LEA. It is possible that a rise in the number of female headteachers, which would lead to a reduction in such opportunities, might therefore not be entirely welcomed by some of the heads.

The headteachers were positive about their gender in terms of their approachability. They felt that people, particularly girls, mothers and female members of staff, could approach them more freely than they might a man. In addition they considered that they had the freedom to empathise with families and be sympathetic in a way that most men could not. Although the general assumption that the leader and manager is male may prove a handicap for the female manager, there is the other side of the coin, the freedom of the female manager to behave in a way that is not constrained by the normal stereotypes associated with leaders. It may be that being a woman in management allows some freedom (Hall, 1996) and gives the opportunity to the female headteacher to develop in fresh ways that are unencumbered by the perceptions of others. In addition Grogan (1996) refers to the life experience of women, as wives and mothers, moulding them as administrators; the experience making them different from males in the same positions.

■ Conclusions

The survey of the entire population of female headteachers in England and Wales has contributed in a number of ways to the understanding of the management and leadership of women headteachers in the 1990s. The high response rate to the survey gives confidence in the validity of the findings and allows the possibility of some generalisations to complement existing and future qualitative research.

One of the major findings emerging from the research is the continuing discrimination that has been faced by women who are now senior managers in education. The experience of isolation and instances of sexism from peers, recounted by the headteachers, indicate that they are operating in a context which may be inimical to success unless women are prepared to adapt to the prevailing values. These might include opting for a single state, childlessness, or working harder and longer than any competitors, male or female.

Many of the headteachers in the survey reported on their experience of resentment on the part of males and some females at being subject to female leadership. However, the majority also identify ways in which being a woman leader frees them from the stereotypes of male leadership. Both of these factors exemplify the differences in the context within which male and female headteachers operate, indicating the relevance of gender to the study of leadership and management.

The research strongly endorses the view that most women manage their schools in a way that can clearly be identified as consultative and people orientated. The majority of the headteachers, particularly those under 50, chose adjectives that identified them as collaborative and caring. The choices also endorsed the importance placed on teamwork and on 'power to' rather than 'power over'. However, they do not claim to be democratic, rather they say that the final responsibility for decisions rests with them. In reviewing effective management in schools, Bolam *et al.* (1993) commented that the headteacher of an effective school:

> Has consultative 'listening' style; is decisive and forceful but not dictatorial; is open to other people's ideas; and is easily accessible to staff. (Bolam *et al.*, 1993, p. 119)

The headteachers' choices of adjectives to describe their management style and values generally reflected and endorsed the findings of previous research. The predominant management style was collaborative and people centred. However, there is a small proportion of the heads for whom this is not true. About 15 per cent of the heads may be adopting, consciously or unconsciously, a style of management and leadership that may have more in common with elements of the more stereotypical 'masculine' style which involves a more directive way of operating. The survey also endorses the tendency for women to be educational leaders, placing stress on the learning of their students rather than on the importance of administrative tasks. The values that the headteachers chose were indicative of the values of educational leaders, 'achievement and respect'.

Whilst the quality of leadership may best be judged within the context of the individual school, the majority of the surveyed heads operate in a manner that largely coincides with concepts of effective leadership in education. It was noted in the introduction that the under-representation of women in senior management in education represents an issue of equity. Since women tend to operate in a collaborative manner that is likely to empower others and endorse values of educational leadership, their under-representation also indicates a loss of potentially effective leadership in schools.

References

Adler, N.J. (1994) 'Competitive frontiers: women managing across borders', *Journal of Management Development*, Vol. 13, No. 2., pp. 24–41.

Adler, S., Laney, J. and Packer, M. (1993) *Managing Women: Feminism and Power in Educational Management*, Open University Press: Buckingham.

Bem, S.l (1974) 'The measurement of psychological androgyny', *Journal of Consulting and Clinical Psychology*, Vol. 42, No. 2, pp. 155–62.

Blackmore, J. (1989) 'Educational leadership: a feminist critique and reconstruction', in Smyth, I. and John, W. (eds.) *Critical Perspectives on Educational Leadership, Deakin Studies in Education Series 2*, Lewes: The Falmer Press.

Bolam, R., McMahon, A., Pocklington, K. and Weindling, D. (1993) *Effective Management in Schools: A Report for the Department for Education via the School Management Task Force Professional Working Party*, London: HMSO.

Bush, T. (1995) *Theories of Educational Management* (second edition), London: Paul Chapman Publishing.

Coleman, M. (1996) 'The management style of female headteachers', *Educational Management and Administration*, Vol. 24, No. 2, pp. 163–174.

DfEE (1997) *Statistics of Education: Teachers in England and Wales 1997*, London: Government Statistical Service.

Evetts, J. (1994) *Becoming a Secondary Headteacher*, London: Cassell.

Ferrario, M. (1994) 'Women as managerial leaders', in Davidson, M.J. and Burke, R.J. (eds.) *Women in Management: Current Research Issues*, London: Paul Chapman Publishing.

Gold, A. (1996) 'Women into educational management', *European Journal of Education*, Vol. 31, No. 4, pp. 419–433.

Goldring, E. and Chen, M. (1994) 'The feminisation of the principalship in Israel: the trade-off between political power and cooperative leadership', in Marshall, C. (ed.) *The New Politics of Race and Gender*, London: The Falmer Press.

Grace, G. (1995) *School Leadership*, London: The Falmer Press.

Gray, H.L. (1989) 'Gender considerations in school management: masculine and feminine leadership styles', in Riches, C. and Morgan, C. (eds.) *Human Resource Management in Education*, Milton Keynes: Open University Press.

Gray, H.L. (1993) 'Gender issues in management training', in Ozga, J. (ed.) *Women in Educational Management*, Buckingham: Open University Press.

Grogan, M. (1996) *Voices of Women aspiring to the Superintendency*, Albany: State University of New York Press.

Gross, N. and Trask, A. (1976) *The Sex Factor and the Management of Schools*, New York: John Wiley and Sons.

Hall, V. (1996) *Dancing on the Ceiling: A Study of Women Managers in Education*, London: Paul Chapman Publishing.

Hall, V. and Southworth, G. (1997) 'Headship', *School Leadership and Management*, Vol. 17, No. 3, pp. 151–170.

Hill, M.S. and Ragland, J.C. (1995) *Women as Educational Leaders: Opening Windows, Pushing Ceilings*, Thousand Oaks, CA: Corwin Press, Inc.

Hustler, D., Brighouse, T. and Ruddock, J. (eds.) (1995) *Heeding Heads: Secondary Heads and Educational Commentators in Dialogue*, London: David Fulton.

Jirasinghe, D. and Lyons, G. (1996) *The Competent Head: A Job Analysis of Heads' Tasks and Personality Factors*, London: Falmer Press.

Jones, A. (1987) *Leadership for Tomorrow's School*, Oxford: Blackwell.

Kruger, M.L. (1996) 'Gender issues in school headship: quality versus power?' *European Journal of Education*, Vol. 31, No. 4, pp. 447–461.

Ouston, J. (1993) *Women in Educational Management*, Harlow: Longman.

Ozga, J. (ed.) (1993) *Women in Education Management*, Buckingham: Open University Press.

Ribbins, P. (ed.) (1997) *Leaders and Leadership in the School, College and University*, London: Cassell.

Ribbins, P. and Marland, M. (1994) *Headship Matters*, Harlow: Longman.

Riehl, C. and Lee, V.E. (1996) 'Gender, organisations, and leadership', in Leithwood, K., Chapman, J., Corson, D., Hallinger, P. and Hart, A. (eds.) *International Handbook of Educational Leadership and Administration*, Boston: Kluwer Academic Publishers.

Shakeshaft, C. (1989) *Women in Educational Administration*, Newbury Park: Sage.

Teacher Training Agency (1998) *National Standards for Headteachers*, London: TTA.

Wallace, M. (1989) 'Towards a collegiate approach to curriculum management in primary and middle schools', in Preedy, M. (ed.) *Approaches to Curriculum Management*, Milton Keynes: Open University Press.

Weindling, D. and Earley, P. (1987) *Secondary Headship: The First Years*, Windsor: NFER-Nelson.

Part 3

Leading People and Teams in Organisations

8

Leading Teachers' Professional Development

Mieke Clement and Roland Vandenberghe

Introduction

Schools and school leaders are experiencing a growing pressure to deliver high quality education. And there exists consensus that teachers should be encouraged and supported within the school context to develop profession-ally in order to deliver this (Little, 1992). It has generally been accepted that teachers' professional development is not simply a matter of individual char-acteristics (see also Kelchtermans and Vandenberghe, 1994). It cannot be disconnected from the context within which it takes place. In the early '90s Huberman (1993) – following the research tradition of (life-)stage theories – described the stages of professional development. The attention he paid to the subjective meanings teachers attach to this process, allowed him to indi-cate which working conditions at the school level favour professional development. Teachers have a greater chance to enjoy an harmonious career, if they work in a school context that encourages some experimentation with-out the threat of punishment if one is not successful. Besides that the possibility to take on new tasks without loss of wages and access to the expertise of colleagues in and outside the school are important organisa-tional triggers for professional development (Huberman, 1993; Hawley and Valli, 1999; Vandenberghe *et al.*, 1999).

Research in the teacher-thinking tradition also reveals which elements of the school culture contribute to teachers' professional development as reflective practitioners. Lieberman (1994) states that norms of collegiality, trust and openness are crucial. Teachers should be stimulated to reflect critically on their practice in collaboration with colleagues. A collaborative school culture with

Source: School Leadership & Management, Vol. 21, no. 1, 2001, pp. 43–57. Edited version.

shared leadership and professional networking holds the best prospects – according to Lieberman – for the development of teachers' knowledge and beliefs. The conclusions that can be drawn from research in the socialisation-tradition follow the same line. A case study of four beginning teachers by Wildman *et al.* (1989) points at the factors that play a role in teachers' socialisation. Among others, the colleagues and the school context are described as important determinants of this process. The way classes are ascribed to teachers, the leadership style, the curriculum and the collegial relationships among the teachers all have an influence on their socialisation.

Research of workplace conditions (Kirby and Colbert, 1992; Louis and Smith, 1990; Rosenholtz, 1989; Smylie, 1994) helps to summarise which organisational characteristics foster teachers' professional development. Generally, a distinction is made between structural and cultural workplace conditions.[1] Structural workplace conditions refer to the organisational, structural measures one can take in order to foster teacher's professional development. Teachers should be able to participate in the decision making process so that they can exert some influence on the organisation of their work. The feelings of control and satisfaction that originate from this participation contribute to teachers' willingness to develop professionally. Even more, participation in decision making also encourages teachers to collaborate and this can create opportunities for professional development. A last structural workplace condition worth mentioning is the evaluation of teachers. It is argued that the evaluation should be frequent and specific in order to foster development. Teachers should get accurate information about the impact and effects of their work. This leads to feelings of efficacy and to a greater commitment to professional development. For that matter the evaluation should be 'investing' also. It should reward teachers for development, for taking risks and for change, instead of only looking for successes of the past. A good evaluation should encourage teachers' professional development by confronting them with new challenges or tasks.

Cultural workplace conditions refer to the values of the school with regard to professional behaviour and professional development. Many authors point at the importance of a problem solving approach in the school. When this is part of the school culture, teachers are encouraged to reflect on their teaching practice. They feel safe to experiment with innovations and improvements. If they encounter certain problems or when the school has to react to new societal requirements, the team reacts as a whole, starting from a collective sense of responsibility. An individual's problem is seen as a problem of the school. Another important cultural workplace condition is collective goal-setting. Clear and shared goals create common expectations; they foster professional solidarity. They make it possible for teachers to weigh the quality of their own teaching against a collective norm and consequently give impulses for teachers to improve their practice. Finally, collegiality is considered important. Smoothly running collaborative relationships lead to a greater involvement and a stronger sense of responsibility for the quality of the education from the teachers. Collegiality challenges teachers' professionally because colleagues function for one another as a source of feedback, support and alternative ideas.

Evidently school leaders seem to be best situated within the school organisation to create these conditions (Leithwood, 1992; Staessens, 1993; Vandenberghe, 1992; van den Berg and Vandenberghe, 1999). They are supposed to play a crucial role in teachers' professional development (Glanz and Neville, 1997; Hallinger and Heck, 1996; Leithwood, 1994; Parray and Hall, 1992; Sheppard, 1996). Yet, if they commit themselves to create these workplace conditions it remains an open question whether they would be successful. The description of 'what works' that can be found in the literature does not always reveal why nor how certain workplace conditions exert such a positive influence on teachers' development. In order to find out how school leaders can influence teachers' professional development positively through the creation of workplace conditions, it is necessary to answer other questions such as:

1 How do teachers assess the school (leader)'s influence on their professional development, what meaning do they attach to their school leader's influence on their professional development?
2 How can we understand the impact of the school leader on this process? Through which specific processes and mechanisms do the workplace conditions the school leaders create, contribute to teachers' professional development?

In order to answer these research questions in this chapter we will focus on a workplace condition that is considered extremely important for teachers' professional development: collegiality. We will confine the discussion to the collegial relationship between the school leader and the teachers. After a brief description of the methodology, a general account is given of the way teachers experience the impact of the school leader on their professional development. Then we present the results that enable the understanding of the origins of this appreciation. As such we will describe the very specific processes behind the school leaders' influence on teacher's professional development. We also follow the recommendations by Greenfield (1999), stating that we should get closer to the participants in the leadership relationship and arguing for a symbolic interactionist approach paying full attention to the meanings, perspectives and purposes underlying the social relations between school leaders and teachers.

Methodology

The data reported here are part of a study that consisted of three phases in which, respectively, the exploration of the research themes, the development of a substantial theory and the external validation of the theory were the main focus (see Clement, 1995; Clement and Vandenberghe, 2000).

The results discussed in this chapter refer to the first and second phase of the study. In the first phase 39 teachers of 11 elementary schools were interviewed in a semi-structured way. The interview explored the teachers' perception of their personal professional development and of the professional interactions with the other team members. In the second phase an extensive case study was made of two of these schools in order to analyse the relations between the concepts explored in the first phase and the patterns that could be discerned in these relations. The researcher spent five weeks in each of the schools and interviewed 23 teachers and the two school leaders.

In order to analyse the research data a two step strategy was used. First a 'vertical' analysis of the data was made. In order to gain insight in the what, how and why of teachers' perceptions of their professional development and of the settings, the interviews, observational notes, documents and research diary fragments were carefully analysed. First all the data were coded, then they were displayed in matrices (see Miles and Huberman, 1994) so that they could be compared systematically. The second step of the analysis, the 'horizontal' analysis, dealt with the comparison among teachers (for the first phase) and settings (for the second phase). A case-oriented approach was adopted here. The typical patterns found in each setting were compared with one another to 'discover whether a pattern found in one site plays out in others as well, suggesting a common scenario' (Huberman and Miles, 1989: 64).

The analyses were validated in a communicative way (Kvale, 1994). Teachers were invited to read and comment upon the vertical analysis of their interview. The 'story' of each school was presented to the school leader and three 'key informants' (and if they agreed the whole team). Two main questions guided this validation process (1) do you agree with the facts as they are reported; and (2) do you agree with the interpretation of these facts developed by the researcher? Using this criterion, we followed Yin (1989: 144), who states: 'The informants and participants may still disagree with an investigator's conclusions and interpretations, but these reviewers should not disagree over the actual facts of the case.'

Results

How do teachers assess the school leader's influence on their professional development?

The data demonstrate that teachers evaluate the contribution of the school leader to their professional development in three ways.

Some teachers are not impressed by the contribution of their school to their professional development. They are convinced that the working conditions do not support their professional development. Collegial interactions are limited to social small talk. In the rare cases colleagues do collaborate, the 'rule of privacy' (Lieberman and Miller, 1990) is not broken. One is allowed to pass on some teaching materials or to complain about the school or the pupils in very general terms. It is however not accepted to discuss with colleagues specific teaching methods or problems. The school leader does not seem able to change these patterns. The teachers get the feeling their school leader does not trust them. He does not launch interesting discussions. He does not monitor (personal) initiatives teachers take. He rather focuses on general projects that are not linked to teachers' daily professional concerns. A teacher comments: 'During one year the focus is on that subject (for instance mathematics) and during the following year another subject is the central theme of our discussions during the team meetings. You try to do something about it because the school leader asks you. We do it because we have to. You have to report it in your classbook. It annoys me, really, but I do it because I have to.'

A second group of teachers expresses the opinion that interesting possibilities for professional development in school can exist. They can respond to some proposed activities they label interesting, but there is no pressure to engage. These teachers feel stimulated by their colleagues. They offer new ideas in a climate of openness and trust. The school leader sustains this culture by passing through relevant information, by allowing teachers to participate in in-service training, by buying relevant professional journals, by discussing interesting innovations at meetings. Above all, the teachers appreciate the school leader's trust. With respect for their professionalism the school leader makes an offer that the teachers can freely engage in (or not) and that is monitored at a distance: 'And then there is our school leader . . . She really is very good. She's terribly interested in innovations and she always tries to motivate you to implement them. Yet at the same time she lets you free. She knows you're experimenting with something and she trusts you. She stimulates you and she understands nothing can be perfect right from the start. She accepts that.' To put it in the terms of Wideen (1992), the school leader supports teachers' professional development through organisational and structural conditions. A leadership in which the norms and expectations with regard to professional development are clearly communicated makes these conditions even stronger.

Finally there is a group of teachers that is convinced that their school stimulates and orientates their professional development. These teachers feel challenged by their colleagues. Teaching methods and problems are discussed frequently. Colleagues are available to offer help when one has some difficulties. Teachers point to the fact that they can learn from one another during meetings. The school leader is very explicit in what he expects from the teachers. They know which requirements they have to respond to. They are obliged to take certain responsibilities (like for instance leading a meeting, preparing a discussion about an innovation, making a plan for the implementation of an innovation). A teacher comments: 'We work very hard during our team meetings. For instance, we were confronted with this new theme of traffic education. We talk about it at the meeting and then afterwards I really bury myself in it. If it wouldn't have been a point of attention at the meeting, one wouldn't start thinking about it. But now this traffic education gets its shape. Every year we deal with something else and we work very hard.'

These data confirm the hypothesis that teachers' professional development does not only depend upon their individual commitment. Several workplace conditions also play a substantial role. The teachers' perception of the way the school leader functions appears to be an important parameter for the assessment of the contribution of the school to the process of professional development. This perception shows remarkable resemblance to the principal styles Hall *et al.* (1982, 1984) discerned. The school leaders of the first group show a rather limited vision of how their school and staff should change in the future, typical for 'responders', whereas the school leaders of the third group seem to have clear, decisive, long range politics and goals characteristic of 'initiators'. At this point, it remains however an open question which specific patterns and processes in the functioning of the school leader explain this impact. To answer this question we need full descriptions of the functioning of the workplace conditions that foster professional development. An indepth description of the way school leaders and teachers shape these conditions will help us to understand their impact.

In the following section we present the results of two case studies of two suburban Flemish elementary schools. Both are mixed, middle sized schools, with 438 and 280 pupils. The school leader of Heathlandpool has 12 years experience as a school leader, the school leader of Writerscourt only 3 years. Both were elected from their team to become school leader. We focus on the workplace condition 'collegiality' and confine ourselves to the relationship between the school leader and the teachers. After a brief description of the workplace condition we explore why it does (or not) favour teachers' professional development.

Through which specific processes and mechanisms do the workplace conditions school leaders create contribute to teachers' professional development?

Collegiality as a test-case

As described in the introduction, collegiality is generally considered an important workplace condition to foster professional development. In earlier studies collegiality was presented as a solution for all problems schools were confronted with (like lack of continuity over the years, lack of commitment to innovations, staff turnover . . .). More recent research made clear however that a more differentiated view on this workplace condition is necessary (Little, 1987). Fullan and Hargreaves (1992) and McLaughlin (1994), among others, have described the strength of collaborative cultures that leave room for help, support, trust and openness. Yet at the same time they have pointed to the importance of the appreciation within such cultures of teachers' autonomy (see also Clement and Vandenberghe, 2000).

The following description of the interactions between the school leader and the teachers at Heathlandpool and Writerscourt confirms that collegiality not only is a varied workplace condition (as Little [1990] demonstrated), but also that it cannot be disconnected from the way teachers' autonomy gets its place.

Analyses of the relationship between the teachers and the school leader of **Heathlandpool** clearly demonstrate a richly varied collegiality. The teachers and school leader tell each other stories during the breaks and in the corridors. These stories can have the character of noncommittal small talk: teachers and school leaders discuss the weather, their family business or politics. Often these stories grow to a sharing of ideas with regard to the school. The teachers appreciate the fact that they can discuss easily educational issues with the school leader. In general they don't find it difficult to ask for help. The school leader actively provides help. She passes through information to teachers who are interested in a certain topic. She gives some tips and advice for excursions, she comments on a preparation of a lesson, she gives advice with regard to the results of the pupils. What is essential for this collaboration is that it creates opportunities for the teachers and the school leader to share their personal opinions and beliefs about teaching. Yet at the same time the collegiality between the school leader and the teachers leaves enough room for teachers to work independently. They don't have the feeling that the collaboration with their school leader impeded them in maintaining their identity. One could rather say that their autonomy offers opportunities for collegial exchanges. Teachers' personal initiatives are often a start to ask for help or to share some ideas. But collegial interactions are also often a source of inspiration for autonomous work.

Interactions between the school leader and the teachers at **Writerscourt** are of a totally different nature. Teachers are not inclined to label their collegial interactions with the school leaders in a positive way. They have the feeling that they cannot get any help from him. According to the teachers he does not have an open mind for what they do in their classroom. A teacher says: 'He never has a chat with you. I regret that.' The teachers also have the feeling that they cannot share personal opinions with their school leader. A teacher points out it would be unthinkable to discuss an article he considered very interesting about the pressure on pupils to achieve the best results. The school leader doesn't encourage collaboration because of a lack of follow up. During team meetings one can often note that the intention is formulated to elaborate certain projects with a small group of interested colleagues. Yet, after the meeting everybody, the school leader included, seems to forget the discussion and the proposals. It seems to be very difficult at Writerscourt to get engaged with the whole team to work out the idea of one colleague. The school leader is not perceived here as the one who could play a motivating role. The teachers are left to their own devices. Their autonomous work does not form a start for collegial interactions with the school leader and – vice versa – the very scarce collegial exchanges do not offer new impulses for their autonomous work.

Learning opportunities and learning space: the missing links

These data illustrate that collegiality between school leaders and teachers can take different forms. One could also suppose that the teachers of Heathlandpool would consider the contribution of their school leader to their professional development as stimulating or at least inviting, while the teachers of Writerscourt would label it as irrelevant. Using the principal change facilitator style-concept, one would label the school leader of Heathlandpool as an initiator, whereas the school leader of Writerscourt shows characteristics of a responder. Yet the description of the workplace conditions as such, nor the labelling of the school leader's change facilitator style reveal how exactly the (lack of) influence of the school leader and the conditions he creates on teachers' professional development can be understood. The case study results demonstrate that two important concepts play a crucial role. The creation of learning opportunities and learning space determines whether a workplace condition – i.e. collegiality – favours professional development. One can say that all workplace conditions should incorporate learning opportunities and learning space (see also McLaughlin and Yee, 1988). Not only should workplace conditions be characterised by the presence of learning opportunities, i.e. every possible stimulus, challenge, support and feedback that offers teachers the opportunity to acquire skills and to experiment with innovations or to implement new teaching activities. Workplace conditions should also be designed in such a way that they offer teachers an adequate learning space. Teachers should get the chance to effectively do something with the opportunities they get.

Indeed, when learning opportunities and learning space are closely tuned to each other, learning experiences in several domains originate. These learning experiences are the milestones for their professional development. The data gathered in Heathlandpool and Writerscourt illustrate this point.

Looking at the relationship between the school leader and the teachers at **Heathlandpool**, one can conclude that the majority of the interactions between the school leader and the teachers is dominated by the creation of learning opportunities. In answer to specific questions or in general, teachers receive interesting information: 'We find it in our personal box then. You take a look at it and maybe it is interesting. We get it all, everything about which she thinks "O, that could be interesting", is copied and put in our box.' The teachers can ask the school leader for feedback about their pedagogical activities or on the way they interact with their pupils. Sometimes, the school leader comments spontaneously on teachers' work. Another way to confront teachers with learning opportunities consists in giving them some specified tasks: the school leader assigns tasks in order to prepare the team meetings. The teachers are supposed to read some texts that are discussed during the meeting in small groups. Themes like the new curriculum for some subjects, the organisation of the school, mastery learning, the frequency and meaning of assignments for pupils, a project about the environment, children with calculation problems, how to correct tests and assignments and so on offer stimuli to reflect on and improve one's professional practice. The school leader's attention to create professional challenges for her teachers is also obvious in her encouragement to take some in-service courses.

Not only are teachers in their collegial relationship with the school leader confronted with learning opportunities, they also have learning space at their disposal to use these learning opportunities. Organisational measures are taken so that teachers can do something with the opportunities they get. From a structural point of view the accurately organised consultation is very important in this respect. Two times a week teachers teaching the same grade are 'class free' so that they can collaborate. This gives them time and space to get involved with learning opportunities. At the cultural level it is important that teachers are recognised as professionals who can decide for themselves what to do with the opportunities offered. A teacher states: 'She demands things from us, but not too much. I believe we're rather free, because she is not always there to control you.' The so-called lack of control is not so much perceived as a lack of interest, but rather as a sign of trust: 'You can do whatever you want, as long as you can account for it. She lets you free. You can experiment, you can do everything . . .'

What happens within the relationship between the school leader and the teachers of Heathlandpool looks very much like 'empowering behaviour'. This school leader created opportunities for teachers to reflect upon and improve their teaching behaviour by supporting and facilitating critique and by making it possible for teachers to act upon their critique.

In general the teachers of **Writerscourt** agree that there are almost no learning opportunities in their relationship with the school leader. They hardly get any feedback on their work. There are no requirements set. They don't have to account for what they do.

One can discern two patterns with regard to learning opportunities and learning space. On the one hand there seems to be little attention for the creation of learning opportunities. On the other hand potential learning opportunities are not fully exploited because they are not supported by an adequate learning space.

Conclusion

It has been accepted for quite a while that school leaders can and should play a role in teachers' professional development. It has been argued that effective school leaders move beyond task-oriented and administrative leadership (Evans and Teddlie, 1995; Leithwood and Mongomery, 1983). They invest in instructional and educational leadership (van den Berg and Vandenberghe, 1988). Their main focus is to create a working context that encourages teachers to scrutinise and reflect upon their own teaching behaviour (Reitzug and Burrello, 1995). Their commitment to create favourable workplace conditions is seen as a guarantee that schools will be/stay able to react adequately to new societal and educational challenges through the development of teachers. The literature leaves no doubt as to what workplace condittitions contribute to this development. Collegiality, for instance, seems to be crucial. Up until now, however, the reasons why collegiality between the school leader and the teachers is favourable for professional development were formulated only in a rather general, almost taken for granted way. A description of the specific interactions between school leaders and teachers helps us to better understand this influence. In Heathlandpool the collegiality between the school leader and the teachers is richly varied and does not deny teachers' autonomy. This constellation makes it possible not only that many learning opportunities originate, but also that the teachers can use a learning space to work with these opportunities. The result is that teachers are convinced that they learn a lot in their relationship with the school leader. The teachers of Writerscourt report very few learning experiences in their relationship with the school leader. An explanation can be found in the fact that the collegial interactions between both are very scarce. Autonomy is the dominant way of functioning. The data also illustrate the point that the influence of collegiality on professional development is so poor because there are no learning opportunities created and because the scarce learning opportunities that do exist, are not supported by a learning space.

The results of both case studies make clear that a close look at the partici-pants in the leadership relationship and at the way they are interacting helps us to understand why school leaders can contribute to teachers' professional development through the creation of workplace conditions. Creating learning opportunities and learning space and tuning them both seems to be the key for success for school leaders. Doing this they act along the principles of transfor-mative leadership (van den Berg and Vandenberghe, 1999) 'in which they inspire the team and support individual teachers. As such they really invest in people. As van den Berg and Vandenberghe (1999) demonstrated, this is one of the most efficient strategies to implement innovations successfully.

Note

1 The difference between structural and cultural workplace conditions is somewhat artificial. All structural workplace conditions have a cultural aspect and vice versa.

References

Clement, M. (1995) *De Professionele Ontwikkeling van Leerkrachten Basisonderwijs. De Spanning Tussen Autonmie en Collegialiteit (ongepubliceerd doctoraatsproefschrift). (Primary School Teachers' Professional Development. The tension between autonomy and collegiality)*, Leuven: K.U. Leuven: Centrum voor Onderwijsbeleid en-vernieuwing.

Clement, M. and Vandenberghe, R. (2000) Teachers' professional development: a solitary or collegial (ad)venture? *Teaching and Teacher Education*, 16, 81–101.

Evans, L. and Teddlie, C. (1995) Facilitating change in schools: is there one best style? *School Effectiveness and School Improvement*, 6 (1), 1–22.

Fullan, M.G. and Hargreaves, A. (1992) *What is Worth Fighting for in your School?* Buckingham: Open University.

Glanz, J. and Neville, R.F. (1997) *Educational Supervision: Perspectives, Issues and Controversies*, Norwood: Christopher-Gordon.

Greenfield, W.D. Jr. (1999) *Moral leadership in schools: Fact or fancy* (paper presented at the annual meeting of the AERA, Montréal).

Hall, G.E., Rutherford, W.L. and Griffin, T.H. (1982) *Three Change Facilitator Styles: Some Indicators and a Proposed Framework*, Austin, TX: The University of Texas, Research and Development Center for Teacher Education.

Hall, G.E., Rutherford, W.E., Hord, S.M. and Huling-Austin L.L. (1984) Effects of three principal styles on school improvement, *Educational Leadership*, 41 (5), 22–29.

Hallinger, P. and Heck, R.H. (1996) Reassessing the principal's role in school effectiveness: a review of empirical research, 1980–1995, *Educational Administration Quarterly*, 32 (1), 5–44.

Hawley, W. and Valli, L. (1999) The essentials of effective professional development: a new consensus, in Darling-Hammond, L. and Sykes, G. (eds.) *Teaching as the Learning Profession: Handbook of Policy and Practice*, San Francisco, CA: Jossey Bass.

Huberman, A.M. (1993) Steps toward a developmental model of the teaching career, in Kremer-Hayon, L., Vonk, H.C. and Fessler, R. (eds.) *Teacher Professional Development: A Multiple Perspective Approach*, Amsterdam: Swetz & Zeitlinger.

Huberman, A.M. and Miles, M.B. (1989) Some procedures for causal analysis of multiple-case data, *International Journal of Qualitative Studies in Education*, 2 (1), 55–68.

Kelchtermans, G. and Vandenberghe, R. (1994) Teachers' professional development: a biographical perspective, *Journal of Curriculum Studies*, 26 (1), 45–62.

Kirby, P.C. and Colbert, R. (1992) *Principals who empower teachers* (paper presented at the annual meeting of the AERA, San Francisco).

Kvale, S. (1994) *Validation as communication and action, On the social construction of validity* (paper presented at the annual meeting of the AERA, New Orleans).

Leithwood, K. (1992) The principal's role in teacher development, in Fullan, M. and Hargreaves, A. (eds.) *Teacher Development and Educational Change*, London: Falmer.

Leithwood, K. (1994) Leadership for school restructuring, *Educational Administration Quarterly*, 30 (4), 498–518.

Leithwood, K. and Mongomery, D.J. (1983) The role of the elementary school principal in program improvement, *Review of Educational Research*, 52 (3), 309–339.

Lieberman, A. (1994) Teacher development: commitment and challenge, in Grimmett, P.P. and Neufeld, J. (eds.) *Teacher Development and the Struggle for Authenticity. Professional Growth and Restructuring in the Context of Change*, New York: Teachers College.

Lieberman, A. and Miller, L. (1990) The social realities of teaching, in Lieberman, A. (ed.) *Schools as Collaborative Cultures: Creating the Future Now*, London: Falmer.

Little, J.W. (1987) Teachers as colleagues, in Richardson-Koehler, V. (ed.) *Educators' Handbook: A Research Perspective*, New York: Longman.

Little, J.W. (1990) The persistance of privacy: autonomy and initiative in teachers' professional relations, *Teachers College Record*, 91 (4), 509–536.

Little, J.W. (1992) Teacher development and educational policy, in Fullan, M. and Hargreaves, A. (eds.) *Teacher Development and Educational Change*, London: Falmer.

Louis, K.S. and Smith, B. (1990) Teacher working conditions, in Reyes, P. (ed.) *Teachers and their Workplace. Commitment, Performance and Productivity*, Newbury Park, CA: Sage.

McLaughlin, M.W. (1994) Strategic sites for teachers' professional development, in Grimmett, P.P. and Neufeld, J. (eds.) *Teacher Development and the Struggle for Authenticity. Professional Growth and Restructuring in the Context of Change*, New York: Teachers College.

McLaughlin, M.W. and Yee, S. (1988) School as a place to have a career, in Lieberman, A. (ed.) *Building a Professional Culture in Schools*, New York: Teachers College.

Miles, M.B. and Huberman, A.M. (1994) *Qualitative Data Analysis. An Expanded Sourcebook*, Thousand Oaks, CA: Sage.

Parray, F.W. and Hall, G.E. (eds.) (1992) *Becoming a Principal. The Challenges of Beginning Leadership*, Boston, MA: Allyn & Bacon.

Reitzug, U.C. and Burrello, L.C. (1995) How principals can build self-renewing schools, *Educational Leadership*, 52 (7), 48–50.

Rosenholtz, S.J. (1989) *Teachers' Workplace. The Social Organization of Schools*, New York: Longman.

Schofield, J.W. (1990) Increasing generalizability of qualitative research, in Eisner, W.E. and Peshkin, A. (eds.) *Qualitative Inquiry in Education. The Continuing Debate*, New York: Teachers College.

Sheppard, B. (1996) Exploring the transformational nature of instructional leadership, *The Alberta Journal of Educational Research*, 42 (4), 325–344.

Smylie, M. (1994) Redesigning teachers' work: connections to the classroom, in Darling-Hammond, L. (ed.) *Review in Research of Education* (20), Washington DC: American Educational Research Association.

Staessens, K. (1993) The professional culture at 'The Cornflower', in Kieviet, F.K. and Vandenberghe, R. (eds.) *School Culture, School Improvement and Teacher Development*, Leiden: DSWO.

Vandenberghe, R. (1992) *Creative management of a school: a matter of vision and daily interventions* (paper presented at the second National Management Congress, Rand Afrikaans University, Johannesburg).

Vandenberghe, R., Dierynck, R. and Joris, C. (1999) Nog steeds enthousiast voor de klas (Still enthusiastic teachers), *Impuls*, 29, 153–160.

van den Berg, R. and Vandenberghe, R. (1988) *Onderwijsvernieuwing op een Keerpunt (Educational Improvement at a Turning Point)*, Tilburg: Zwijsen.

van den Berg, R. and Vandenberghe, R. (1999) *Succesvol leiding geven aan onderwijsinnovaties. Investeren in mensen (Successful Management of Educational Innovations. Investing in People)*, Alphen aan den Rijn: Samsom.

Wideen, M.F. (1992) School-based teacher development, in Fullan, M. and Hargreaves, A. (eds.) *Teacher Development and Educational Change*, London: Falmer.

Wildman, T.M., Niles, J.A., Magliaro, S.G. and McLaughlin, R.A. (1989) Teaching and learning to teach: the two roles of beginning teachers, *Elementary School Journal*, 89 (4), 471–493.

Yin, R.K. (1989) *Case Study Research: Design and Methods*, Newbury Park, CA: Sage.

9

Leadership Role: Morale, Job Satisfaction and Motivation

Linda Evans

Introduction

My research has focused on identifying and explaining the factors that affect job-related attitudes in schoolteachers (Evans, 1997a, 1998) and in academics (Evans and Abbott, 1998) and has revealed the complexity and intricacies of three specific job-related attitudes: morale, job satisfaction and motivation. My findings pointed to factors that are considerably more influential on these attitudes than those generally identified by assumption and common-sense reasoning. This chapter picks up what my research-informed analyses have led me to attribute as morale-, job-satisfaction- and motivation-influencing factors, identifying leadership as a key factor. Taking this as a starting point, it then applies a comparative analysis of research findings from two studies that used different categories of research subjects, in order to delve deeper into examining precisely what, fundamentally, affects job-related attitudes among education professionals.

A Fifth Stage of Elucidation

I have identified what may be considered to be four levels of understanding, or stages of elucidation, represented by work in the field of job-related attitudes. These range from a first level of understanding that has as its basis conventional wisdom and common-sense, but oversimplistic, reasoning. This level is exemplified by arguments that are typically promulgated by the media, such as those which equate job satisfaction with centrally initiated policy and conditions of service, including pay. At the other end of the range is the fourth level:

Source: *Educational Management & Administration*, Vol. 29, no. 3, 2001, pp. 291–306.
Edited version.

one of in-depth analysis and recognition of the need for conceptual clarity and precision. This level of understanding, recognizing the inaccuracies associated with crude generalization which ignores individualism, focuses upon the lowest common factor in relation to determinants of job satisfaction among individuals. Analysis at this fourth level seeks commonalties and generalization, but ones which are accurate, because they are free from contextual specificity. This level has contributed much to elucidation not only of what job satisfaction and morale are, but of what, fundamentally, are their determinants. Suggested determinants of job satisfaction are, typically, individuals' needs' fulfilment, expectations' fulfilment or values' congruence.

To these I have added a fifth stage of elucidation. If we accept that the rationale for undertaking any piece of research must not simply be to develop theory, but also to apply that developed theory to policy and practice, then information that, for example, teachers' or academics' job satisfaction is dependent upon their job-related needs or expectations being met is useful, but needs supplementing if it is to be applied meaningfully. The fifth level applies the lowest common factor analysis of level four to context-specific exemplars. In the case of my research into schoolteachers' job-related attitudes these are teaching-specific exemplars, and with the academics whom I studied the exemplars are specific to their work.

My research findings revealed schoolteacher morale, job satisfaction and motivation to be influenced much less by externally initiated factors, such as salary, educational policy and reforms and conditions of service, than by factors emanating from the more immediate context within which teachers work: school-specific or, more precisely, job-specific factors. As a result, leadership emerged as a key attitudes-influencing factor. Underpinning this, three factors were highlighted as being influential upon morale, job satisfaction and motivation: realistic expectations, relative perspective and professionality orientation. Relative perspective is the individual's perspective on her/his situation in relation to comparable situations. In the context of work situations, for example, relative perspectives may incorporate consideration of previous posts – in whole or in part – or of other institutions, or of colleagues' situations. The current job-related situation is perceived and evaluated in relation to other jobs or occupations, former jobs, knowledge of the situations of colleagues in other institutions or departments. Relative perspective also includes consideration of the work-related situation in relation to the rest of one's life. This consideration includes the relative prioritization of work and personal life.

Realistic expectations are influenced by relative perspective. They do not necessarily reflect individuals' ideals; rather, they reflect what the individual *realistically* expects from her/his work-related situation.

Through an iterative process, professionality orientation both influences and is influenced by realistic expectations and relative perspective. Professionality is not the same as professionalism. It is not a very widely known term and I am frequently asked by fellow academics, as well as schoolteachers, to explain it and its distinction from professionalism. It appears to have been introduced over 20 years ago by Hoyle (1975), who presented a continuum of teachers' professionality ranging from 'extended' to 'restricted'. I have defined professionality as: 'an ideologically-, attitudinally-, intellectually-, and epistemologically-based stance, on the part of an individual, in relation to the practice of the profession to which s/he belongs, and which influences her/his professional practice' (Evans, 1999).

I have highlighted intra-institutional disparity as one of the key findings of my research into schoolteachers' attitudes to their work (Evans, 1997a, 1998), arguing that it reflects a complex combination of individuals' professionality orientations, realistic expectations and relative perspectives. Essentially, my research findings have led me to the interpretation that it is perceived proximity to their conception of their job-related ideal that underpins individuals' job-related attitudes. This ideal may not necessarily have been conceptualized as such, but its dimensions begin to take shape through individuals' conceptions of their preferences and priorities. It is also dynamic; being liable to fluctuation and modification. Job-related ideals – or, put another way, ideal jobs – reflect individuals' current values, needs and expectations. These are influenced by relative perspective, and they underpin professionality orientation and realistic expectations. Since these vary from individual to individual, even within one professional group, what satisfies one teacher may not necessarily satisfy another, and the school that suits one may not suit another.

When the lowest common factor analysis, to which I refer above, was applied to teaching-specific exemplars leadership emerged as a key attitudes-influencing factor, since it shaped teachers' work contexts and had the capacity, through policy and decision-making, to enable or constrain and to determine individuals' proximity to their ideal jobs. Leaders, I have argued (Evans, 1999), are capable of filling teachers with enthusiasm or making them dread going to work every morning; more significantly, they may exacerbate the problems created by the imposition of centrally initiated policy or they may buffer teachers against them. My samples of schoolteachers reported diverse and wide-ranging levels of morale, job satisfaction and motivation which could, for the most part, be attributed to the influence that leadership imposed on individuals' working lives. My sample of academics, on the other hand, reported generally more uniform and, compared with the schoolteachers, considerably higher levels of morale, job satisfaction and motivation.

▌ The Research

This chapter draws upon the findings of two separate studies: a composite study of morale and job satisfaction among primary school teachers in the UK, and a study of the effectiveness of teaching and learning in higher education.

Composite study of teacher morale and job satisfaction

This comprized four studies, carried out from 1988 to 1992, each having a different focus within the broad, overall, remit of identifying and examining factors which influence teacher morale and job satisfaction. Pseudonyms are used in all references to my samples. A more detailed description of the research design of this study, including samples of core interview questions and details of the questionnaire used, as well as sample details, is provided in Evans (1997b, 1998).

The effectiveness of teaching and learning in higher education

The main aim of this study was to acquire greater understanding of how teaching in higher education may be effective in meeting what both students and tutors perceived as their needs. Data were collected through semi-structured interviews with 20 tutors and 36 students from a university which is recognized for its strong research focus. This is an old university. The sample of tutors and students represented four different degree courses. Interviews with tutors incorporated discussion of what they perceived to be their job-related ideals and needs, as well as issues influencing morale, job satisfaction and motivation. A more detailed description of the research design of this study, including interview schedules and processes of analysis, is provided in Evans and Abbott (1998: 19–27).

■ Continuing the Story: Applying a Comparative Analysis

It was the disparity between the two different samples, schoolteachers and academics, in relation to reported levels of morale, job satisfaction and motivation, that prompted me to want to delve deeper into analysing influences on these job-related attitudes. The schoolteacher sample reported diverse and wide-ranging levels, which were generally attributable to leadership, while the academics, who seemed unaffected by leadership, had, for the most part, comparatively higher levels of morale, job satisfaction and motivation.

An outline of the research findings from both studies is presented in Table 9.1. The starting point in trying to understand better the nature of, and the influences on, morale, job satisfaction and motivation among education professionals was to examine what accounts for commonalities and differences between and within the two samples. A reasonable assumption would be that, since the schoolteachers represented four different institutions, and the academics only one, the distinction between the two samples in relation to the range of levels of job-related attitudes is institutional. This is not the case, however. While it could be claimed that, if my sample of tutors is representative, the university in question was one that fostered positive job-related attitudes among its academic staff, it was certainly not the case that any of the four institutions represented by my schoolteacher sample sustained staff morale, job satisfaction and motivation levels that were sufficiently uniform to warrant its being categorized as a 'high morale' or a 'low morale' school. Within each of the four primary schools morale, job satisfaction and motivation levels varied; in some cases dramatically, and in other cases less significantly.

Table 9.1 *Outline of general trends, within each of the two samples, emerging from the research findings relating to schoolteachers' and academics' job-related attitudes*

	Schoolteachers	Academics
Morale, job satisfaction and motivation levels	Diverse	General uniform
Description of levels	Wide-ranging: from very high to very low	Narrow in range: from high to very high
Key factors influencing diversity of levels within sample	Professionality orientation Prioritization of job	Length of service at the university
Key factors influencing morale, job satisfaction and motivation levels	Institutional leadership Institutional organization Institutional policy and practice Collegial relations	Compatibility with institutional ethos Link between teaching and research
General sources of positive job-related attitudes	Teaching Decisional participation Collegiality Interpersonal relations	Research Training Collegiality
General sources of negative job-related attitudes	Institutional policy Management decisions Interpersonal relations	Teaching Institutional policy Departmental policy
Specific sources of positive job-related attitudes	Passing on skills/knowledge Personal efficiency Leading INSET Collegial camaraderie Involvement in institutional policy/decision-making Recognition from respected colleagues	Academic freedom Recognition from the academic community Contributing to advancing knowledge/understanding Passing on skills/knowledge Mentoring colleagues
Specific sources of negative job-related attitudes	Poor management Ineffective leadership Incompatibility with institutional professional climate	'Low level' administrative responsibilities Teaching 'low calibre' students Teaching loads Responsibility for teaching general courses unrelated to own research

My interpretation that proximity to an 'ideal job' determines job satisfaction, morale and motivation levels was borne out by the academics' study. Out of the full sample of 20, six tutors admitted that they already, or very nearly, had what they considered to be their ideal jobs and these tutors reported very high levels of job satisfaction, motivation and morale. Of the remainder, the majority, who reported generally high levels of job satisfaction, motivation and morale, perceived their work as incorporating many elements of their 'ideal job'. The small minority that were rather more – though not excessively so – dissatisfied, applying their relative perspective to the evaluation of their situation, felt that their work had lost many of those elements that had made it, for them, more 'ideal' than it currently was.

Yet, while I have dismissed the notion of 'high morale' or 'low morale' institutions, it is clear from my findings that there is a very strong institutional dimension to the job-related attitudes of both schoolteachers and academics. Since it is within the contexts in which individuals work that the job-related needs that both underpin and reflect their job-related ideals are able to be met, the institution is immensely influential on levels of job satisfaction, morale and motivation. The nature of this influence is individualized, because job-related needs and ideals are diverse. It is a question, not of a model of general motivational, or morale-friendly, institutional policies and ethos, but of the degree of match between individuals and their institutions: what I have referred to elsewhere (Evans, 1998) as round pegs and square holes, or, as Vancouver and Schmitt (1991) describe it, 'person–organization fit'. In this comparative analysis I try to identify more precisely the constituent features of a good match.

Uncompromising Contexts: The Basis of a Good Match

Most of the academics' and some of the schoolteachers' cases represent good matches. Common to all of these cases was the individual's general acceptance of institutional policy and practice. This was a genuine acceptance, rather than what Lacey (1977) terms strategic compliance, but it did not preclude specific areas of contention; it was an overall, rather than a wholehearted and total, acceptance. Similarly, mismatches were represented by cases of individuals' overall dissension of institutional policy and practice.

The bases of acceptance or dissension of institutional policy and practice were a complex and dynamic interrelated combination of individuals' ideologies, values, knowledge, understanding, expectations and prioritizations – all of which are constituent elements of professionality. With reference to my research into schoolteachers' job-related attitudes I have previously (Evans, 1998) identified as the basic determinant of the degree of individual–institution match the extent to which there is ideological compatibility between school leaders – in particular, headteachers – and teachers. Leadership, then, I reasoned, is one of the most potent influences upon morale, job satisfaction and motivation.

Moreover, in uncovering this relationship between perceptions of leadership and teachers' attitudes to their jobs, I found that my research findings corroborated those of others (Ball, 1987; Hayes and Ross, 1989; Nias, 1980, 1989; Nias *et al.*, 1989; Rosenholtz, 1991; Veal *et al.*, 1989). In particular, in one of the earliest studies of teacher morale – a questionnaire survey of nearly 1800 American teachers – Chase became aware of this relationship: 'When teachers' expectations are fulfilled with regard to the leadership of administrators and supervisors, their morale soars; when their expectations are disappointed, morale takes a nose dive' (1953: 1). However, in the light of analysis of the findings of my study of academics, I now consider it an oversimplified and inadequate interpretation that morale, job satisfaction and motivation are significantly influenced by leadership. I do not reject my original identification of leadership as a significant influence on job-related attitudes; rather, I qualify it. I present a fuller interpretation of precisely *why* it is so influential and of the nature of its influence.

Comparison of the job-related factors that were applicable to my two samples, schoolteachers and academics, highlighted leadership as a potentially significant one, since I was struck immediately by the disparity in relation to the extent to which leadership impacted upon the working lives of each of the two samples. Among my sample of schoolteachers, which, in this respect, seems to be typical of the profession as a whole as it still is today, institutional leadership was a dominant feature of individuals' working lives. This was the case even where leaders were considered ineffective or inadequate. The nature of teachers' working lives within the social and administrative structure of the school is very leader-dependent. In the developed western world at the turn of the millennium, frequent policy changes and reforms aimed at improving standards, and an emphasis on accountability, meant that effective teaching in schools and colleges could not be done unilaterally. It now involves collegial cooperation and interdependence and institutional coherence of policy and practice, all of which require coordination on the part of one or more leaders. Leadership which is deficient because it fails to provide the necessary coordination therefore impacts as much upon teachers' working lives as does effective leadership. Among my sample of academics, however, leadership featured considerably less prominently in relation to individuals' working lives. The nature of these academics' work was such that most of it seemed to be leader-independent and able to be carried out with a high degree of autonomy. Perhaps one reason for this is that research constituted a large proportion of the academics' work, and this is an activity which may generally be carried out effectively independently of institutional or departmental leadership. Authoritarianism and hierarchism, which underpin the structure of institutional organization in the compulsory education sector, were not evident in the day-to-day business of academic life, as it was reported by my sample.

Of the schoolteachers whom I interviewed and observed, those who reported low levels of morale and job satisfaction and, in some cases, motivation, attributed their negative attitudes to poor leadership and management in their schools. From the evidence outlined so far, therefore, it is reasonable to assume that leadership is an important factor that needs to be incorporated into consideration of what influences job-related attitudes among education professionals: negative attitudes are associated with contexts where leadership features prominently, positive attitudes are associated with contexts where there is much more leader-independence. Is the solution to problems of low morale and job satisfaction among schoolteachers, therefore, to get rid of headteachers and give teachers as much freedom and autonomy as academics appear to have? There is, after all, a precedent for this; schools in Zurich currently do not have headteachers and teacher morale there is reported to be high (Baker, 1998; BBC, 1998).

The issue is not so simple and straightforward. First, school leadership did not necessarily have a detrimental effect on the job-related attitudes of my teachers; there were a few examples of relative indifference on the part of teachers to their headteachers' leadership and management, as well as several examples of leadership that was attributed as fostering very positive job-related attitudes. Second, academics' working lives are not as leader-independent as they may appear. My comparative analysis is complicated by the existence of two levels of leadership that were applicable to the academics: departmental and institutional. Although departmental leadership appeared to impact only negligibly upon their day-to-day working lives (five departments were represented by my sample), the academics were essentially influenced by institutional leadership, since it determined the wider, pervasive ethos within which they operated and which they accepted, and which, in turn, was reflected in policy- and decision-making that impacted upon their work (the university in question had a distinct ethos reflecting a strong, explicit research culture). Third – and this is, I suggest, one of the most significant revelations to arise from my comparative analysis – leadership is not, *fundamentally*, in itself, an attitudes-influencing factor. Rather, it is the medium through which are transmitted the values and ideologies represented by the contexts in which people work. My current definition of a work context is: 'the situation and circumstances, arising out of a combination and interrelationship of institutionally- and externally-imposed conditions, that constitute the environment and culture within which an individual carries out her/his job.' What influences job-related attitudes is the extent to which these contexts are acceptable to individuals, on the basis of the degree of congruence between their own values and ideologies and those that shape the work contexts. Leadership is *seen to be* an attitudes influencing factor because it imposes considerable influence on these work contexts, either actively or, in the case of ineffective, laissez-faire leadership, by default.

The precise nature of the values and ideologies that underpin individuals' conceptions of what, for them, are 'ideal' jobs was another significant finding to be uncovered by my comparative analysis. In the cases of schoolteachers and academics, job-related ideals incorporated ethical, epistemological, affective, professional, economic and egocentric considerations to encompass views on six specific issues:

- equity and justice
- pedagogy or androgogy
- organizational efficiency
- interpersonal relations
- collegiality
- self-conception and self-image

It is impossible to arrange these issues hierarchically because individuals differed in their prioritizations of them. Nevertheless, all six were incorporated into every conception of an 'ideal' job.

The basis of a good match is an 'uncompromising context': a work context that does not require individuals to compromise their ideologies as reflected by their views on the six issues listed above. An 'uncompromising context' is one that accommodates individuals' views on these six issues – particularly those that they consider most important. Within my two samples the nature of individuals' views on each of these issues was wide-ranging.

Equity and justice

Situations and circumstances that were considered to be unfair were identified as sources of dissatisfaction by schoolteachers and academics. Precisely what constituted unfairness varied considerably from one individual to another, reflecting differences arising from professionality orientation, relative experience and realistic expectations. The range of perceived unfairness included situations and circumstances that discriminated against the individual him/herself, discriminated against others, afforded unmerited advantages to others and differentiated where it was felt there should be uniformity or commonality.

Pedagogy or androgogy

This issue concerned individuals' perceptions of the quality of educational provision within their institutions or departments. Views related to teaching methods, course/curriculum content, teacher–learner relations and departmental or institutional aims, general policy and culture in relation to teaching and learning. Dissonance between individuals' views and those reflected in policy and practice within their institutions or departments potentially contributed towards 'compromising contexts'. For some, potential 'compromising contexts' were those in which could be found examples of educational provision that reflected views dissonant from their own. For others, only if dissonant views imposed constraints on their own practice were their work contexts considered 'compromising'.

Organizational efficiency

'Uncompromising contexts' were those in which the day-to-day running of their institutions or departments generally came close to matching individuals' views on organizational efficiency. Conversely, perceived inefficiency potentially contributed towards creating 'compromising contexts'. As with pedagogical or androgogical issues, for some individuals 'compromising contexts' were those in which examples of perceived organizational inefficiency could be found. For others, 'compromising contexts' were only those in which perceived organizational inefficiency impacted upon their own working lives.

Interpersonal relations

Though it was evident among both groups, this issue was considerably more prominent among the sample of schoolteachers than among that of academics. This probably reflects the generally more communal nature of schoolteachers' working lives in relation to the rather more isolated nature of academics' day-to-day lives. Indeed, the importance within teachers' working lives of staffroom relations has been highlighted in several studies (Nias, 1985; Nias *et al.*, 1989; Woods, 1984, 1990). 'Compromising contexts' were those in which the extent and/or the nature of workplace interpersonal relations failed to match individuals' 'ideals'; 'uncompromising contexts' were those that accommodated individuals' views. This issue involved not only collegial relations but also relations with clients, ancillary staff and governors.

Collegiality

This overlaps with interpersonal relations, but is also sufficiently distinct from it to merit separate categorization. Collegiality refers to the work-related product or output of workplace interpersonal relations. It includes features such as the degree and quality of: teamwork, cooperative ways of working, consultation and interdependence and support among colleagues. 'Uncompromising contexts' were those in which individuals' perceptions of the level and/or quality of collegiality that prevailed within their institutions or departments approximated to their 'ideals'. 'Compromising contexts' were those in which there was incongruence between these two.

Self-conception and self-image

This issue represents, in a sense, an amalgamation of the five issues already listed, yet it also goes beyond them. It concerns the extent to which individuals' work contexts supported, reinforced and even shaped their perceptions of themselves, both personally and professionally. 'Compromising contexts' were those that created dissatisfaction with individuals' self-conceptions and self-images, by, for example, requiring them to act in ways that were contrary to their nature or to their ideologies and beliefs. 'Uncompromising contexts' were those in which self-conceptions and self-images were able to be sustained, or even enhanced, in accordance with the demands and requirements of the job. A bad match was one where individuals were, in order to perform their jobs, required to be someone that they were unhappy being, in some way and to some extent. A good match was one in which the job might be considered to bring out the best in someone.

These six issues clearly matter to schoolteachers and academics. In general, a good match, therefore, is a work context that does not compromise the individual's professionality. What education professionals evidently want is to be able to practise, unhindered, within a context that is compatible with their needs, expectations, values and ideologies.

Implications for Policy and Practice in Educational Management and Leadership

Since it is at institutional level that morale, job satisfaction and motivation are influenced most of all, it is at this level that they are best able to be enhanced and improved. Mercer and Evans (1991: 297) recognize that, although there are limits to what may be achieved, institutional leaders and managers do have scope to redress the negative effects upon teachers' attitudes to their work of government-imposed policy and rhetoric. They refer to school managers' failure to address the issue of job satisfaction among staff as 'professional myopia':

> There appears to be an element of short-sightedness on the part of senior staff who have the responsibility for ensuring the highest quality of performance from teachers . . . there is a great and perhaps largely unnecessary loss to the teaching profession.

My own research, too, has illustrated the capacity that educational leaders and managers have for buffering their staff against potentially demoralizing, dissatisfying and demotivating externally imposed changes (Evans, 1999), and anecdotal evidence based upon a secondary school headteacher's first-hand experience corroborates this: 'Many teachers face poor prospects, low morale and even lower pay levels, but treat them right and they'll move mountains for you' (Stephens, 1998).

Quite apart from this compensatory role, institutional leadership and management can do much to foster positive job-related attitudes by helping to create and sustain work contexts that are conducive to high morale, job satisfaction and motivation. This chapter has presented evidence of what such work contexts involve and of the nature of the influence of leadership upon job-related attitudes. It is to the provision of work contexts that are congruent with individuals' values, ideologies and expectations in relation to the six issues identified that leadership may most effectively contribute. This is not simple and straight-forward to achieve because, as I have pointed out, these values, ideologies and expectations vary from individual to individual. The leader who, in the interests of raising morale and increasing job satisfaction and motivation, wants to shape uncompromising contexts clearly has her/his work cut out. How, then, may work contexts be shaped in order to cater for diversity? How may individual, rather than simply a majority of, needs be met? I suggest two approaches that are not mutually exclusive and may, therefore, be combined: a 'teacher-centred' approach to educational leadership, and a contractual approach.

I have introduced my 'teacher-centred' approach elsewhere (Evans, 1998: 160–71; 1999: Ch. 6). Essentially, it parallels – and takes its name from – a child-centred approach to teaching. I present it as an educational management and leadership ideology that is predicated upon acceptance that leaders and man-agers have as much responsibility towards the staff whom they lead and manage as they do towards the pupils and students within their institution, and that this responsibility extends as far as endeavouring to meet as many individual needs as possible, within the confines imposed by having to consider more corporate needs. The 'teacher-centred' leader behaves towards the staff whom she/he leads with as much care and solicitude and interest in their welfare as would a 'child-centred' teacher towards the pupils in her/his care. In some respects, 'teacher-centred' educational leadership resembles what Sergiovanni labels 'ped-agogical leadership' – certainly, there is overlap between the two:

> Pedagogical leadership differs from bureaucratic, visionary and entrepreneurial leadership in that it is capital intensive but not in an economics sense. Instead of increasing material value, pedagogical leadership adds value by developing various forms of human capital. (Sergiovanni, 1998: 38)

'Teacher-centred' leadership focuses on the individuals that make up a staff, rather than a staff unit as a whole; it treats individuals differently and is responsive to the diversity that constitutes 'the staff'. The 'teacher-centred' leader would try to develop a work context that, underpinned by a professional culture of tolerance, cooperation, compromize and consideration for others, is as 'uncompromising' as possible for as many individuals as possible for as much of the time as possible. Diametrically opposed to this approach is author-itarian leadership that reflects the leader's own stance – his/her values, ideologies, expectations and aspirations – and that promotes these and tries to enforce them within institutional policy- and decision-making.

My second suggestion, the contractual approach, is not an ideology but quite simply an approach to leadership and management that may reflect any ideol-ogy. It sits perfectly easily with authoritarian leadership, but it may also go hand-in-hand with 'teacher-centred' leadership. It would involve institutional and departmental leaders setting out their stalls and making explicit their ways of operating; indicating clearly not only their expectations of teachers but also the nature of the managerial and leadership service that they would be prepared to provide. This may even include the formulation of a 'contract' of commitment, or what is effectively a service level agreement. By this process principals, head-teachers and departmental heads, for example, could list what they consider to be specific key features of their management and leadership in the form of an outline of behaviour to which they expect to adhere. This 'contract' would be reviewed annually in the light of comments from members of staff. It would be accepted as a code of behaviour to which a particular specific headteacher would aspire, or endeavour to sustain, rather than a legally binding agreement or even a promise carved in stone. It would be linked to statements of institutional values, ethos and general policy, but all these would have to come much closer to reflect-ing reality than does much of the rhetoric that is typically included in many school or college prospectuses, mission statements and development plans. It would require leaders to lay their cards on the table and allow teachers, in turn, to see what kind of a hand they could expect to be dealt if they accepted a spe-cific post. I base this idea on evidence from my research that the academics in my sample held much clearer ideas than did the schoolteachers of what their work was to involve, and what was expected of them and required of them to be suc-cessful. Unlike the schoolteachers, they all recognized the ideological basis of the degree of match between themselves and their work contexts. They were able to identify the distinct institutional culture and ethos that determined the context in which they worked and which influenced their job-related attitudes through the extent to which it was assimilated. They all 'knew the score' and understood the implications for their working lives of the specific features and facets of this culture. Their morale was higher, and their job-related attitudes more positive, generally, than those of the schoolteacher sample. It is not unreasonable to attribute this – at least in part – to their being generally better matched to their work contexts because they had a better idea of what to expect from them.

If morale, job satisfaction and motivation are influenced by the degree of match between individuals and the contexts in which they work, and in particu-lar, as my research has shown, in relation to six specific issues, then the process of achieving a good match ought to be left much less to chance than it seems to be. On the whole, academics seem to be in the position of knowing, broadly, what they are letting themselves in for when they take up an appointment; what they can expect of the work-related context in which they will find themselves when they become a member of a university staff. Schoolteachers, on the whole, are much less secure in this respect. Since there are many more variables involved, compatibility with their new work-related contexts is generally much more of a 'hit and miss' affair. What is perhaps needed, then, is a more thorough selection process, not just on the part of schools appointing new staff, but also on the part of staff seeking new posts. Teachers would potentially be able to select the schools where they work with a view to ideological compatibility, thus increasing the likelihood of their job-fulfilment, through their job-related needs being met. Similarly, schools may recruit new members of staff with the same considerations of compatibility and, in doing so, increase the likelihood of perpetuating their individual institutional culture and ethos.

Conclusion

This comparative analysis has revealed leadership to influence job-related attitudes not directly, as I believed a year ago, but in an indirect way, through its capacity for shaping work contexts that either match, or are at odds with, what individuals want in relation to: equity and justice, pedagogy or androgogy, organizational efficiency, interpersonal relations, collegiality and self-conception and self-image. It is this degree of match that fundamentally affects how people feel about their jobs. Whether they realize it or not, it is their work contexts – not their leader – upon which people are essentially reliant, and analysis of the findings of a parallel study, encompassing a wider perspective than that afforded by examination of the schoolteacher study only, demonstrated this to be the case. Yet, this revelation does not diminish the responsibility of educational leaders towards those whom they lead, in relation to fostering positive attitudes; it depersonalizes it and it also delineates it. Understanding what matters to people, and, in particular, knowing precisely what are the key issues upon which the acceptability of an individual's work context depends are crucial to effective leadership. This chapter has contributed to that knowledge and understanding.

References

Baker, M. (1998 'Pay Alone is Not the Key, Mr Blunkett', *The Times Educational Supplement* (11 Dec.): 8.

Ball, S.J. (1987) *The Micro-Politics of the School*. London: Routledge.

British Broadcasting Corporation (1998) *Scrutiny*, broadcast Monday 26 October, BBC 2.

Chase, F.S. (1953) 'Professional Leadership and Teacher Morale', *Administrator's Notebook* 1(8): 1–4.

Evans, L. (1992) 'Teacher Morale: An Individual Perspective', *Educational Studies* 18(2): 161–71.

Evans, L. (1997a) 'Understanding Teacher Morale and Job satisfaction', *Teaching and Teacher Education: An International Journal of Research and Study* 13(8): 831–45.

Evans, L. (1997b) 'Addressing Problems of Conceptualization and Construct Validity in Researching Teachers' Job Satisfaction', *Educational Research* 39(3): 319–31.

Evans, L. (1998) *Teacher Morale, Job Satisfaction and Motivation*. London: Paul Chapman.

Evans, L. (1999) *Managing to Motivate: A Guide for School Leaders*. London: Cassell.

Evans, L. and Abbott, I. (1998) *Teaching and Learning in Higher Education*. London: Cassell.

Hayes, L.F. and Ross, D.D. (1989) 'Trust versus Control: The Impact of School Leadership on Teacher Reflection', *International Journal of Qualitative Studies in Education* 2(4): 335–50.

Hoyle, E. (1975) 'Professionality, Professionalism and Control in Teaching', in V. Houghton *et al.* (eds.) *Management in Education: The Management of Organizations and Individuals*, pp. 314–20. London: Ward Lock Educational in association with Open University Press.

Lacey, C. (1977) *The Socialization of Teachers*. London: Methuen.

Mercer, D. and Evans, B. (1991) 'Professional Myopia: Job Satisfaction and the Management of Teachers', *School Organization* 11(3): 291–301.

Nias, J. (1980) 'Leadership Styles and Job Satisfaction in Primary Schools', in T. Bush, R. Glatter, J. Goodey and C. Riches (eds.) *Approaches to School Management*, pp. 255–73. London: Harper & Row.

Nias, J. (1985) 'Reference Groups in Primary Teaching, Talking, Listening and Identity', in S. Ball and I.F. Goodson (eds.) *Teachers' Lives and Careers*, pp. 105–19. Lewes: Falmer Press.

Nias, J. (1989) *Primary Teachers Talking: A Study of Teaching as Work*. London: Routledge.

Nias, J., Southworth, G. and Yeomans, R. (1989) *Staff Relationships in the Primary School: A Study of Organizational Cultures*. London: Cassell.

Rosenholtz, S. (1991) *Teachers' Workplace: the Social Organization of Schools*. New York: Teachers College Press.

Sergiovanni, T. (1998) 'Leadership as Pedagogy, Capital Development and School Effectiveness', *International Journal of Leadership in Education* 1(1): 47–53.

Stephens, T. (1998) 'It All Sounds Obvious, But . . .', *Guardian Education* (15 Dec.): 33.

Vancouver, J.B. and Schmitt, N.W. (1991) 'An Exploratory Examination of Person–Organization Fit: Organizational Goal Congruence', *Personnel Psychology* 44(2): 333–52.

Veal, M.L., Clift, R. and Holland, P. (1989) 'School Contexts that Encourage Reflection: Teacher Perceptions', *International Journal of Qualitative Studies in Education* 2(4): 315–33.

Woods, P. (1984) 'The Meaning of Staffroom Humour', in A. Hargreaves and P. Woods (eds.) *Classrooms and Staffrooms*, pp. 190–202. Milton Keynes: Open University Press.

Woods, P. (1990) *Teacher Skills and Strategies*. London: Falmer Press.

10

Workload and the Professional Culture of Teachers

Helen Timperley and Viviane Robinson

In this chapter, we take a somewhat controversial position and argue that the increased workload and stress associated with a self-managing environment can be attributed, in part, to the ways in which teachers organize themselves. Teachers not only suffer from workload problems but also create them, and their greater involvement in systemic reform, as recommended by Fullan (1996), may not lead to the desired coherence of reform efforts. Our argument centres on the premise that organizing principles developed to meet the challenges of managing single-cell classrooms, such as individualism, autonomy (Bush, 1995; Fullan, 1993; Little, 1990; Smyth, 1996) and strong subject department identity (Johnson, 1990; Lee *et al.*, 1993; MacLaughlin and Talbert, 1990; Siskin, 1994), impede the systemic thinking (Senge, 1992; Sterman, 1994) required for developing coherence in reforms which go beyond the unit of the classroom or department. When reform requires a systemic response, these organizing principles are likely to result in increased workload through fragmentation, duplication of effort and the addition of new tasks to those already existing.

We develop this argument by drawing on the relevant literature about how teachers organize their work, identifying, in particular, the autonomy accorded to individuals and departments and the relatively uncritical support which teachers offer to their colleagues. We then suggest how these organizing principles may reduce coherence and exacerbate workload and propose that a greater emphasis on systemic thinking is needed if teacher involvement in school-wide initiatives is to be successful and manageable. Finally, we illustrate our argument through a previously unpublished school-based case study in which a group of teachers in a school with a high degree of self-management undertook a major school-wide initiative.

Source: Educational Management & Administration, Vol. 28, no. 1, 2001, pp. 47–62.
Edited version.

■ Autonomy and Collegiality

Organizational theorists have long identified schools as loosely coupled systems in which the various components, while responsive to one another, preserve their own identity through some degree of separateness (Weick, 1976). This relative independence of operation provides teachers with the autonomy to make individual judgements to deal with the uncertainty and complexity of classroom environments. While functional for the relatively independent operations of single-cell classrooms (Lee *et al.*, 1993; Weick, 1976), autonomy can place limitations on the coherence of school-wide initiatives when it comes to mean 'freedom from scrutiny and the largely unexamined right to exercise personal preference' (Little, 1990: 513). If each individual decides independently how he or she will act, how does the school as an organization develop coherent responses to organizational issues?

Recent research on secondary-school organization has given a central role to the department, for it is from that unit, rather than from the school as a whole, that teachers derive their professional identity and their understanding of teaching and learning (Hargreaves and MacMillan, 1995; Lee *et al.*, 1993; MacLaughlin and Talbert, 1990; Siskin, 1994, 1997). Although strong departmental identity may be appropriate when addressing departmental issues, school-wide initiatives require teachers to think and coordinate their efforts across departmental boundaries. As Siskin (1997) concludes from her case studies of three principals attempting to develop coherence in their school-wide visions, 'Departmental divisions confront reformers with powerful barriers to school-wide communication and community' (Siskin, 1997: 621).

Teachers are often encouraged to balance individual and departmental autonomy with greater collegiality as a way of promoting professionalism (Darling-Hammond, 1990; Firestone, 1996), of improving decision-making through sharing expertise (Wallace and Hall, 1994; Weick and McDaniel, 1989) and of providing coherence in systemic reform (Fullan, 1996; Hannay and Ross, 1997). Empirical examination of collegial processes in schools, however, show that the benefits of collegiality rarely live up to expectations because norms of mutual and uncritical support take precedence over enhancing the validity of information fundamental to quality decision making (Argyris, 1990; Bush, 1995; Lipman, 1997; Timperley and Robinson, 1998). For example, Little (1990) observed that supportive collegial norms often preclude discussions about curriculum or instructional practice when such discussions might imply concerns about a colleague's competence.

Implications for workload

How do these norms of departmental and individual autonomy and supportive collegiality impact on teachers' workload in a self-managing environment? It is assumed that a self-managing school will develop a school-wide vision and practices consistent with that vision (Fullan, 1996; Siskin, 1997; Hannay and Ross, 1997). Developing such a vision in a loosely coupled system is fraught, however, because alignment of strategic activities requires coordination among staff who are accustomed to a high degree of independence. Teachers who think and act within their own bounded single-cell classrooms or departments are likely to create the fragmentation and resulting overload portrayed by Fullan (1996) as they duplicate, or even compete with, each other's efforts. Such fragmentation is almost inevitable when systemic considerations, such as the interrelationship among individual and departmental initiatives are neglected.

Potential compounding of workload is also likely to occur when supportive collegiality and autonomy result in a reluctance to discuss the merits of current curricula or instructional practice for fear of possible exposure to implied judgements of competence (Little, 1990). The absence of such discussion leaves those seeking to introduce new initiatives with limited options for discontinuing what currently exists. New initiatives, therefore, are likely to be added to existing workloads unless individuals privately decide on discontinuation of the old.

Systems Thinking

We propose that if teachers are to be effective contributors to school-wide initiatives in a self-managing environment without increasing their workloads unreasonably, then they must go beyond the bounded thinking and action required for managing individual classrooms and departments to that which is more systemic. Sterman (1994: 291) identifies system thinking as, 'the ability to see the world as a complex system, in which we understand that "you can't just do one thing" that "everything is connected" '. A key skill Sterman identifies for engaging in such thinking is to create maps of the structure of an issue through eliciting the knowledge and beliefs which actors bring to its discussion and resolution. Senge (1992) refers to this process as surfacing and testing mental models in ways that identify and challenge an individual's leaps of abstraction between what actually occurs and the inferences that are made.

In uncertain environments, such as schools, individuals are likely to have very different mental models of the structure of an issue because its complexity and ambiguity will support varied causal interpretations. Sterman (1994) claims that individuals are more likely to improve their understanding of the systems they have created if they engage in a dialogue which tests their assumptions of causal structure of the issue.

Organizing principles that neglect considerations beyond a department, or preclude discussion of the merits of current practice, impede the processes Sterman (1994) and Senge (1993) describe as fundamental to systems thinking. For example, awareness of the systematic implications of individual or departmental practice is inevitably limited if teachers interact only with departmental colleagues, for they are likely to hold similar views about curriculum knowledge and how it should be organized (Siskin, 1997). Similarly, if supportive collegial norms preclude discussion of issues of instructional practice, how can models of existing instruction be challenged? When systemic rather than individual or departmental initiatives are mounted, organizing principles more compatible with systems thinking need to be employed.

In the remainder of this chapter, we pursue the issue of how teachers both create and suffer from workload problems, through a school-based case study at a suburban high school which we call 'Phoenix College'. This case illustrates how a group of teachers, representative of different departments in the school, set about improving the achievement of minority students. We argue that norms of departmental and individual autonomy led to the development of parallel structures and the addition of new tasks for this already overworked group. The problem of workload was compounded by a norm of collegiality which precluded public criticism of practices which were privately judged inadequate. In the absence of voluntary withdrawal of such practices, the new initiatives inevitably added to the teachers' workload.

The Case Study

Phoenix College, a large secondary school in New Zealand, had a high degree of autonomy from central authorities in the management of both its operational and teacher salary budget. The instructional programme was constrained by centrally mandated curriculum objectives, but decisions about how to organize that instruction were largely the school's responsibility. The school wanted to improve the achievement of its Pacific[1] students who comprised 18 per cent of its enrolment. Despite its reputation for academic success, Pacific students were disproportionately represented in the school's non-academic programme and were underperforming academically. Three years prior to the research, the principal and the school's only Samoan teacher had attempted to address the problem by developing a multi-pronged initiative designed to improve the attendance and performance of Pacific students.

Initially, Phoenix College was one of six schools involved in a research study on how schools solve complex administrative and curricular problems. Our findings from this earlier phase of the research showed that, although Pacific student achievement had improved over the previous three years, the effectiveness of some aspects of the initiative was compromised by unresolved differences among key staff about how best to assist these students. In response to this analysis, the school decided to establish a taskforce with a brief to examine reasons for improved Pacific achievement and to determine how it could be improved further. This case study focuses on the work of this taskforce.

Method

Our initial involvement during the first phase of the research took place over a period of six months and culminated in a research report and feedback to the key staff involved in the Pacific student achievement initiative. The second phase of the research, which is the subject of this chapter, involved intensive data collection over the subsequent eight months, with follow-up data gathered for a further three months.

Data-collection methods comprised audio-taping and observing 10 meetings of the taskforce. Twenty-one audio-taped interviews with the principal, task-force members and other relevant staff were completed by the first author and a research assistant. In addition, many informal conversations took place before and after formal meetings and over the telephone. Numerous documents were analysed, including taskforce minutes, archival documents of the school's initiatives to improve Pacific student achievement over the previous three years and trends in public examination results.

Data analysis was inductive and continued throughout the duration of the case study. It was informed by problem-based methodology (Robinson, 1993) in which the first step was to identify the taskforce's key practices. Since we sought to explain those practices by connecting them to organizational norms existing in the school, we reconstructed the values, beliefs and practical considerations that underlay them. This reconstruction, summarized in Figure 10.1, took into account both the practitioners' explanations of their practices and the frequently unstated beliefs and values that appeared to the researchers to underpin them. Given the possibility for error in this process, the accuracy of all reconstructions was checked with the relevant practitioners in feedback interviews.

Pacific Student Achievement Initiative

The work of the taskforce is briefly described in terms of the way it was structured and the processes it typically employed in its meetings. These descriptions are followed by discussion of the organizing principles that explain its operation and achievements.

Structure of initiatives to improve Pacific student achievement

Over a period of three to four years the number of programmes and initiatives to assist Pacific students at Phoenix College increased from three to 13. During this period, no programmes were discontinued or evaluated for their effectiveness, more were simply added on to those already existing. Pacific students had traditionally received assistance from three established school programmes that catered for students with English language or other learning difficulties. These included a non-academic Home Room programme, in which students were taught the core curriculum by one teacher, and two withdrawal and in-class English support programmes. These programmes are identified in Table 10.1 as 'Established Programmes'. A multi-pronged initiative to improve Pacific student achievement, developed three years prior to the research, included parents, staff and students in seven new initiatives, such as a homework centre, parent support groups and staff training in teaching students for whom English is a second language (see Table 10.1). Student achievement in public examinations was showing a gradual improvement but still well below that of other ethnic groups. The new taskforce for Pacific student achievement, the focus of this research, was set up to examine ways to further improve Pacific student achievement. These new initiatives focused on improving home–school relationships, identification procedures for student placement, and classroom teaching and learning. In effect, this added three new initiatives to those programmes and initiatives already in operation.

Table 10.1 *Initiatives to assist Pacific students at Phoenix College*

Programme and initiatives	Time since established	Cumulative no. of initiatives
Established programmes: Home Room, in-class and withdrawal English support	>3 years	3
Pacific student achievement initiative: Included staff professional development, parent involvement and student support through counselling and a homework centre	3 years	10
Taskforce: Included home–school relations, identification procedures for student placement, classroom teaching and learning	new	13
Home Room taskforce: Included home–school relations, identification procedures for student placement, classroom teaching and learning, Home Room environment	new	14

Taskforce processes

The taskforce was established by calling a meeting of volunteers: 17 staff attended the initial meeting with a similar number coming to a second meeting two weeks later. Approximately 50 per cent of attendees were common to both meetings. At this second meeting, it was decided to establish a seven-member group who would organize the other volunteers. Initially, the taskforce selected five areas for intervention that were subsequently reduced to three. In deciding the focus of their activities, taskforce members made no mention of any of the other 10 initiatives that were already in place. When interviewed about this omission, some members explained that they were unaware of these previous initiatives. Other members were aware of them, concerned about their ineffectiveness, but reluctant to disclose their judgement. Several of the latter group believed that they could compensate for this ineffectiveness by introducing new, more effective schemes.

Taskforce members were busy people. Their competing commitments resulted in only one of the eight meetings being attended by all members of the group. Invariably, some members arrived late and others had to leave early. The members accepted this intermittent attendance as inevitable because they could all identify with the pressures of trying to meet conflicting commitments.

As the year drew to a close, five months after the initial meeting, little had been accomplished. The Samoan chairperson, Maria, was to go on leave the following year and a new chairperson was appointed. Plans were made to meet and report in the new year but these plans never happened. The explanation given to the researcher was that the new chairperson was overcommitted and unable to undertake the necessary organizational responsibilities.

Explaining the Workload Problems

In the remainder of this chapter we offer an analysis and explanation of why members of the taskforce undertook their work in this way. To anticipate, they developed structures and processes independent of any consideration of task efficiency or impact on their workload. Eventually, these processes became so inefficient that the group failed to make any substantive recommendation on how to assist Pacific students in the school.

One obvious explanation for the limited achievement of the taskforce is the competing priorities, the timetable clashes and the constant interruptions that are an endemic feature of any large secondary school. The committee and co-curricular responsibilities of staff far exceeded the time they were able to allocate to such duties. Such an explanation is too simple, however, because the staff simultaneously suffered from and created these pressures. They unintentionally created these pressures by adding on new activities without reducing the number of those already existing, by developing parallel structures to solve similar problems, by relying on volunteers with high workloads to undertake key tasks and by uncritically accepting all suggestions for how Pacific students might be assisted.

We offer three explanations for the teachers' actions. First, their bounded non-systemic thinking left them largely unaware that they had created an uncoordinated proliferation of many different initiatives. Second, the norm of professional autonomy reduced their capacity to hold one another accountable for the quality and efficiency of the various initiatives that were in place or for the efficiency of the taskforce processes. Thirdly, the norm of supportive collegiality led staff to uncritically support the genuine desire of colleagues to help Pacific students by volunteering to participate in yet another initiative. The relationship between these explanations, the practices of the taskforce and their achievements is summarized in Figure 10.1.

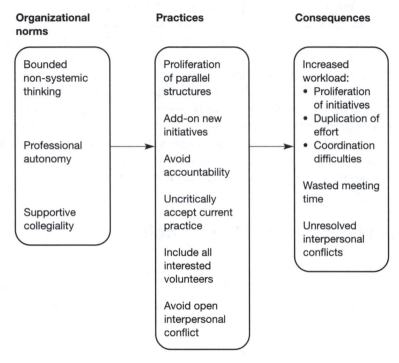

Figure 10.1 *The relationship between organizational norms and school practice*

Bounded non-systemic thinking

Strong departmentalization is an established feature of the organization of secondary schools in the United States (Hargreaves and MacMillan, 1995; MacLaughlin and Talbert, 1990; Siskin, 1994, 1997) and appears equally applicable to the New Zealand context. Departmentalization allows teachers to identify and associate with colleagues with whom they must work most closely. It becomes a limitation, however, when initiatives require systemic thinking and action beyond departmental boundaries, as in the case of the Pacific student achievement taskforce, because the complex interconnections between departments become a constraint on the change process. Potentially, the taskforce's structure allowed for consideration of these interconnections by having cross-departmental representation on its management group. This representation, however, was insufficient to ensure the systems thinking and actions required to cross departmental boundaries.

The most salient example of the limitations of departmentalization was the relationship between the taskforce and the Home Room Department that catered for students with special learning needs. Teaching in this department involved the integration of core subjects with few expectations that the students would sit public examinations. For the last few years, 90 per cent of students in this department had been Pacific. Several members of the taskforce expressed concerns about the education offered to the students and these concerns were reflected in their selection of issues to be investigated. At most meetings of the taskforce, concerns about the Home Room Department were referred to indirectly, but in the following example the staff representative from the Home Room Department challenged another taskforce member about his implied criticism of the department. He replied to this challenge by stating:

> OK, the impression I got from visiting and speaking to others is that a certain amount of work that appears to have been done in the Home Room is work that looks neat in books and occupies time. It doesn't necessarily achieve an education in that it's fine to have kids copying out of a book, but I don't know if that fits with the type of learning that needs to [happen].

Similar concerns were expressed by others about student placement: 'Well, the questions are, "Why is it that the Home Room Department has such a high percentage of Pacific Islanders in it? Why is that happening?" '

Respect for the autonomy of the Home Room Department, however, prevented taskforce members from taking any substantive action to either investigate their concerns further or influence change. Answers to the questions raised were not pursued. Respect for departmental autonomy also compounded workloads when a group of Pacific parents made a formal complaint about the Home Room Department. The senior management of Phoenix College chose to manage this complaint by setting up a second taskforce (see Table 10.1) to examine issues of student placement, teaching and learning, home–school communication and the environment of the Home Room Department. The first three issues were identical to those targeted by the taskforce for Pacific student achievement and had been included in the latter primarily because of its concern about the Home Room Department. Half the memberships of the two taskforces were common to both.

Although Maria, the Samoan chairperson, and one other member of the management group suggested both taskforces be combined, the staff member from the Home Room Department and Paul, the deputy principal, opposed this suggestion. He expressed his concerns this way:

> If we suddenly went in and said we're going to target the Home Room Department,
> . . . I think you'll get a very strong reaction from others who aren't here. They may
> see it as another go at the Home Room Department, whatever the intention was. In
> terms of what people in the department have said to me about what they're feeling
> at the moment, it's a reality that would have to be managed.

Other taskforce members accepted Paul's argument and his offer to work in a liaison role between both groups to keep them informed of each other's activities. The reporting never happened because he chose to work privately with the head of the Home Room Department and taskforce members did not challenge this independent decision. As a result, neither taskforce influenced change. When asked by the researcher for his reasons for working in this way, Paul explained: 'Josie [the Head of Department of the Home Room Department] has been territorial. I mean she has put up some barriers.'

Interviews of taskforce members established that they both accepted the head of department's right to be territorial and the limitations this placed on their capacity to influence the programme, despite their privately expressed concerns about racist selection procedures and inadequate teaching. The consequences of this arrangement for workloads were that those members belonging to both groups now had twice as many meetings to attend. Even data-collection methods were duplicated, with both taskforces surveying the same Pacific parents about home–school communication. The workload demands involved in distributing and collecting the questionnaires precluded either taskforce from collating or using the results of their surveys.

Departmental autonomy is insufficient to explain the duplication of effort and proliferation of parallel structures that occurred at Phoenix College, however, because in most instances the separate initiatives were not department based. At a deeper level, the way in which the management group set about its work reflected an inability to think and act systemically (Senge, 1992; Sterman, 1994). This inability was particularly evident in the addition of new initiatives to assist the Pacific students. The seven initiatives and three programmes identified in Table 10.1 already existed at the time the taskforce was established. Only one of those programmes, the Home Room Department, was ever referred to in the taskforce's deliberations, yet several taskforce members committed considerable time to them. The taskforce's selection of new areas for attention effectively added three more initiatives to those already in place.

The above description could be interpreted as a problem unique to a disorganized school or the taskforce itself not be seen as representative of other school operations. Our response to the first explanation is that the school was considered to be the most effective and well managed in the district by both parents and education authorities. Applications for student places far exceeded the number available and the principal served on a national taskforce to address educational achievement issues because of this reputation as an effective educational manager. The operation of the taskforce itself was not unique in the school and the way it was set up was typical of general school operations. Both the principal and the senior management knew of the existing 10 initiatives and had reservations about the effectiveness and expense of some of them. Despite this knowledge, no requirement was placed on the group to rationalize these previous efforts. Similarly, the idea of setting up the second taskforce on the Home Room Department came from the principal. He knew of the duplication of effort but considered a separate group would more appropriately respect the autonomy of the Home Room Department and its head.

Professional autonomy

In addition to the compartmentalized thinking and action evident at the organizational level, strong professional norms of autonomy (Bush, 1995; Fullan, 1993; Little, 1990; Smyth, 1996) and equality of authority (Timperley and Robinson, 1998) influenced the operation of the taskforce. In Figure 10.1, these norms are summarized as professional autonomy. Teachers' work requires them to have considerable autonomy to make individual judgements (Lee *et al.*, 1993) and accountability in schools is sometimes rejected through a fear that the professionalism of teachers will be undermined (Willms and Kerchoff, 1995). These norms of non-accountable autonomy at Phoenix College, however, contributed to much of the extra workload experienced by members of the management group of the taskforce because members failed to hold their colleagues to account for not actioning agreed decisions and accepted current practice even when privately critical of its effectiveness.

Tasks agreed to at one meeting were often not carried out, a process which contributed to limited progress and wasted time at subsequent meetings. For example, on two occasions meeting dates were set, but those responsible for arranging release time from classroom duties failed to do this, with the result that few members were able to attend. Similarly, taskforce members agreed to co-opt other interested staff to develop an action plan for each of the three subgroups. By the end of the year only the home–school communication subgroup under Maria's leadership had begun to formulate such a plan and put it into action with the parent survey. The inaction of other subgroups was not challenged. Similarly, the failure of the new chairperson to reconvene the taskforce in the new year was not raised. When asked about the reasons for accepting the lack of action, members of the taskforce management group expressed a reluctance to interfere with what they believed to be professional decisions about how to manage personal workloads. In effect, each member made autonomous decisions about their own contribution and the consequences of these decisions were treated as undiscussable.

The failure of taskforce members to hold each other to account could have been counteracted by the actions of the school's management team. Phoenix College did have formal accountability mechanisms but these did not serve to make any members of the taskforce management group accountable for their actions. For example, the principal delegated responsibility for the taskforce to

Paul, the deputy principal responsible for learning support. Paul subsequently delegated this responsibility to Maria, so she could have relevant management experience. Neither the principal nor his deputy, despite their awareness of the lack of progress, held the taskforce as a group, or any individual within it, accountable for the lack of action.

Respect for professional autonomy and a reluctance to hold each other to account contributed not only to the organizational difficulties but also to the compounding of multiple components of the initiative. Group members were reluctant to express publicly their negative judgements about some aspects of the initiative already in place. Some members of the taskforce were particularly critical of three of the seven initiatives for which Maria was responsible that had been established three years prior to the taskforce. The school management, together with two other members on the taskforce, for example were concerned about the amount of time she spent counselling individual students. Maria, on the other hand, believed that removing barriers to student achievement through individual counselling was an effective use of her time. As she expressed it to the researcher: 'You need to look at the student as a person, the student as a learner in the school environment. . . . As a counsellor, I look at the barriers to learning.'

Rather than express their concerns directly, taskforce members would periodically ask questions of her such as: 'How much time do you spend counselling students?' 'What do you think is important in your role?' Maria answered these questions in accordance with her own beliefs about the benefits of counselling, unaware of the questioners' privately expressed reservations about counselling as an effective use of her time. The reluctance of the members of the taskforce to engage with matters of individual professional judgement mirrored Little's (1990: 510) description of teachers showing 'little inclination to engage with peers . . . in ways that may jeopardize self-esteem and professional standing'. As a result, the management group were limited to making recommendations about the addition of new components, and stymied in reviewing the worth of those already existing.

Supportive collegiality

The value of working in collegial groups is both acclaimed as a way for teachers to benefit from the support and expertise of their colleagues (Cunningham and Gresso, 1993; Weiss and Cambone, 1994) and portrayed as a mechanism for teachers to pool their ignorance (Hargreaves, 1984) and avoid the difficult issues that may limit quality decision making (Argyris, 1990; Timperley and Robinson, 1998). In the taskforce, the supportive and inclusive attributes of collegiality prevented evaluations of current initiatives or the exercise of mutual accountability.

Norms of supportive collegiality also explained the inclusion of all interested volunteers in the work of the taskforce and the avoidance of open interpersonal conflict (Figure 10.1) The desire to be inclusive was graphically portrayed by the taskforce's decision to expand its membership from seven to ten at its third meeting. Despite the coordination problems evident in the first three meetings, the group decided to expand its membership to include three other staff who had earlier expressed an interest in joining. The initial decision to restrict the management group to representatives of key areas in the school had caused considerable unease among the members, because it had led to the exclusion of the three staff who did not fit this brief. At the third meeting of the group, one member raised this:

> Tom: I was impressed by the enthusiasm of those who volunteered to be in this group at the larger meeting. And then I was surprised how few of them [were] in this group – some of those people weren't here. . . . To start with a group this small is crazy, particularly if you have the enthusiasm from those other people who carry things through.
>
> Maria: Phillippa, Don and Susan offered to be in this group.
>
> Tua: I reckon we pull them on.

In making this decision, taskforce members did not pause to think how an expansion of the group might affect its functioning, in particular, the time spent in coordination and the potentially increased intermittence of attendance. Although all three new members attended the fourth meeting, their subsequent attendance also became erratic.

The desire to be collegially supportive also led to an avoidance of conflict and an increasing workload in ways described above. For example, Paul advocated the establishment of parallel taskforces on the basis that the involvement of the Pacific student achievement taskforce in the Home Room Department was likely to produce a 'very strong reaction from others who aren't here'. Similarly, failure to examine the worth of current aspects of the initiative were partly motivated by a desire to avoid conflict with Maria who believed in the worth of the initiatives she had established. At various times over the previous three years, Paul had attempted to redirect Maria's activities, not openly, but indirectly, by making it difficult for her to continue those he had reservations about. He used mechanisms such as timetabling her for activities other than counselling and cutting the funding for the poorly attended homework centre. Each time he had been overruled after Maria had directly approached the principal for reinstatement of previous conditions. These conflicts had not been openly discussed.

Inevitably, the tensions associated with these previous incidents manifested themselves within the taskforce, initially by an apparent inability to coordinate their efforts to arrange meeting times and staff release. Other taskforce members recognized the cause of these organizational problems but preferred to accept their continuation over discussing and resolving them. As one member said,

Yeah' there's been a lot of baggage carried into this committee, and its primarily between Maria and Paul, the communication between them. And the rest of us are getting pulled into it, and getting involved in that. Some of us sure as hell don't want to be involved in that, because that's not what we're here for.

This member's reluctance to discuss and resolve the ongoing conflicts and the effects it was having on group functioning was shared by others in the taskforce. Collegiality did not extend to assisting others to work out their differences. This preference for avoiding rather than resolving conflict is not restricted to teachers, but has long been recognized in the literature, 'When a problem arises . . . the safest policy is to delay dealing with it, rather than trying to do away with it' (Machiavelli, 1519, in Bondanella and Musa, 1979: 240–1).

We have previously critiqued the limitations of collegiality when it is interpreted, as appeared to be the case at Phoenix College, as avoiding mutual accountability and discussion of difficult interpersonal issues (Timperley and Robinson, 1998). We have proposed that, if the potential for collegial groups is to be realized, it must be interpreted more rigorously to reflect a commitment to learning together about developing effective solutions to problems. A major implication of this position is that collegial groups must focus on their progress towards solving the problem, and identify and resolve personal and interpersonal issues that might limit their ability to do so. The taskforce lost sight of the problem they were trying to solve, that is, to improve Pacific student achievement, and allowed unresolved interpersonal conflict to limit their effectiveness.

The ineffectiveness of the taskforce could have been challenged by senior management by requiring the group to develop both an effective solution to the problem of Pacific student achievement and a way of working together that would facilitate this solution. By failing to place these requirements on the group, senior management inadvertently created conditions that allowed the taskforce to continue with ineffective processes.

Interrelationship between explanations

Although we have discussed separately each of the explanations for the way in which the taskforce set about compounding workloads for its members, they are inevitably interwoven. No single organizing principle accounted for any one practice or consequence identified in Figure 10.1. For example, we have suggested that respect for professional autonomy led taskforce members to add on new initiatives rather than to review the worth of those already existing. An essential part of systems thinking, however, is to create maps of the structure of an issue and to publicly test the validity of the assumptions underlying such maps (Senge, 1992; Sterman, 1994). It is not possible to undertake such an exercize if norms of supportive collegiality and professional autonomy preclude challenge of current practice. Thus, the interpersonal, professional and organizational norms and practices contributed both separately and in combination to the ineffectiveness of the taskforce and to workload stress.

Conclusions

In this chapter, have argued that increased workload and stress associated with a self-managing environment can be attributed, in part, to the ways in which teachers organize themselves with few demands from management to do things differently. Occupational norms of departmental and professional autonomy (Lee *et al.*, 1993; MacLaughlin and Talbert, 1990; Siskin, 1994, 1997) and supportive collegiality (Lipman, 1997; Little, 1990), while adaptive for managing the environment of a single-cell classroom, limit the systemic thinking required for school-wide initiatives. Workload is increased through fragmentation, duplication of effort, proliferation of new ideas and a reluctance to challenge colleagues. Without a change in these occupational norms, meaningful teacher involvement in school-wide initiatives is inevitably limited because workloads are not infinitely expandable.

We do not dispute the benefits of direct teacher involvement in school-wide reform efforts because it is teachers who must implement change, and their input helps them to make sense of what is happening and holds possibilities for improving the reform effort itself (Fullan, 1996; Hannay and Ross, 1997). The challenge to school managers is to facilitate the realization of the potential benefits without increasing workloads to unacceptable levels.

We suggest that the answer to this question lies primarily in teachers and school managers identifying what is required to engage effectively in school-wide reform efforts and to distinguish how this is different from classroom teaching. The operation of the Phoenix College taskforce was limited by their adoption of organizing principles more suited to managing single-cell classrooms than to managing school-wide reform. As a result, taskforce members spent many hours trying to organize themselves and fit their ever-increasing commitments into finite time schedules, rather than dealing with the complex issue of Pacific student achievement.

The role for managers in this process is to conceptualize the shifts required for teachers to be involved effectively at a systemic level, and then to create the conditions to facilitate these shifts. The first condition is creating the demand for the teachers to engage in systemic thinking. Such a demand may take the form of a requirement to map the school's current response to the problem and demonstrate how this map interrelates with other aspects of the school system (Sterman, 1994). At Phoenix College such a map would have revealed the existing 10 initiatives to assist Pacific students and raised questions about their efficiency and effectiveness.

Senge (1992) advocates that the inferences participants bring to such a task should be publicly defended and tested because it is through dialogue that faulty assumptions can be contested and alternatives debated. This type of public testing does not typically form a part of classroom teachers' professional lives where the performance demand is for competent classroom practice, rather than for systematic reflection on and defence of the assumptions underlying that practice.

A second condition for effective teacher involvement that does not unreasonably increase workloads is the reformulation of what it means to be collegial. If groups of teachers are to contribute to solving organizational problems, they need to be constantly mindful of their progress towards a solution and to hold each other accountable for that progress (Timperley and Robinson, 1998). Part of this condition involves taking joint responsibility for resolving the personal and interpersonal issues that may limit progress, including the implications of their joint actions for each others' workloads. This interpretation of collegiality is very different from that advocated in much of the literature (Cunningham and Gresso, 1993; Weiss and Cambone, 1994) or that practised in many schools (Hargreaves, 1994; Little, 1990) where collegiality means working together and supporting one another.

The challenge for management is to create the demand for collegial groups to develop solutions to the identified problems and to provide the conditions that will maximize the probability for success. Phoenix College management believed that they had created these conditions by formulating the problem to be solved and providing any requested release from classroom teaching. The conditions that were missing were the demand for a solution within a reasonable timeframe and the assistance to resolve the personal and interpersonal issues that were limiting the development of an effective solution.

▌ Notes

The authors wish to acknowledge the cooperation of Phoenix College staff and their preparedness to examine and learn about their own practice.

1. Pacific students in this context refers to those whose families have migrated to New Zealand from various South Pacific Islands, including Samoa, Tonga, Fiji, Tokelau and Nuie.

▌ References

Argyris, C. (1990) *Overcoming Organizational Defenses: Facilitating Organizational Learning*. Boston, MA: Allyn & Bacon.

Bondanella, P. and Musa, M., ed. and trans. (1979) 'The Discourses', in *The Portable Machiavelli*. New York: Viking Press.

Bush, T. (1995) *Theories of Educational Management*. London: Paul Chapman.

Campbell, R.J. and Neill, S.R. (1992) *The Use and Management of Secondary Teachers' Time after the Education Reform Act 1988*. Warwick: Warwick University.

Cunningham, W.G. and Gresso, D.W. (1993) *Cultural Leadership: The Culture of Excellence in Education*. Boston, MA: Allyn & Bacon.

Darling-Hammond, L. (1990) 'Teacher Evaluation in Transition: Emerging Roles and Evolving Methods', in J. Millman and L. Darling-Hammond (eds.) *The New Handbook of Teacher Evaluation: Assessing Elementary and Secondary School Teachers*. Newbury Park, CA: Sage.

Firestone, W.A. (1996) 'Images of Teaching and Proposals for Reform: A Comparison of Ideas from Cognitive and Organizational Research', *Educational Administration Quarterly* 32: 209–35.

Fullan, M. (1993) *Change Forces: Probing the Depths of Educational Reform*. London: Falmer.

Fullan, M. (1996) 'Turning Systemic Thinking on its Head', *Phi Delta Kappan* 77: 420–3.

Hannay, L.M. and Ross, J.A. (1997) 'Initiating Secondary School Reform: The Dynamic Relationship between Restructuring, Reculturing, and Retiming', *Educational Administration Quarterly* 33 (suppl.) Dec.: 576–603.

Hargreaves, A. (1984) 'Experience Counts, Theory Doesn't: How Teachers Talk about their Work', *Sociology of Education* 57: 244–54.

Hargreaves, A. (1994) *Changing Teachers, Changing Times: Teachers' Work and Culture in the Postmodern Age*. Toronto: Ontario Institute for Studies in Education at the University of Toronto.

Hargreaves, A. and MacMillan, R. (1995) 'The Balkanization of Secondary School Teaching', in L.S. Siskin and J.W. Little (eds.) *The Subjects in Question: Departmental Organization and the High School*, pp. 141–71. New York: Teachers College Press.

Johnson, S.M. (1990) 'The Primacy and Potential of High School Departments', in M.W. McLaughlin, J.E. Talbert and N. Bascia (eds.) *The Contexts of Teaching in Secondary Schools: Teachers' Realities*, pp. 123–40. New York: Teachers College Press.

Kyriacou, C. (1987) 'Teacher Stress and Burnout: An International Review', *Educational Research* 29: 146–52.

Lee, V.E., Bryk, A.S. and Smith, J.B. (1993) 'The Organization of Effective Secondary Schools', *Review of Research in Education* 19: 171–267.

Leithwood, K., Menzies, T., Jantzi, D. and Leithwood, J. (1996) 'School Restructuring, Tranformational Leadership and Amelioration of Teacher Burnout', *Anxiety, Stress and Coping: An International Journal* 9: 199–215.

Lipman, P. (1997) 'Restructuring in Context: A Case Study of Teacher Participation and the Dynamics of Ideology, Race, and Power', *American Educational Research Journal* 34: 3–28.

Little, J. (1990) 'The Persistence of Privacy: Autonomy and Initiative in Teachers' Professional Relations', *Teachers College Record* 91: 509–36.

MacLaughlin, M.W. and Talbert, J.E. (1990) 'The Contexts in Question: The Secondary School Workplace', in M.W. McLaughlin, J.E. Talbert and N. Bascia (eds.) *The Contexts in Question: The Secondary Schools: Teachers' Realities*. New York: Teachers College Press.

O'Connor, P.R. and Clark, V.A. (1990) 'Determinants of Teacher stress', *Australian Journal of Education* 34: 41–51.

Pithers, R.T. and Fogerty, G.J. (1995) 'Occupational Stress among Vocational Teachers', *British Journal of Educational Psychology* 65: 3–14.

Robinson, V.M.J. (1993) *Problem-Based Methodology: Research for the Improvement of Practice*. Oxford: Pergamon Press.

Senge, P.M. (1992) *The Fifth Discipline: The Art and Practice of the Learning Organization*. Milsons Point, Australia: Random House.

Siskin, L.S. (1994) *Realms of Knowledge: Academic Departments in Secondary Schools*. Washington, DC: Falmer Press.

Siskin, L.S. (1997) 'The Challenge of Leadership in Comprehensive High Schools: School Vision and Departmental Divisions', *Educational Administration Quarterly* 33: 604–23.

Smyth, J. (1996) 'Evaluation of Teacher Performance: Move Over Hierarchy, Here Comes Collegiality!', *Journal of Education Policy* 11: 185–96.

Sterman, J.D. (1994) 'Learning in and about Complex Systems', *Systems Dynamics Review* 10: 291–330.

Timperley, H.S. and Robinson, V.M.J. (1998) 'Collegiality in Schools: Its Nature and Implications for Problem Solving', *Educational Administration Quarterly* 34 (suppl.): 608–29.

Wallace, M. and Hall, V. (1994) *Inside the SMT: Teamwork in Secondary School Management*. London: Paul Chapman.

Weick, K.E. (1976) 'Educational Organizations as Loosely Coupled Systems', *Administrative Science Quarterly* 21: 1–19.

Weick, K. and McDaniel, R. (1989) 'How Professional Organizations Work: Implications for School Organization and Management', in T.J. Sergiovanni and J.H. Moore (eds.) *Schooling for Tomorrow: Directing Reforms to Issues that Count*. Boston, MA: Allyn & Bacon.

Weiss, C. and Cambone, J. (1994) 'Principals, Shared Decision Making, and School Reform', *Educational Evaluation and Policy Analysis* 16: 287–301.

Whitehead, A.J. and Ryba, K. (1995) 'New Zealand Teachers' Perceptions of Occupational Stress and Coping Strategies', *New Zealand Journal of Educational Studies* 30: 177–88.

Willms, J.D. and Kerchoff, A.C. (1995) 'The Challenge of Developing New Educational Indicators', *Educational Evaluation and Policy Analysis* 17: 113–31.

Wisniewski, L. and Gargiulo, R.M. (1997) 'Occupational Stress and Burnout among Special Educators: A Review of the Literature', *The Journal of Special Education* 31: 325–46.

Wylie, C. (1997) *Self-Managing Schools Seven Years On: What have we Learnt?* Wellington: New Zealand Council for Educational Research.

11

Teacher Stress in the Low-Trust Society

Geoff Troman

In modern societies the antithesis of trust is a state of mind which could best be summed up as existential angst and dread. (Anthony Giddens, *The Consequences of Modernity*, 1990, p. 138.)

Introduction

Stress is a pervasive feature of contemporary life. The context of the escalation of stress is the 'globalization of capital and communications, the rapid growth of information and technological developments, changed modes of economic production, economic crisis and increasing moral and scientific uncertainty' (Woods *et al.*, 1997, p. 1). The extent of occupational stress and stress-related illness, particularly in Western societies, is now well established by social research (Newton *et al.*, 1995; Bartlett, 1998). The annual cost of stress to the Education Service in 1998 has been estimated at £230 million (Brown and Ralph, 1998). It is argued that while stress is a problem among the caring professionals, it is generally of particular concern in the teaching profession (Kyriacou and Sutcliffe, 1979). For instance, a study of teachers' job satisfaction revealed 'unhappiness' being experienced at a personal level (Gardner and Oswald, 1999). The wholesale restructuring of national education systems that began in the 1980s has been linked with teacher stress (Dunham, 1984; Travers and Cooper, 1996; Dinham and Scott, 1996; Woods *et al.*, 1997; Brown and Ralph, 1998).

The nature of stress in teachers' work was noted by Nias (1996). In her editorial introduction to a special edition of the *Cambridge Journal of Education*, devoted to the topic of teacher emotions, she stated:

Source: *British Journal of Sociology of Education*, Vol. 21, no. 3, 2000, pp. 331–53. Edited version.

in this edition teachers' most extreme and negative feelings appear when they talk about their colleagues, the structures of schooling or the effect of changing educational policies upon them . . . the most intensive, hostile and deeply disturbing emotions described in these articles came not from encounters with pupils or students, but with other adults, particularly colleagues, parents, school governors and inspectors. It is not clear why this shift should have occurred, nor whether it simply reflects a change in research priorities. It does, however, open up a fresh area of discussion and reflection for practitioners and academics alike. (Nias, 1996, p. 300).

This chapter is a contribution to the discussion Nias has initiated.

Many complex macro, meso and micro factors are at work in the production of stress in teaching (Woods, 1995). Teaching work in the primary school, for example, has changed radically during the past decade. Classroom teaching now constitutes only part of the teachers' work. Other tasks, extra but closely related to teaching, involve work in planning and administration with colleagues, and work with parents and the community (Campbell and Neill, 1994; Webb and Vulliamy, 1996). These factors might indicate that, for some teachers, relationships are giving rise to emotional and psychological problems in their work and lives.

The works of Woods (1995), Jeffrey and Woods (1996), Menter *et al.* (1997), Troman (1997) and Woods *et al.* (1997) clearly note the negative effects of the intensification of work and managerialism on primary teachers and collegial relations in the primary school. Evans (1992), in a rare study of primary teacher morale and job satisfaction, found the situation-specific variables of headteacher behaviour and staff relationships to be key factors influencing the teachers' satisfaction/dissatisfaction with teaching.

I will argue in this chapter that while all the above social processes are undoubtedly involved in teacher stress and the breakdown in staff relationships, labour process theory may have a limited explanatory power (Hargreaves, 1993) in revealing all that is involved in the stress process and changing cultures of teaching. Using a case study of primary teachers who are experiencing stress and stress-related illness in their work, I look beyond labour process arguments to consider changing trust relations in high modernity and relate these to the institutional and personal levels of schooling. The chapter focuses on teacher experience of trust and distrust in their work, and the consequences of this for individuals and staff relationships.

Methods

Most research on teacher stress has adopted large-scale survey methods. By contrast, our research is qualitative in nature and my approach is ethnographic. I agree with Seddon (1998, p. 1) when she argues that:

> Ethnography . . . provides a window into the practical realities of people's work and lives. It shows the constraints and contradictions that they face and reveals the way they respond to large-scale social changes.

The research employs semi-structured and open-ended, in-depth, life history interviewing. A local authority Occupational Health Unit engaged in counselling local authority employees experiencing stress helped identify teachers to invite them to take part in the research. Attendance at the Unit for counselling, receiving medical treatment for stress-related illness and having a prolonged period off work provided an operational definition of stress for our research. Those individuals who were willing to co-operate in the research provided us with an opportunity sample. Some of the respondents gave me further contacts with friends who were receiving support from the Unit which provided a small snowball sample.

The eventual sample consisted of 20 teachers, 13 women and seven men. These worked, or had worked, in schools representing a range of urban and rural locations. The gender proportions and ages represent those found in the teaching profession generally, in that they are predominantly women and a large majority is 40 years of age or older (Wragg *et al.*, 1998). A range of positions is represented although the majority are teachers (mostly subject co-ordinators) in mid to late career. There are three headteachers (two male, one female) and two newly qualified teachers (female). A range of adaptations was evident including teachers on sickness absence, those who had returned to work and some who had left teaching. The teachers who participated were interviewed in their homes between two and five times over a 2-year period. This adds a longitudinal dimension to the research.

The quotations presented in this chapter provide insights into the teachers' perspectives. However, no attempt is made to claim that these perspectives are the only possible interpretation of events. In addition, an organizational study of two large urban primary schools involving observation and interview was conducted. One is a self-defined 'low stress' school that has recently received a highly favourable OFSTED report and has low teacher absence rates, low staff sickness rates, low staff turnover, and high teacher morale. The other, a self-defined 'high stress school', is currently under 'special measures', having been defined by OFSTED as a 'failing' school. Its is experiencing high levels of teacher stress, high staff turnover and high absence rates.

Trust and Relationships

Trust between individuals and groups provides the basis for social order, it is the mortar of solidarity and integration (Durkheim, 1956). Elster (1989) argues that social order is characterized by the predictability of social life and is maintained by the existence of habitual rules and social norms. A normal and routine life would not be possible without 'an implicit and unconsidered trust that everyday life does not carry major threats' (cited in Misztal, 1996, p. 68). Hence, trust facilitates stability, co-operation and cohesion.

Educational relationships cannot be established and maintained without a strong bond of trust existing between teacher and pupils. Hargreaves (1998a, p. 5) argues that teaching is an 'emotional practice' involving trustful relationships with others. Trust is of prime importance in teaching, for the presence of trust ensures that 'creative individuals are allowed greater freedom and autonomy' (Alexander, 1989, p. 142).

Trust and Society

It is important to complement the existing psychologically based body of stress research with a perspective that embraces the 'social' aspects of stress and stress-related illness (Fineman, 1995) and 'addresses the relationship between the (current) social environment and individual subjective experience' (Handy, 1995, p. 8). This relationship was demonstrated consummately by Durkheim (1897), showing that the most individual of acts, suicide, has a social basis. This current stress research engages with the 'core sociological issues of the relationship of the individual to society, of agency and constraint, control and order' (Pollard, 1992, p. 119).

It is necessary here to seek inter-relationships between the micro, meso and macro levels of analysis rather than treating them as discrete (Kelchtermans, 1995a). As Hargreaves (1998b, p. 422) argues, these levels are not 'tightly insulated from one another' and 'structure and agency are relationally connected'. In work on the social construction of teacher stress, we must avoid analyses that 'force a false separation of self, structure and situation into different sites of experience' (Hargreaves, 1998b). What is really important, Hargreaves argues, is that we seek to understand how 'structures exert their effects and with what consequences and implications for the self, in different places and times'.

Giddens' work on the dialectical relationship between the individual and the globalization of capital, information and human relationships is of importance here. His extensive conceptual development of the nature of trust relations in high modernity, for example, draws 'recursive links between changes in society and individual dispositions' (Misztal, 1996).

Trust cannot be understood without making reference to the allied concept of risk. Giddens (1990, p. 31) argues that 'where trust is involved, in Luhmann's view, alternatives are consciously borne, in mind by the individual in deciding to follow a particular course of action.' Trust operates in environments of risk, in which varying levels of security (protection against dangers) can be achieved.

Giddens (1990, p. 34) defines trust as,

> confidence in the reliability of a person or system, regarding a given set of
> outcomes or events, where that confidence expresses a faith in the probity or
> love of another, or in the correctness of abstract principles.

For Giddens, trust in pre-modern societies was based on 'personal trust (trust
in persons–facework commitment) secured by kinship, community, religion
and traditions' (Mitsztal, 1996, p. 90). 'However, trust in late modernity
(owing to the decline/fragmentation of traditional institutions, and the
increased division of labour and specialisation) is based also on the abstract
systems (faceless commitments) of *symbolic tokens* (media of interchange,
such as money) and *expert systems* – that is systems of technical and professional knowledge where trust is based in a body of knowledge' (Misztal,
1996, p. 90). However, Giddens argues that in a period of high modernity,
where social relations have become *disembedded* from local contexts and
'recombined across time–space distances' (Giddens, 1990, p. 53), there is '*a*
renewed *re-embedding* and growing importance of personalised trust, based
on deliberately cultivated face-to-face relationships' because they are more
psychologically rewarding than trust in abstract systems (p. 88).

Giddens also uses the concepts '*basic*' or '*elementary*' trust, often using
them interchangeably. *Basic* trust is connected with the genesis of our '*onto-
logical security*', i.e. our confidence in the continuity of personal identity.
Elementary trust is connected with the 'predictability of daily encounters'
(Misztal, 1996, p. 91). 'Without the development of *basic trust* (initially with
parents, family, friends) people may experience existential anxiety, and lack
of confidence in the continuity of their self-identity and the constancy of
their environment.'

With the breakdown of kinship, community, religion and tradition, trust
needs to be *negotiated*:

> Trust in persons is not focused by personalised connections within the local
> community and kinship networks. Trust on a personal level becomes a project,
> to be 'worked at' by the parties involved, . . . trust has to be won, and the means
> of doing this is demonstrable warmth and openness (Giddens, 1990, p. 121.)

However, Giddens argues that in the high-risk society' (Beck, 1992), the consequences of the antithesis of trust are anxiety and dread. These are the
'debilitating effects of modern institutions on self-experience and the emotions' and are brought about through the absence or fracturing of trust
(Giddens, 1990, p. 100).

The High-Risk Low-Trust Society

We live in a *risk culture* (Giddens, 1990, 1991); consequently, there is a crisis of trust in society involving the breakdown of trusting relationships and the growth of distrust not only within intimate and personal relationships, but also towards institutions (Castells, 1997). In globalization, the social and geographical mobility of modern societies 'tends to erode trust and credibility by undermining the bonds of solidarity' (Misztal, 1996, p. 96). Distrust is evident in the low-trust management styles in Western societies. The presence of conflict and a lack of mutual loyalty and responsibility between workers and bosses are features of low-trust workplaces (Fox, 1974; Kramer & Tyler, 1996).

Distrust of professionals is widespread. In education, reforms were introduced in the context of a public 'discourse of derision' and were based on a profound distrust of teachers (Grace, 1991; Ball, 1991; Helsby, 1999). The moral panic concerning falling educational standards has continued to encourage the public's distrust of teachers. The regulatory body of OFSTED inspections and league tables, whose aim is to restore confidence and trust in education and minimize the risk of failure, by the regulation and contol of teachers' work and processes of schooling, have themselves become the object of distrust by some teachers.

The Nature of Trust Relations in Schooling

Hargreaves (1998a, p. 1) argues that teaching is a 'profoundly emotional form of work' – 'teaching activates, colours and otherwise affects the feelings and actions of others with whom teachers work and form relationships'. The following section of the chapter examines the nature of *'face-work'* (Goffman, 1959) and trust *negotiations* within an *expert system*, primary schooling, and in *'access points'* where *experts* (teachers), lay people and regulatory bodies meet and engage in trust *bargaining*.

The organization of the section is dictated by the analysis of interview data. Experiencing 'vulnerability' and 'giving trust' and 'wanting to be trusted' were key themes running though respondents' testimonies in the stress research. The focus here, therefore, is on categories of trust–distrust and the negative impact on the individual physical and emotional well-being of individual teachers and their personal and collegial relations. The section is arranged as shown in Table 11.1.

Table 11.1 *Trust–distrust categories*

Trust	Distrust
Intimacy	Alienation
Togetherness	Antagonism
Supportive	Undermining
Mutuality	Isolation
Security	Insecurity
Acceptance	Suspicion

Intimacy–alienation

Some of the teachers experienced a breakdown in close and intimate personal relationships leading to alienation at home and at work. The majority of the teachers appeared to enjoy trusting and supportive intimate relationships that enabled them to cope with their illness. But for some chronic strains involved difficulties in or a break up of a personal relationship. In some cases, stressful domestic events were paralleled with stressful circumstances at work. Mary thought she was 'untypical' of other stressed teachers in that she viewed her domestic situation as the prime factor in her stress illness. She was untypical in the sense that her intimate relationship had ended in extremely violent and acrimonious circumstances. However, her case shows graphically the negative impact of an inter-relation of influencing factors arising in both professional and personal lives. Stress from school would spill over into the home and exacerbate the stress being experienced as a result of her relationship with her partner in turn, stress from home would spill into her workplace.

Togetherness–antagonism

All of the respondents were quite clear of the importance of close staff relationships – 'togetherness'. Human exchanges in genuinely collaborative teacher cultures made work more pleasant and served to reduce stress. Pressures of intensification led to antagonist relationships between teachers and pupils. Elizabeth found the work of integrating children with emotional and behavioural difficulties (EBD) and catering for the full range of pupil achievement in a context of financial cuts and large classes very stressful. In these circumstances, she was clearly finding it difficult to form warm and trusting relationships with many of the pupils.

Some of the teachers were locked into a stress cycle where exhaustion contributed to worsening teacher/pupil relationships, which in turn induced further exhaustion and impacted on teacher efficacy:

> *Susan*:   I'm exhausted and being exhausted is actually affecting my performance in the classroom. Because I'd started to notice that certainly by the end of the week I was getting to a stage where I just was not functioning as I would be running low on fuel. Things were getting to me that wouldn't have got to me on a Monday.

Pupils may read the signs (for example, teacher body language, linguistic 'tetchiness') and 'suss out' (Beynon, 1984) the teacher is not operating as effectively as usual, and try and maximize their own 'interests at hand' (Pollard, 1985) in escalating misbehaviour. An outcome of this process is the erosion of warm teacher/pupil relationships.

Some of the teachers of my research had good reasons to distrust some of their pupils. Unlike Nias' (1996) teachers, mine reported many incidents in which the hostile behaviour of pupils had been the source of stress and impacted negatively on school collegiality.

Many writers have argued that teachers derive their job satisfaction from the psychic rewards of teaching (Lortie, 1975; Rosenholtz, 1989; Hargreaves, 1998a). Central among these is the development of close relationships and 'emotional understanding' (Hargreaves, 1998a). In the examples we have seen as part of our research, there seems little space for this type of emotional work.

Supportive–undermining

All the teachers recognized the importance of trusting relationships and human and professional support from colleagues. They particularly valued a supportive and encouraging attitude from the headteacher. Support for the teachers' professionality was sometimes perceived to be not forthcoming. Indeed, some headteachers were felt to undermine the teachers' sense of efficacy and professionalism.

All the teachers stated that they could not work effectively without the support of their headteachers. However, this was seen as often being denied them. Susan, for example, requested support in dealing with an incident in her class and wanted her headteacher to discipline a pupil who was involved:

> And before I know it I'm having it turned round. She said, 'You must not lead other people to think ill of the children and you must be very careful what you say'. And I'm thinking, 'I came in here with a child that another LSA [Learning Support Assistant] has seen do something to another child, and not only had she seen him do it once but seen him do it twice. And he's sitting out there and I'm expecting you to tear him off a strip and I'm the one who's being torn off a strip'. And I went out extremely confused and extremely unhappy. And basically resolving never ever to go in there with a problem again because as far as I'm concerned I have not been supported at all.

Hargreaves (1998a, p. 10) argues that when a teacher asks a colleague for help 'they place their confidence and perceived competence on the line. Their professional persona and sense of self is put at risk' (Dadds, 1993). A consequence of this kind of interaction experienced by Susan is what Giddens (1990, p. 98) argues is:

> a suspension of trust in the other as a reliable, competent agent, and a flooding in of existential anxiety that takes the form of hurt, puzzlement and betrayal together with suspicion and hostility.

Some headteachers were viewed by their staff as incompetent and provoked negative emotions (Blase and Anderson, 1995). They did not value positive human relationships in or outside work. As Judith explained:

> We were treated badly. It didn't matter that we had any lives.

These headteachers were perceived as not giving support by providing positive feedback on the work of their staff. Elizabeth felt affirmed by a glowing report from OFSTED on her work. She had never previously received praise from her headteacher, who would 'not know what a good job I was doing, but even if she did wouldn't say anything nice'.

Mutuality–isolation

In some of the study schools, there was genuine mutuality in the sense that the teachers were mutually dependent on each other in dealing with difficulties in their work and lives. In other study schools individuals were becoming socially isolated from their colleagues and positive social relationships. In some schools, collaboration had become compulsory in order to aid restructuring. But, in practice, this form of collaboration sometimes took the form of 'contrived collegiality' (Hargreaves, 1994). Some of the schools in the stress research had adopted what on the face of it was collegial arrangements for planning and decision-making. However, the trust invested in the teachers was, in some cases, heavily bounded. It was a circumscribed trust. For example, in Susan's school, collegial decision-making was expected by management but the issues involved were rather trivial:

> *Susan:* I think it's bureaucracy gone mad . . . I do not: understand why I have to be in a meeting which discusses the kitchen staff – discusses things that I as an ordinary class teacher do not need to know about. I mean for goodness sake there's a senior management in the school, senior management in schools are the people who need to know about these things. I am a normal class teacher. I do not need to know about these things. I need to be sent a memo about them, but I don't need to sit there when I could be doing other things.

Other studies (Evans 1992; Brown and Ralph, 1998) have shown that a source of stress in teaching was that teachers were not included in decision-making in their schools. Attendance at meetings involving the type of experience already described was one source of Susan's stress. She argued that management organized what to her were meaningless meetings in order to satisfy OFSTED that collective decision-making took place in the school. Thus, they were of symbolic rather than practical value.

Financial cuts that involved the removal of non-contact time for staff had brought about emotional turbulence in staff relationships and a breakdown in trust between teachers and managers in the school where Ralph was deputy head:

> We had at the time a full time member of staff giving non-contact time to all the staff throughout the school. And if she was ill or her daughter was ill – in my job we have diaries on each of the staffroom notice boards to go and write up, 'Lorraine (cover teacher) won't be in. Cover your own classes for the day'. And there were staff who on the one hand would be becoming emotional in tears, but also would stand there and scream and shout: 'I need my non-contact time.' 'This isn't right.' I mean shouting. And it would be at me. As if it's my fault because I'm the message bearer . . . I find being shouted at by staff stressful. I know it's part of my role as deputy to handle staff who are feeling stressed and whatever. And at times I'm tempted to turn round and say: Oh shut up. But you can't do that.

Duties, pastoral work and planning for teaching stressed Ben:

> What really got me more than anything else I think is not being able to take a break during the day. I mean the morning break was about fifteen minutes. By the time you'd sort of got the kids out and shushed the stragglers out the corridor, you were lucky if you had time to drink your coffee before it was time to start again. And at lunchtime – the so called hour's break – you were usually getting things ready for the afternoon or looking after a child. You got about ten minutes to gobble down your sandwiches.

With the intensification of work, teachers have less time in 'back regions' (Goffman, 1959) such as staffrooms in which to socialize with colleagues. There is, therefore, less informal personal interaction of the kind that induces personal trust. Social relationships in primary schooling, as a result, are becoming more formalized through such organizational structures as 'contrived collegiality' (Hargreaves, 1994).

Security–insecurity

Security refers to feelings of confidence in the face of risks or danger. Some of the teachers experienced threats to their physical and psychological security.

Teaching was once seen as a secure occupation – a job for life (Lortie, 1975; Woods, *et al.*, 1997). However, this is increasingly not the case as short-term contracts and part-time working arrangements proliferate (Lawn, 1995).

Some heads, in their business manager roles, and faced with new forms of governance and unfamiliar aspects of management such as personnel matters in the context of financial cuts, have brought about a separation of managers and teachers in some schools. In some cases, existing micro-political tensions had been exacerbated by the restructuring of education.

The atmosphere of distrust undermines collegiality. Heterogeneity is increasingly evident in the workforce of primary schools with a core of permanent teachers and a periphery of part-time and temporary contract teachers (Lawn 1995). The impact of this arrangement is divisive rather than integrative.

Olivia's head had formerly been a friendly colleague but was now responding to pressures for her to be more managerial in her approach, and was creating a climate of criticism and using a range of what Olivia described as 'bullying' strategies:

> So the original team work had long since gone by now . . . that all changed. Now she's undermining my status, she's setting me an impossible workload, she's not acknowledging any value in the work that I do . . . creating a critical atmosphere. I mean, I hated any meeting with her because I knew it was going to be a catalogue of what I hadn't done . . . Suddenly changing – goal posts changing like nobody's business. Suddenly changing her position which created insecurity. You suddenly realized that what you thought was the unwritten rule of procedure she would suddenly change and we were doing something else.

Here Olivia has a lack of 'elementary trust in the possible intentions of others' (Giddens, 1990, p. 82). For an individual to feel psychologically secure, they need continuity and reliability in personal relationships (Giddens, 1990, 1991).

Acceptance–suspicion

The 'official' distrust of teachers embodied in the new accountability systems was a source of stress in Marion's work and life. Before experiencing stress, and later burnout, Marion seems to have had a moral commitment to her pupils, parents and colleagues. With the impending OFSTED inspection, legal accountability took over and the opposing values of OFSTED looked certain to provide a 'head-on-collision' with Marion's values. Accountability took on a life of its own 'just doing things for someone else to read'. Accountability was the source of a great deal of compulsion in her work – 'I had to do it'. In the early stages of illness (at home), she tried to catch up with 'accountability' paperwork for the inspection. She also wrote lists of household tasks she had completed in order to be accountable to her husband. Now retirement is seen by her as an escape from legal to self-accountability: 'And there is still a great need to justify my existence. But it's only to me. No one is expecting me to say what I've been doing and account for my day, minute by minute.'

Mistrust of teachers' professionality meant they experienced multiple accountability pressures:

> And then it came to the inspection. We heard about the inspection and then – I mean the amount of paperwork that one has to do then is just crazy. And I'd said that I needed more time to do this. And again it just wasn't possible really to fund it. And I could feel it all happening again. I could see all the signs; the irritability, the crying.

A number of the teachers had become ill prior to the inspection and were absent from school when it took place. Mary explained that:

> In the week just before I had the breakdown, the OFSTED inspection was looming, also appraisals, SATs and parents' evenings. It was unfortunate but all those came at one point. So it was just overwhelming, I just couldn't cope with it and woke up in the middle of the night sobbing uncontrollably.

The teachers felt they needed to produce much documentary evidence to provide proof of their professionalism. Ben and his school received an excellent OFSTED report but found the build up to it contributed to intensification and was extremely stressful:

> It was just hell really. And I felt that all the staff were very stressed, particularly at the time we had the inspection in January. The amount of preparation for that – we were a school who were well prepared for it I think. But it was still planning. . . The amount of work involved in preparing for the visit was enormous. So we did all this extra work on top of the normal work which was taking up our evenings and our weekends.

Good parent–teacher relationships require high levels of trust. However, in the stress research, the parents were sometimes distrustful of the teachers. For instance, Merryl, as head of a small school, experienced stressful conditions involving changed powers of governors and parent power (Merryl fearing the withdrawal of pupils, with the inevitable impact on the budget of a small school):

> The governing body were very much people who would come and talk, would say things had to be done, and then go away and leave me to do it. There was one governor who was supportive and helped me draft policies but the others were not supportive. And there was one particular governor – I've never ever met a woman like her before and I never want to again. I understand she was

actually invited onto the governing body before I started because she was regarded to be safer in the system than outside criticizing. It was thought that if she had some responsibility for the school she couldn't do as much damage.

Ralph had experienced the joint impact of pupils' manipulation and parent power, and felt that teachers were increasingly distrusted by pupils:

> I have seen a difference in parent's interactions with staff in recent years. Parents are much more prepared to be critical. Much more prepared to come in if they feel that something unfair or unjust or inappropriate has happened. Often based on either misinformation or partial information. There was a time, and I'm aware that I was on the tail end of it, but previously if you were in trouble at school and the chances were if you went home and told your parents you'd be in trouble at home as well. That's not the case now. There are many more, if you're in trouble at school, 'Oh that's not fair!'

Conclusion

Giddens' (1990, 1991) theoretical framework is useful for viewing the nature of trust negotiations in schools. However, it requires empirical underpinning and development. The theory, by conflating agency with structure, takes us away from dualist conceptions of society to enable accounts of the social world in which:

> The self is not a passive entity, determined by external influences; in forging their self identities, no matter how local their specific contexts of action, individuals contribute to and directly promote social influences that are global in their consequences and implications.

Not all of the teachers in this study worked at schools in which distrust had become physically and emotionally damaging. Some enjoyed positive personal and collegial relationships in their work. However, the majority did not. There were also examples of teachers' resistances to oppressive work regimes leading to changes being made to the 'system' at school level, which brought about improvements in the psychic lives of the teachers. All this is consistent with Giddens (1990, 1991). For viewing events not as deterministic outcomes of social forces, but as a dialectical process between agency and structure, 'change is an ever present possibility' (Shilling, 1992, p. 80). However, in late modernity, there is no certainty or inevitability; closure is difficult.

Giddens (1990, p. 6) recognizes that modern institutions 'hold out the possibility of emancipation but at the same time create mechanisms of suppression, rather than actualisation, of self'. However, the evidence from this study can be used to question the theory. For instance, it does not, in my view, fully consider the contexts within which the trust negotiations between individuals and groups are taking place, or the extent of existential anxiety and dread that is generated in these interactions. Giddens does not, it seems, fully engage with issue of the 'degrees of freedom that differentially-placed agents have within a concrete structural situation' (Willmott, 1999). Actors in this case study, although not always devoid of agency, were heavily 'constrained and in situations where the educational system contextually limits what can be done, by whom and where' (Willmott, 1999). Manifestations of power and authority that are strongly evident in the empirical account do not seem adequately explained by the theoretical account.

In terms of education policy, it is always possible that problems experienced at the implementation stage may react back on the context of influence thus leading to policy reformulation. However, rather than policy-makers listening to teachers' views on their changed work, there now seems to be a consensus and political will among the two major political parties that school improvement is to be sought by further tightening the control of teachers' work.

Apart from the personal (emotional and physical) and economic costs to the system resulting from the breakdown of personal relationships described in this chapter, there is a further consequence. The participants in primary education are now engaged in the mutual surveillance and documenting of each others[1] activities as the social relations of the primary school become more formalized. Management monitor and appraise teachers and keep files on teachers' behaviour and performance. Attempts to gain security are sought in legal and quasi-legal ways. The 'bullied' teachers of this research keep dossiers that record 'bullying' incidents and they attend all meetings (not just disciplinary) with management accompanied by a 'professional friend' to act as a witness and note taker. Evidence compiled in this way can later be produced at an industrial tribunal. Security seeking can also be seen in the proliferation of contracts. Management tightly specify the tasks to be accomplished in employment contracts and job descriptions. Whether or not this work is being produced and its quality is then established by monitoring, appraisal and teacher competency schemes and inspection by OFSTED, parent–teacher relations are formalized through the introduction of home/school contracts. The unions and teachers involved in this study seek regulations and legislation on Health and Safety in the workplace that addresses such issues as occupational stress and workplace harassment.

We know from the teacher development literature that school improvement is 'only likely in schools where risk-taking is encouraged within an atmosphere of basic trust and support' (Goodlad, 1984) and where teachers are 'given the basic security of being trusted and valued' (Hargreaves, 1998a, p. 10).

Yet the picture of the work cultures of low-trust schooling presented in my analysis, like Helsby's (1999, p. 65), is:

clearly the antithesis of the vision of the 'new work order' which promises to motivate staff and to unleash their capacity to be innovative and entrepreneurial in responding to customer needs.

In the UK, measures intended to increase teacher motivation, job satisfaction and morale, and to make teaching a more attractive and 'modern' profession by the introduction of firmer appraisal and performance-related pay are, if the analysis in this chapter is correct, likely to bring about the opposite effects. These proposals seem set to increase divisiveness and lead to further erosion of trust between the participants in primary schooling.

 # References

Alexander, J. (1989) In: T. Parsons (ed.) *The Modern Reconstruction of Classical Thought*, London: Routledge and Kegan Paul.

Ball, S.J. (1988) Staff relations during the teachers' industrial action context, conflict and proletarianization, *British Journal of Sociology of Education*, 9, pp. 289–306.

Ball, S.J. (1994) *Education Reform: A Critical and Post-structural Approach*, Buckingham: Open University Press.

Beck, U. (1992) *Risk Society*, London: Sage.

Beynon, J. (1984) Sussing-out teachers – pupils as data gatherers, in: M. Hammersley and P. Woods (eds.) *Life in School*, Buckingham: Open University Press.

Bartlett, D. (1998) *Stress: Perspectives and Processes*, Buckingham: Open University Press.

Brown, M. and Ralph, S. (1998) Change-linked stress in British teachers. Paper presented to the British Educational Research Association Conference, September, Queen's University Belfast.

Campbell, R.J. and St. J. Neill, S.R. (1994) *Primary Teachers at Work*, London: Routledge.

Castells, M. (1997) *The Power of Identity*, Oxford: Basil Blackwell.

Dadds, M. (1993) The feeling of thinking in professional study, *Educational Action Research*, 1, pp. 287–303.

Dearing, R. (1994) *The National Curriculum and its Assessment, Final report*, London: SCAA.

DES (1992) *Curricular Organization and Classroom Practice in Primary Schools: A Discussion Paper*, London: DES Information Branch.

Dinham, S. and Scott, C. (1996) *The Teacher 2000 Project: A Study of Teacher Satisfaction, Motivation and Health*, Nepean: University of Western Sydney.

Lortie, D. (1975) *The School Teacher: A Sociological Study*, Chicago, IL: University of Chicago Press.

Misztal, B.A. (1996) *Trust in Modern Societies*, Cambridge: Polity.

National Governor's Association (1989) *Results in Education*, Washington, DC: NGA.

Newton, T., Handy, J. and Fineman, S. (eds.) (1995) *Managing Stress: Emotion and Power at Work*, London: Sage.

Nias, J. (1989) *Primary Teachers Talking: A Study of Teaching as Work* , London: Routledge.

Nias, J. (1996) Thinking about feeling: the emotions in teaching, *Cambridge Journal of Education*, 26, pp. 293–323.

Nias, J., Southworth, G. and Yeomans, R. (1989) *Staff Relationships in the Primary School*, London: Cassell.

OFSTED (1994) *Primary Matters: A Discussion on Teaching and Learning in Primary Schools*, London: OFSTED.

OFSTED (1995) *The Handbook for the Inspection of Nursery and Primary Schools*, London: OFSTED.

OFSTIN (1997) *A Better System of Inspection*, Hexham, Northumberland: OFSTIN.

Pearlin, L.I. (1989) The sociological study of stress, *Journal of Health and Social Behaviour*, 30, pp. 241–256.

Pollard, A. (1985) *The Social World of the Primary School*, London: Holt, Reinhart and Winston.

Pollard, A. (1992) Teachers' responses to the reshaping of primary education, in: M.Arnot and L. Barton (eds.) *Voicing Concerns: Sociological Perspectives on Contemporary Educations Reforms*, Wallingford: Triangle.

Rosenholtz, S.J. (1989) Workplace conditions that affect teacher quality and commitment: implications for teacher induction programs, *The Elementary School Journal*, 89, pp. 421–39.

Seddon, T. (1998) Capacity building: a strategy for educating between state and market. Paper presented at the *Ethnography and Education Conference*, September, University of Oxford.

Shilling, C. (1992) Reconceptualising structure and agency in the sociology of education: structuration theory and schooling, *British Journal of Sociology of Education*, 13, pp. 69–88.

Travers, C.J. and Cooper, C.L. (1996) *Teachers Under Pressure: Stress in the Teaching Profession*, London: Routledge.

Troman, G. (1997) The effects of restructuring on primary teachers' work: a sociological analysis. Unpublished Ph.D. thesis, Buckingham: The Open University.

Webb, R. and Vulliamy, G. (1996) *Roles and Responsibilities in the Primary School: Changing Demands, Changing Practices*, Buckingham: Open University Press.

Willmott, R. (1999) Structure, agency and the sociology of education: rescuing analytical dualsim, *British Journal of Sociology of Education*, 20, pp. 5–21.

Woods, P. (1995) The intensification of the teacher's self. Presented at the *Conference on Teacher Burnout*, Marbach, November.

Woods, P., Jeffrey, B., Troman, G. and Boyle, M. (1997) *Restructuring Schools; Reconstructing Teachers: Responding to Change in the Primary School*, Buckingham: Open University Press.

Wragg, E.C., Wragg, C.M., Haynes, G.S. and Chamberlin, R.P. (1998) *Teaching Competence Project, Occasional Paper 1*, Exeter: University of Exeter School of Education.

12

The Influencing Role of Subject Leaders in Secondary Schools

Judith Aubrey-Hopkins and Chris James

Introduction

The importance of the head of subject department in secondary schools in England and Wales, or subject leadership (SL) as it has been redefined (TTA, 1998), is widely recognised and, as a consequence, the people who fulfil this role are the focus of attempts to improve leadership practice (NAfW, 1999; DfEE, 2000). However, approaches, such as the implementation of policies on SL professional development and the management of the performance of teachers, take place in the context of existing practice in which there is little understanding of the influencing role of SLs on their department members. This chapter explores the role of the SL and reports empirical research findings about the influencing aspects of it. It begins by considering the main themes from the literature on the leadership role of SLs.

The Role of the Head of Department

The first theme that emerges is the recognition of SLs' line management responsibilities and their potential to influence teaching and learning in whole areas of the school curriculum (see, for example, Everard, 1986). Research into the role identifies SLs as the 'driving force behind any school . . . the key to improving the quality of the learning process' (Earley and Fletcher-Campbell, 1989, p. 215). The SL's potential to influence classroom practice is significant because it is at that level that there is the greatest effect on pupil achievement (Scheerens,

---

Source: Commissioned.

1992). Indeed, the literature specifically links the role of the SL to improving pupil achievement (see, for example, OHMCI, 1995; Brown and Rutherford, 1998; Harris, 1998; Bolam and Turner, 1999; Busher *et al.*, 2000). As the role demands that SLs are close both to those they lead and to the locale of pupil learning, the lines of leadership, management and accountability are typically short. There is, however, a tension here between closeness to department members and the requirement to influence them on the one hand and a desire to retain distance and to respect their autonomy on the other (Ernest, 1989).

A second theme is the complex and demanding nature of the role (Bolam and Turner, 1998; Glover and Miller, 1999). SLs are expected to be 'leading professionals' (Bennett, 1995; Busher *et al.*, 2000) and to act as exemplars to their department members and other colleagues (Earley and Fletcher-Campbell, 1989). For SLs new to post establishing their teaching competence is a priority (Bullock *et al.*, 1995). But the role entails much more than 'being a good teacher'. The management responsibilities of the role (TTA, 1998) and increasing educational accountability extend the role's complexity and challenging nature.

The third theme is the wide range of contexts for subject leadership and the problems this variation creates for generalising and theorising about the SL role. Bennett (1995) draws attention to four particular factors that play a part in creating this diversity: subject epistemology, department membership, the SL's individual competence and expertise and the concept of teaching underpinning the SL's practice. The different structure of subject areas (Busher and Harris, 1999) is also source of variation. Bolam and Turner (1999) suggest that the factors influencing the SL's leadership actions include those associated with the SL, the task, the subordinates and the organisational situations, each of which can vary considerably.

Investigating the Influencing Role of SLs

It is taken as axiomatic that the SL's role entails influencing the practice of department members. During that influencing process, power will be brought to bear and will be experienced by department members as attempts to change their practice. Thus, in exploring the role of SLs, the notions of power, influence, leadership and role are linked and their relationship provides a conceptual framework for the investigation. This relationship is now considered.

Sources of power in organisations arise, *inter alia*, from having control of scarce resources, having credibility, stature, prestige, possessing the ability to control uncertainty and from the creation of legitimacy for certain ideas, values and demands through the process of symbol construction and value use (Hardy, 1994). Decision-making power, first characterised by Dahl (1957), is the exercise of power to make decisions that are binding on others. Non-decision-making power, first advocated by Bacharch and Baratz (1963), prevents alternatives and options reaching the decision-making agenda. Symbolic power (Lukes, 1974) achieves political acquiescence by consciously shaping values, preferences, cognitions and perceptions in order to legitimise demands and to ensure that grievances or issues are not articulated or transformed into challenges. The choice of organisational structure, the co-option of others and the manipulation of commitment, norms and information may all be used to create legitimacy. Whilst decision-making and non-decision-making dimensions of power are instrumental in nature and affect the ability to resist, symbolic power shapes attitudes and the will to resist (Hardy, 1994). All three are forms of sovereign power and are largely consciously mobilised to influence others. Influence is the essence of leadership (Yukl, 1998) and for the purpose of this conceptualisation, we see the practice of leadership as a process of influencing others to take up and enact a role (James and Connolly, 2000). In that process the leaders themselves are influenced and their leadership role shaped because of the reciprocal experience of the exercise of power. Hardy (1994), drawing on the ideas of Foucault (1975), also identifies system power in organisations, which is not mobilised consciously and resides in the unconscious acceptance of the values, traditions, cultures and structures of a system. System power pervades all organisational relations.

Typically, textbook definitions of role draw attention to expected behaviours, the position of the role within the structure of the organisation and role function. An individual may occupy multiple roles and may be affected by role conflict (for example, role incompatibility, overload and underload) which, itself, may result in role stress (Merton, 1968; Mullins, 1993). Although definitions of role tend to portray roles as static and predetermined, Giddens (1979) argues for a more dynamic interpretation asserting that social systems are not composed of roles but are constituted as socially reproduced practices which both create and are created by social systems. None the less, the notion of role provides a useful heuristic device to describe reproduced practices associated with position and structure and, for the purposes of this research, is a useful unit of analysis. Our use of the term does not preclude the acceptance that individuals may be moved both consciously and unconsciously to assume organisational roles by political influences, in which the emotional experience of taking up a role may play an important part (French and Vince, 2000).

The delineation of a set of practices in which an individual or group engages, or the behaviours that are part of a role, presupposes the existence of some kind of boundary that distinguishes what is included in the set of practices or behaviours and what is not. From an open-systems theory standpoint, the management of a system boundary preserves what is within the boundary (the core), gives the core the resources necessary to do its work and maintains a continuous interaction with the environment (Czander, 1993).

Inadequate boundary management fails to bring in appropriate resources or allows inappropriate ones to enter. It may also allow valuable resources to leave the core or fail to ensure that the system produces resources that are appropriate for the environment. Violations of the boundary are expressed as organisational conflicts and have the potential to escalate into major events, which is why there may be reluctance to protect role boundaries (ibid.). Thus, for an individual or group, the management of the role boundary is associated with emotion as is the taking up and enacting of a role in organisations, especially educational organisations (James, 1999). The way in which an educational leadership role is defined (the espoused role) and leadership practice (the role in use) may be different (James and Vince, 2001). The differences may result from the emotional experience of taking up a role and the defences against unwanted role-associated emotions.

Research Design

The research reported here sought to construct, interpret and theorise secondary school SLs' experience of influencing the educational practice of their department members. Data were collected by means of semi-structured tape-recorded interviews with 17 SLs whose job titles were heads of mathematics (four), English (four), modern foreign languages (three), science (three), history (two) and Welsh (one). The interviewees worked in different mixed comprehensive schools in South Wales. With one exception, all the schools catered for pupils in the 11–18 age range. Pupils in the seventeenth school were aged between 11 and 16 years. Four of the schools worked in Welsh medium and all the schools had significantly changed their practice to improve pupil achievement (Connolly et al., 2000). All the SLs were recommended as 'good SLs' by their headteachers and/or the local authority specialist advisers. The interviews' questions explored the ways in which the SLs considered that they effected the practice of department members generally as well as their influence on particular individuals. The main findings from the data are now considered.

The Emergent Themes

Communication

Communication is at the heart of attempts to influence practice. The SLs communicate through meetings, weekly bulletins, notice boards and written notes to staff. Formal discussions between the SL and individual department members typically occur when the department member's practice is giving concern although such discussions are rarely successful (see below). Regular formal discussions between the SL and individual members of the department for other purposes (for example, to discuss their work or professional development) tend not to be used unless the SL had a wider, whole-school responsibility, for example for staff development, or when the SL was new to post.

SLs regard department meetings as an important opportunity to influence their colleagues. The content of the meetings varied, as did the balance between administrative matters, the discussion of aspects of teaching and learning and the sharing of good practice. In some instances, department administration and pedagogy were dealt with in separate meetings.

Informal communication occurs in a variety of places and at various times – during breaks and lunchtimes, when passing colleagues in the corridors, during informal visits to classrooms, during shared journeys to school and via ancillary staff. Informal communication was characterised by brevity and happenstance and relied on sound relationships between the SL and department members. The SLs put significant emphasis on informal contacts as a successful mode of influence.

The SLs sought to resolve problems in communication that might be exacerbated by the physical separation of the 'institutional bases' of department members. In some instances meetings were held at the various bases where the pupils' work and resources could be used as a stimulus for the discussion of pedagogy. In others, the relocation of the institutional bases was a priority following the SL taking up his or her post. Heads of federal departments, for example science (Busher and Harris, 1999), valued being based close to the teaching rooms of the heads of the separate subject departments.

In general, communication was aimed at ensuring collective cognate action rather than shaping individual practice. Communication to mould the ways of working of individual department members appeared problematic (see below), and inclusive collective strategies were used as a way of ensuring appropriate individual action. Communication was sometimes targeted at the whole department in order to influence the work of an individual. The following quotation illustrates an SL's use of this strategy, with the implicit threat of public exposure for a particular teacher should there be failure to conform: 'If you say "well in two weeks time we are going to take in all Year 9 books and have a look at them", then that teacher will make sure that those books are marked as well as anybody else's.'

Delegation

Analysis of the data reveals the problematic nature of delegation and uncertainty about whether it influences practice. There is a tension between the SLs' desire to delegate and the willingness of department members to accept delegated tasks. Some department members accept delegated tasks willingly while others are less keen. In some instances, perceived willingness to accept delegated tasks was a stimulus for the SL to delegate. Delegation is made more difficult in departments where there is a high turnover of staff and where members of staff are inexperienced or lacking in confidence. SLs are also unwilling or unable to delegate tasks because of the apparent inability of department members to carry them out competently. In the words of one SL referring to the second in department:

> Whenever it comes to administrative things he shuts off, so all I've got him doing in my department is in charge of the administration of in-school examinations and the minutes of the department meeting. He doesn't do the minutes very well either . . . But asking him to do anything else – he always makes a mess of it, he doesn't do it effectively . . . he's getting on a bit so in the end I think I might as well do it myself.

In other situations, the delegated tasks are taken on but then not carried out. Sometimes, SLs are unwilling to delegate tasks to colleagues who have responsibilities beyond the department.

SLs hope that delegation will improve teaching although they are unable to substantiate it. However, when successful, it appears to give department members additional confidence, extend their role and increase their authority as teachers.

Working with individual members of the department

SLs use a variety of ways to seek to influence underperforming staff. On occasions a direct approach, including setting targets, is used although it can be problematic. It is also not always effective either immediately or in the long term. Other strategies employed include working to develop the relationship with the individual, time-limited action plans and discussion following classroom observation. Attempts to influence individuals are given added authority by recourse to department policies and by referring to examples of work from the other members of the department. Varying degrees of success are claimed. One SL explained:

> You have to be careful that you tackle it in a professional way as opposed to personally. That you say this has to be done because it's policy or *we* need to do this more. But I'm not saying that I succeed each time but definitely this is what I've found to be the best way to approach the problem.

A significant task for SLs is working with the anxieties of staff members that are typically expressed as a lack of confidence. SL strategies for working with this group included giving praise, deferring to the member's expertise, establishing a mentoring style of relationship, involvement in shared decision-making and the joint creation of schemes of work.

For a variety of reasons including age, personal problems, not wanting to antagonise colleagues, sometimes SLs do not address the undeperformance of department members whose practice needs to be improved. They seek to build on strengths rather than focus on weaknesses. One SL explained:

> You have to bear in mind that people haven't quite got the energy as they get older and subsequently they haven't got the enthusiasm so you have to look after those people and you've got to draw things out of them because if they feel you're putting more and more pressure on them they'll turn against you . . . In a way I'm leaving sleeping dogs lie there. I try to get the best out of him under the circumstances . . . So you've got to cajole them, you've got to say it's for the sake of the department.

Despite the importance of improving the practice of inadequately performing department members, the strategies adopted on an individual basis were not generally successful. Symbolic power, through the establishment of group norms, collaboration, teamworking and accepted rituals and routines designed to weaken the inclination to resist (Hardy, 1994) appear to dominate but are not universally successful. However in one department there had been a significant change in teaching methods employed as a result of the use of this influencing practice. The collective authority of the department was significant in ensuring that a 'reluctant' department member was 'dragged on board.'

A number of themes were significant among department members considered to be easy to influence. First, newly qualified teachers frequently initiate requests for advice and guidance. This kind of influencing relationship changed over time although not always without difficulty as a result of the increasing autonomy of the newly qualified teacher. Secondly, SLs feel that they have to limit the activities of their colleagues who are eager – occasionally too eager – to take on additional responsibilities and to try new ideas. Thirdly, sometimes SLs deliberately reconfigure, extend and even transform individuals' roles by giving them additional responsibilities that have implications for the whole department and, occasionally, for the whole school. These themes for the influencing role of the SL are held together by the common thread of role boundary of department members.

Department policies and decision-making

The use of department policies and schemes of work is frequently cited as an important way in which the SLs influence practice. The process of their development is seen as an important way of establishing standard practice across the department and is regarded as a particularly important activity for the SLs new to their posts.

However, SLs are also anxious to ensure individual teachers' autonomy. As one put it: 'What I do is try and change the system and how we look at what we are doing as opposed to changing individuals. You know I think that everybody has a right to teach their own individual way.'

SLs also influence practice through involving colleagues in departmental decision-making. They offer two rationales. First, it ensures engagement in the change processes and, secondly, it enables a greater range of expertise to be brought to bear on departmental problems. Both these rationales appear to have the underlying purpose of establishing legitimacy for decision-making. According to the SLs, involvement in decision-making impacts positively on teaching although they were unable to provide evidence that directly supported this assertion.

Although the notion of involvement was a dominant theme in departmental decision-making, SLs also exercise their decision-making power to influence practice, for example, by taking a decision to effect change that would otherwise have been blocked by members of the department. Non-decision-making power is also evident. One SL refused to allow the discussion of a change proposed by a department member to be included on the department meeting agenda. Regardless of the decision-making process, the SLs took responsibility for the outcomes of decisions including appropriate accountability.

Sharing good practice and working collaboratively

Sharing of good practice as a mode of influence took numerous forms and includes the mutual review of work and the joint production of a portfolio of exemplars of pupil work to illustrate appropriate standards and to support the moderation of assessed pupil work. The SLs took the lead in sharing successful experiences. Typically, part of the department meeting is used for this purpose. The SLs feel that they often benefit on a personal basis from the exchange of successful practice. Peer observation (the observation of one teacher's classroom practice by another member of the department) also features as a way of interchanging ideas.

Sharing good practice was in some instances problematic on the grounds of equity, quality and content. Attempts to share teaching resources occasionally cause conflicts particularly when some colleagues contribute more than others. There are also examples of shared ideas that did not work in practice, shared materials of poor quality and a situation where a shared innovation had to be rejected on health and safety grounds.

Linked to the idea of sharing good practice is the concept of working collaboratively. SLs aspire to, and espouse, it as a form of influence although examples tend to be restricted and episodic in nature. Generally, collaborative teaching is limited mainly because of constraints of time and availability. Initiatives such as pairing teachers in order to overcome an individual's ineffectiveness are generally not successful. SLs attempt to lead collaboration in such activities as the production of teaching resources and marking and moderating assignments. They argue that it extends the range of expertise utilised for departmental tasks and helps to set a common standard. Preparation for school inspection is a significant driving force for collaboration.

Staff development

The broad category of staff development is cited widely as a form of influence. Not unexpectedly, attendance at courses outside the school by members of the department and the SL features prominently. There was evidence of attempts to match course attendance with the needs and/or responsibilities and/or interests of individual department members. Typically, those attending courses are required to share the outcomes with other members of the department. One SL said that attendance at courses helped department members to 'feel confident about trying out new ideas and initiatives'. Professional development through teaching pupils with a range of ages and abilities and delegation of responsibilities are also highlighted. In one case, the department meeting was cited as the main method of development.

Monitoring and evaluation

Monitoring took place both formally in recognised explicit procedures and informally in *ad hoc* ways. In the data, classroom observation was pre-eminent in the formal monitoring procedures with some SLs favouring it, 'It keeps them on their toes. I don't see anything wrong with that'; some accepting it, 'OK, I've got to go in and monitor and that's not something that we really want to do but I think that we can benefit from it'; with others not seeing the need, 'I know my department backwards I don't need to go in and see the way they teach. I can tell from looking at their [the pupils] work what's going on'. The SLs and their departments accepted that the observation of lessons was part of the SL's work. In many instances, observation was formalised with the SL and the teacher agreeing the monitoring focus beforehand, feedback being given after the observation and the preparation of a written report. Typically, all the members of the department were included in this kind of monitoring activity although, in one case, the SL did not monitor the classroom practice of a department member who was a deputy head because she felt uncomfortable doing so. Long-term absence of department members could disrupt the monitoring cycle.

Although monitoring the work of the department through classroom observation was cited as a mode of influence, the SLs were unsure whether such monitoring *per se* had a direct effect on practice. It was the actions taken subsequent to observation and the culture created by monitoring and of which monitoring was a part that were more significant. In one example where a department had undergone considerable change, there was now a culture in which continual monitoring and review were accepted as an integral part of department practice:

> The last couple of years has seen a tremendous amount of change . . . there's a real openness about continual monitoring, reviewing, discussion, about all our processes and practices, I think. There doesn't seem to be any sense of criticism in the department and therefore people are very open to exchange ideas and accept critical comment in a positive way.

For many of the SLs, classroom observation was a way of gathering examples of good practice that could then be discussed and shared. Peer observation was actively encouraged in addition to the formal monitoring of classroom practice by the SL. In some instances, department members observed the SLs' teaching.

In a number of cases, SLs also undertook monitoring by reviewing pupils' work (for example, a whole year group) which was followed by discussions with individual members of staff where practice was not acceptable. In some cases, this kind of monitoring took place at short notice with follow-up collections on some other pretext in order to check up on errant department members. Other members of the department were sometimes involved in the collection and monitoring of books according to their responsibilities.

Informal monitoring was a significant feature of the data. It took place in a variety of ways such as during opportunistic visits to classrooms, through the proximity of the SL's teaching room to those of the members of department or by noting what remained on the blackboard after a lesson. It was difficult for the SLs to find clear evidence when a department member's performance was inadequate. Such teachers were frequently adept at rationalising and/or not taking responsibility themselves for their inadequate performance. As one SL put it: 'They can always explain why they are not underachieving really.' In other cases, department members whose practice was typically inadequate would contrive to teach unusually well during formal monitoring. All these are examples of departmental members exerting their own influence in the face of influence by the SL. These responses by inadequately performing department members were used by the SLs to justify the use of impromptu and informal strategies for monitoring classroom practice.

External influences

External interventions such as inspections or involvement in initial teacher education are also used by SLs to influence practice. Typically, inspections, whether by Estyn (the schools inspection agency in Wales) or as part of a local education authority review, provide legitimacy for the development of policies and schemes of work required for the event. Feedback emanating from the inspection/review process is also used. Although SLs generally feel that an inspection helps them in their attempts to influence ineffective department members, it does not always provide the evidence as expected.

Similarly, departmental participation in initial teacher education supports the SLs' efforts to influence practice. Teachers involved in initial teacher education tend to be more reflective about their practice. Furthermore, student teachers are a source of innovatory ideas and resources. Experience of being observed by students reduces anxiety about monitoring procedures and the additional non-contact time generated when students are proficient enough to take classes on their own provides SLs with more opportunity to observe their colleagues' teaching.

Discussion

The study confirms that the role of SL, with its immediate leadership responsibility for the work of other teachers, is a taxing one. SLs are directly exposed both to the politics of department management and to the scrutiny of their professional performance in a way that others in school leadership positions, such as headteachers and deputy headteachers, may not be but without the *ex officio* authority and experience of those more senior members of staff. SLs are involved day to day in both operational and strategic issues that frequently demand an immediate response. They are in regular and frequent contact with those they lead and they strive to ensure and enhance that contact. The sense of 'no time to manage' (Earley and Fletcher-Campbell, 1989; Bolam and Turner, 1999) and the stresses of 'managing in the middle' (Busher and Harris, 1999) are significant. However, other factors such as increasing levels of accountability and the immediacy, complexity and diversity of the role exacerbate its challenging nature and may, in fact, be more fundamental in its pressures.

SLs influence department members predominantly by establishing norms, expectations and routines. This symbolic power (Lukes, 1974; Hardy, 1994) creates a culture that embodies a control mechanism where shared standards and values instead of bureaucratic restraints guide behaviour (Ouchi, 1982) and SLs use it explicitly and implicitly. The value of agreed norms and expectations in influencing practice resides in the sensitivity and the willingness of department members to respond to them. Various inclusive and collaborative strategies were used to ensure commitment to the norms and the legitimacy of the norms. Agreeing standards appeared to be relatively straightforward at the policy level, but became increasingly problematic and beyond the remit of the SL at the level of the individual teacher's classroom practice. Although it was at this point that the SL preferred to respect the individual teacher's autonomy, the SLs in this study none the less used a range of strategies, some manipulative, to ensure conformance to norms (especially by inadequately performing teachers) at the classroom level. An overarching theme was the difficulties experienced by the SLs in acknowledging teachers' professional freedom and autonomy, influencing their individual performance and creating, maintaining and changing a context of collective expectations and requirements. This task required the sophisticated use of power in which the creation of legitimacy was crucial. Of particular interest was the finding that, within this group of acknowledged 'good SLs', formal managerial strategies such as regular performance reviews with target-setting were used only exceptionally. Where they had been used to address inadequate performance, they had generally been unsuccessful and been discontinued.

Important tasks for the SLs were ensuring that activities undertaken by members of their departments were appropriate, motivating staff and containing the emotions and anxieties associated with the work. The SLs also played a part in changing – even transforming – the nature of the roles of department members. The extent to which the SL was able to penetrate the role boundaries of department members was critical, perhaps more so than the members' actual role capabilities. Only by crossing the role boundaries could the SLs influence their department members and a number of strategies, the legitimacy of which the SLs sought to create, were used to do so. From the data, an 'ideal boundary type' was not the department member whose role boundary was easily crossed. This kind of department member would tend to take on too much and/or lack focus. In these instances, the SL would help the member of staff to manage his or her role boundary more appropriately. Nor was it the department member whose boundaries were impermeable. These department members were particularly problematic for it was almost impossible to influence them. The ideal boundary type appeared to be the department members who managed their boundaries to allow relevant resources to enter and to take on suitable additional responsibilities and who allowed appropriate resources to leave – often in the form of expertise and completed tasks to support individual and collective efforts – thereby enabling others to take up roles that conformed to the purposes of the department.

The conscious and unconscious experience of power as the SLs sought to influence their department members appeared to shape them in their role. In effect, it made them particular kinds of SL with distinctive predispositions and priorities. The influence exerted by department members affected the SL's influencing role, changing its nature and restricting it in some ways and enhancing it in others. An SL's influence will mould his or her colleagues into particular kinds of department member. For example, those to whom delegation is easy become defined as 'helpful' while those unwilling to do so become designated as 'difficult' and such definitions may become fixed and reinforced by subsequent actions. We were conscious in our own enquiry of reinforcing such definitions. When SLs assert their influence to effect change, department members may respond in ways that are not always helpful or hoped for. Poorly performing department members may subvert specific strategies designed to address their inadequate performance in order to resist influence and thereby to configure themselves as 'satisfactory performers'. Deliberate attempts to influence marginally underperforming members of staff may turn them into 'problems' or 'poor-performers' rather than bringing about a desired improvement. The positioning effect of power may present a problem for SLs in their current post as they seek to initiate change and, if they take up a leadership post in another school, their experience may not have prepared them for a new emotional-political setting. Also, attempts to enhance the influence of SLs through, for example, performance management are likely to be implemented in and reflect the existing emotional-political systems of influence and, as with any assertion of power, may have consequences that are neither required nor expected.

References

Bacharch, P. and Baratz, M.S. (1963) Decisions and non-decisions: an analytical framework. *American Political Science Review* 57: 641–51.

Bennett, N. (1995) *Managing Professional Teachers: Middle Management in Primary and Secondary Schools*. London: Paul Chapman Publishing.

Bolam, R. and Turner, C. (1998) Analysing the role of the subject head of department in secondary schools in England and Wales: towards a theoretical framework. *School Leadership and Management* 18(3): 373–88.

Bolam, R. and Turner, C. (1999) The management role of subject department heads in improvement of teaching and learning. In R. Bolam and F. van Wieringen (eds.) *Research and Educational Management in Europe*. New York: Waxmann Munster.

Brown, M. and Rutherford, D. (1998) Changing roles and raising standards: new challenges for heads of department. *School Leadership and Management* 18(1): 75–88

Bullock, K., James, C.R. and Jamieson, I.M. (1995) An exploratory study of novices and experts in educational management. *Educational Management and Administration* 23(3): 197–205.

Busher, H. (1998) Reducing role overload for a head of department: a rationale for fostering staff development. *School Organisation* 8(1): 99–108.

Busher, H. and Harris, A. (1999) Leadership of school subject areas: tensions and dimensions of managing in the middle. *School Leadership and Management* 19(3): 305–17.

Busher, H., Harris, A. and Wise, C. (2000) *Subject Leadership and School Improvement*. London: Sage.

Connolly, M. Connolly, U. and James, C.R. (2000) Leadership in educational change. *British Journal of Management* 11(1): 61–71.

Czander, W.M. (1993) *The Psychodynamics of Work and Organisations*. New York: Guilford Press.

Dahl, R. (1957) The concept of power. *Behavioural Science* 20: 201–15.

DfEE (2000) *Performance Management in Schools*. London: DEE.

Early, P. and Fletcher-Campbell, F. (1989) *The Time to Manage*. Windsor: NFER-Nelson.

Ernest, P. (1989) Head of secondary school mathematics department: a demanding role. *School Organisation* 9: 319–37.

Everard, B. (1986) *Developing Management in Schools*. London: Harper & Row.

Foucault, M. (1975) *Discipline and Punish*. New York: Vintage Books.

French, R. and Vince, R. (1999) *Group Relations, Management and Organisation*. Oxford: Oxford University Press.

Giddens, A. (1979) *Central Problems in Social Theory*. London: Macmillan.

Glover, D. and Miller, D. (1999) The working day of the subject leader and the impact of interruptions on teaching and learning in secondary schools. *Research in Education* 62: 55–67.

Hardy, C. (1994) *Managing Strategic Action: Mobilising Change, Concepts, Readings and Cases*. London: Sage.

Harris, A. (1998) Improving the effective department: strategies for growth and development. *Educational Management and Administration* 26(3): 269–78.

James, C.R. (1999) Institutional transformation and educational management. In T. Bush *et al.* (eds.) *Educational Management: Redefining Theory, Policy and Practice*. London: Paul Chapman Publishing.

James, C.R. and Connolly, U. (2000) *Effective Change in Schools*. London: Routledge Falmer.

James, C.R. and Vince, R. (2001) Developing the leadership capability of headteachers. *Educational Management and Administration* EMA 29(3): 307–17.

Lukes, S. (1974) *Power: A Radical View*. London: Macmillan.

Merton, R.K. (1968) *Social Theory and Social Culture*. New York: Free Press.

Mullins, L.J. (1993) *Management and Organisation Behaviour*. London: Pitman.

NAfW (1999) *Delivering the BEST for Teaching and Learning: The Performance Threshold*. Cardiff: National Assembly for Wales.

OHMCI (1995) *Leadership and Management in Secondary Schools*. Cardiff: OHMCI.

Scheerens, J. (1992) *Effective Schooling: Research, Theory and Practice*, London: Cassell.

TTA (1998) *National Standards for Subject Leaders*. London: Teacher Training Agency.

Yukl, G. (1998) *Leadership in Organisation*. London: Prentice-Hall.

Facilitating the Role of Middle Managers in Further Education

Ann R.J. Briggs

Introduction

This chapter reports on the first phase of research into the leadership roles of middle managers in further education colleges. Its focus is the exploration of the perceptions of a range of middle manager roles from the points of view of staff at three levels of college hierarchy, and it identifies features of their 'environment for management' which facilitate and impede the middle managers in role. In this chapter the term 'environment for management' will be used to denote the underpinning management structures of the college and the management styles within which they operate, together with the attitudes, perceptions and expectations of staff at all levels of the college.

The roles investigated include:

- Heads of curriculum departments, which may comprise one or more subjects
- Managers of student services, learning resources and learning support services
- Heads of individual service departments, for example: Estates, Finance, Personnel

These roles have been chosen as being at the articulating point of management systems, where whole-college strategy is transformed into day-to-day practice through the agency of the middle manager, and where the specialist professional expertise of the role-holders can, in turn, contribute to the formulation of new policy and strategy.

The whole research is being carried out at four English Further Education Colleges: this chapter offers preliminary results from one of the case study colleges.

Source: Research in Post-Compulsory Education, Vol. 7, no. 1, 2000, pp. 63–78. Edited version.

■ Context

Local management for further education colleges, as for schools and universities, leaves each college free to determine how its human and financial resources are best to be deployed to carry out the functions of the institution. The internal management structures of colleges, and the contexts in which they operate, are therefore largely developed in response to local management need, and shaped by the philosophies of those who manage them.

Management systems in further education colleges have been greatly affected by extensive post-incorporation change. Lumby (2001: 82) reports that of the 164 colleges she surveyed, only 4 had not restructured between 1993 and 1999, and that the majority had restructured more than once. New departments were created at incorporation to take over functions which had previously been carried out by local educational authorities. The post-incorporation funding system for many colleges meant reduced resource and 'top-heavy', resource-hungry management structures were re-organised into leaner, tighter systems. This was replicated on a larger scale through college amalgamations, where both market and financial pressures led to rationalisation of provision across urban areas, reducing the number of individual autonomous colleges.

Further education is little researched (Hughes *et al.*, 1996, Lumby, 2001) and management in further education still less. There are therefore fewer empirically-based studies than in the school sector for college researchers and managers to consider. The diversity of the sector may at times limit colleges from imitating each others' systems, yet an understanding of the issues which underlie, delimit and frame the diversity of management practice is valuable.

The nature of middle manager roles

'The strategic data bank of the organisation is not in the memory of its computers but in the minds of its managers,' (Mintzberg, 1990: 166). Mintzberg considers that managers possess delegated authority and status, and he analyses a number of intuitive roles for managers, which together form an integrated whole. These roles fall into three categories: interpersonal, informational and decision roles. Bennett (1995: 138) discusses the origin and nature of the role-holder's decision-making strategies: 'Individuals bring together experience and values into an "assumptive world", or theory in use'. The assumptive world of each manager is individual; it is based on personal values and on the analysis of previous experience, and it will remain largely unquestioned until it fails to represent or resolve a problem. It will then be re-defined to meet the new circumstance. The models offered here by Mintzberg and Bennett are of intuitive management, based upon experience and on subconsciously developed theory. In this scenario, managers may be acting in response to largely subjective judgments as to what their role constitutes, how it is to be carried out, and whether or not it is being performed effectively.

In seeking to clarify the nature of manager roles, Busher and Harris (1999: 307) draw upon the work of Glover *et al.* (1998) to identify four dimensions to the work of academic middle managers in schools. Firstly there is the 'bridging and brokering' role, where the policies and perspectives of senior staff are translated by the middle manager into departmental practice. Busher and Harris define this as transactional leadership. Secondly, there is a transformational dimension, where the middle manager encourages staff to cohere and establish a group identity, creating a collaborative departmental culture where creativity is fostered. A third proposed dimension is where the expert knowledge of the middle manager is used to improve staff and student performance. This implies the existence of a transactional role which has the added dimension of mentoring, and could be described as supervisory leadership. Lastly, there is the dimension of representative leadership, which emphasises the liaison role of the middle manager, both inside and outside the institution, both representing departmental interests, and enabling departmental colleagues to maintain their own liaison networks.

All four of these dimensions could usefully be applied to the role of further education middle managers; some dimensions may be found more strongly associated with particular middle manager roles, and some may be more closely linked with particular management environments.

As Bennett (1995) points out, the term 'middle management' implies a hierarchy, with senior managers creating the vision for the organisation, and middle managers articulating it in practical terms. This system 'assumes a downward flow of authority from the leader, given in order to promote what the leader seeks' (Bennett, 1995: 18). When considering the role of department heads and subject leaders in schools, the concern of many researchers has been whether or not these managers participate in shared decision-making, and to what extent they participate in the strategic management of the school.

Middle managers in further education

In further education colleges, the middle management structure includes personnel who lead college service departments and student service provision, as well as those leading curriculum areas. This situation presents possibilities for a greater range of management functions. The roles to be considered in this study lie at the third or fourth tier of the college hierarchy: on the service/student service side they would typically be at the third tier, answering to a member of the Senior Management Team who is directly answerable to the Principal. On the curriculum side, where lines of management tend to be longer, they are likely to be at the fourth tier, answerable to a Head of Faculty (or similar) who would have a third tier line of management as described above. (See Figure 13.1; roles to be researched are in bold.)

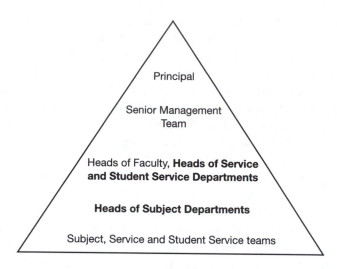

Figure 13.1 *Generalised hierarchy of management in FE colleges*

This 'layer' has been chosen for study because of its distance from the both the apex and base of the traditional college hierarchy. Shain and Gleeson (1998) argue that these managers have a key role in mediating tensions and change and in filtering competing messages from 'above' and 'below'. Such role-holders may not be included on a regular basis in senior management decision-making and policy formation, yet the nature of their role means that they may have considerable 'local' knowledge, power and autonomy. They may be responsible for large areas of curriculum provision, or for key departments within the college. It could be argued that management structures which enable these middle managers to work effectively will be crucial to the effectiveness of the whole college, since they are the ones who, in Bennett's terms (1995: 18) 'articulate the vision': on a day-to-day basis they make the business of the college happen. However, if role is defined by the holder in response to the role set (Kahn *et al.*, 1964), the people who have contact with the role-holder, those who have a stake in the outcomes of decisions, for the middle manager the role sets will include role-holders from the apex to the base of the hierarchy – superordinates, subordinates and fellow middle managers, as well as students and other clients of the college.

Difficulties associated with the role

The middle manager role discussed here could therefore bring with it substantial local autonomy and job satisfaction. It could also result in 'sent role conflict' (Kahn *et al.*, 1964) with the simultaneous occurrence of demands from the groups above, who hold substantial power and who carry the burden of corporate accountability, and from those below, who are substantial in number, and who interact on a daily basis with students and clients. Their own accountability will lie in both directions: they also carry individually the professional accountability for their own specialism, whether that is a curriculum area or an area of service provision, and will feel a major responsibility for carrying out their role in accordance with their own role expectations, based upon their value systems, knowledge and experience.

College service managers are largely judged by the efficiency and effectiveness of their service, whereas those running curriculum departments will mainly be judged by student outcomes. The role of each will intersect with others, for example curriculum heads manage the finance and human resource needs of their department, whilst admissions officers give advice on curriculum matters, and estates managers influence the environment in which both curriculum and student service activities are carried out.

There is thus potentially role ambiguity (Kahn *et al.*, 1964) between the specialists in any given management area, and others whose specialist function intersects with theirs. The day-to-day pressure of management roles and fragmentation of activity described by Mintzberg (1990: 166) – 'management consists of a mass of fragmented and disjointed activities, constant interruption, pressure for immediate answers to questions and solutions to problems' – may result in the expertise of specialists not being fully used. Also, as the primary function of the college is teaching and learning, and responsibility for the product may be seen as taking precedence over responsibility for the process, a hierarchy of middle managers may unofficially develop, where curriculum managers perceive themselves as more important than college service managers and are unwilling to acknowledge and use their expertise.

Methodology

The research reported here is a preliminary analysis of one of four case studies which have been carried out in further education colleges in England. A case study approach was chosen in order to investigate a number of 'singularities' (Bassey, 1999: 47) in enough detail for the environments for management at each college to be understood, for comparisons to be made between them and 'fuzzy generalisations' (Bassey, 1999: 12) to be drawn. It is hoped that a modelling approach can then be applied to the set of case studies in order to understand better the processes at work.

The case study college presented here is a large multi-site general further education college. Each site was formerly a separate college, and the focus of recent years has been on establishing 'one college 'and on systems to promote financial security and student achievement. The most recent FEFC (Further Education Funding Council) inspection confirms that these goals have been achieved.

The generalised hierarchy presented in Figure 13.1 largely applies to this college, but there are variations due to its multi-site setting. Each site, or Centre, is under the overall direction of an Assistant Principal, answering to the Principal and Senior Vice-Principal. Many Subject Heads had responsibility only at the

Centre where they were based, although there were some whose management role spanned several Centres. Service and Student Service Heads have been operating across Centres: at the time of the case study visits, this system was being rationalised to give more 'local' autonomy to Centres, and for most middle managers to have responsibility at only one Centre.

There are five strands to the methodology:

- Interviews with four senior managers, including the Principal
- Focus group interviews with three sets of middle managers: heads of curriculum areas, heads of college services and heads of college student service
- Questionnaire survey of a sample of team members of the managers interviewed in the focus groups
- Observation of a meeting at which a range of senior and middle managers were present
- Documentary analysis of college documents illustrating the management structures in practice

Sampling for the interviews was carried out by means of a preliminary visit, where the aims of the research were discussed with senior managers facilitating the research, and individuals and groups were identified which it was hoped would offer a valid representation of college middle management. Access was limited by the availability of individual managers on mutually convenient days and locations. Sampling for the questionnaires aimed at a general 'snapshot' of opinion, and was chosen with simplicity of operation in mind. Managers attending focus groups were asked to pass on survey forms to up to six men and six women who fell into particular employment categories (eg full-time/part-time). Not all managers had twelve people who could be sampled and surveyed: the number of respondents per focus group was therefore variable.

Questioning patterns at all three layers of the survey were based upon:

1 The perceived role of middle managers
2 Characteristics of effective middle management
3 Factors which support the middle manager in role
4 Factors which impede the middle manager in role
5 Perceptions of the management style of the college overall, and of the respondents' management area
6 Senior and middle managers were also asked about their perceptions and expectations of the roles of the different groups of middle managers, and how well they worked together

A preliminary analysis of responses is presented here, with a focus on research questions 1, 3, 4 and 6.

The Perceived Role of Middle Managers

There was much consistency from the three sets of respondents: senior managers saw the role in terms of transactional leadership: a key operational function, through which strategy was translated into action, with middle managers being responsible for 'staff, students, courses and facilities – and external links'. Middle managers likewise saw themselves as 'bridging the gap', making sure that things got done, taking college objectives and interpreting them, being 'enablers'. Team members saw their Heads as 'bridges and brokers', leaders, information managers and – particularly in the case of service teams – a source of specialist expertise, indicating supervisory leadership. Curriculum teams were least likely to see their Head as a source of specialist expertise, possibly because their Head might not be an 'expert' in the respondent's curriculum area.

There was some reluctance for middle managers to call themselves leaders: 'I shy away from describing myself as leader' but as one Service Head pointed out: 'Senior Management can't lead every area of the College, that's what middle managers are for,' and all groups spoke about setting 'local' targets, nurturing and monitoring teams, creating a group identity – indicators of transformational leadership. 'Leading teams and individuals: I've done plenty of that today, I can tell you!' The 'contingent nature of leadership' (Lumby 2001: 24) is well illustrated in the range of activities and responsibilities described.

Involvement in strategy

Middle managers perceived themselves as operating in an environment which included an element of dispersed leadership, and this included development of strategy at a 'local' level: a Head of Student Service commented: 'We get a couple of lines in the College Strategic Plan: our own planning has to be more detailed, but it depends on where the college is going.' However, difficulties were experienced in the area of strategy, both in its formulation and implementation. A Senior Manager commented that Heads of School and Service are expected to contribute towards strategy, a view supported and accepted by other senior and middle managers; however heads of school had not had responsibility for dealing with funding units, unlike their colleagues in other colleges. College documentation indicates that managers had had training in this area, but were not required to work with unit targets. They were therefore liable to make proposals which were difficult for senior management to address, as they were not 'in the right format'.

This mismatch of role expectations is echoed in comments from middle managers: 'It's frustrating if you have ideas [ie curriculum development] that you can't carry through: you kind of run into a brick wall'; 'Sometimes senior managers just get in the way'; and from team members: 'Inability [of middle manager] to carry through the wishes of the team and make dynamic changes' (member of curriculum team) 'an unwillingness to take consensus to Senior Management.'

If the above examples can be seen as 'translating action into strategy', there are also difficulties concerning translating strategy into action. One focus group member of the Heads of Service demonstrated the ambiguity of her role in the comment: 'I'm never quite sure what level of college I fit in,' commenting that she was sometimes invited to planning meetings, and sometimes not. A Senior Manager commented that the operational details of strategy 'sometimes doesn't get through at all' to course leaders, implying imperfect communication or operation of systems. Team members spoke of their middle managers 'having to implement decisions they have not necessarily been part of making' or 'mediating between those who actually do the work and those who institute unworkable policies'. Interestingly, this latter category was widely seen as comprising not only the college senior management, but national government; this recognition neatly acknowledges the 'bridging and brokering' role carried out by the senior managers themselves.

Authority and clarity of role

Clearly some of the imperfections and frustrations expressed above can be attributed to the size of the institution and the resulting complexity of its management: 'No-one's really cracked being a big, multi-site college' (Senior Manager); 'Support from College management [helps middle managers perform their role well] – delegation of duties and trust of staff.' Members of each of the focus groups were able to identify indicators of whether they were performing their role well: these included external inspection reports, formal and informal feedback from staff at all levels, meeting targets set by themselves and others, lack of complaints; Student Service heads singled out feedback from students as an indicator: 'if we're not getting it right for students, then we should go home.' Responses all pointed to systems which enabled them to assess their own effectiveness on a regular basis.

In the observed meeting between senior and middle managers, middle managers often 'took the floor', either leading discussion on an initiative within their management remit, or contributing 'local knowledge' to matters of cross-college concern. At other times during the meeting, senior managers reported upon procedures which had been discussed and now had to be implemented, making sure that there was common understanding of the actions to be followed. The balance of developmental discussion and agreement to implement appeared to be well understood and accepted.

Intuitive leadership

Data from the focus groups and from the senior managers indicated an intuitive style of leadership, based on what Bennett (1995: 138) termed 'theory in use'. Whilst there was training for managers in specific college functions – timetabling, induction, using IT systems – there was no systematic training for management. There was good evidence of middle managers seeing it as their responsibility to inform themselves about their specialist areas of responsibility, for example keeping up with new legislation or changes in factors impacting upon the curriculum. However, one focus group member summed up his development of management skills in the words: 'I think you take the job on and you kind of analyse in your mind what things need to be done, and you do it in your own way. If you don't know how to do it, you either watch somebody else do it, or you ask someone.' He added the comment: 'What I like about it is that you can do it your way – they're not telling you how to do it.' This method of learning was replicated in the experience of other focus group members, but not all were appreciative of the process, and responses from their team members indicated a strong wish that their managers be taught how to manage.

Liaison between Role-Holders

Discussion in the focus groups indicated that managers wished to liaise with those holding other middle management roles, for the smooth operation of the college. There were occasional indications of conflict between role-holders, for example, policies and practices carried out by the Accommodation and Finance services were not always appreciated or understood, but on the whole there was a desire to work collaboratively.

In order to address some of the difficulties presented by the size and dispersed locations of the college, plans are at present under way to give more autonomy to the individual Centres of the college. Replicating some of the middle manager functions on each Centre should relieve some of the pressures of internal departmental co-ordination at present experienced: 'Co-ordinating activities across five centres – making sure that people are where they're supposed to be, then you get a phone call [from another centre] . . . it's a nightmare'; 'If we were single-sited we'd be in seventh heaven'; 'They hop from one place to another not able adequately to do the jobs well.'

The re-organisation should also promote liaison between middle managers occupying different roles: 'I've often found that if you've got any of the [Service] departments within the college on your site, it's a lot easier to work with them than [through the main site]'; 'You build a relationship with them which is difficult otherwise'; 'When you do get the opportunity to work with [managers in other roles] you get a great deal more insight'; 'You are so busy with your part of college to actually see and know what is going on for other people and where you can actually plug into what they are doing help them.' The dispersal of leadership which is proposed – interestingly following on from 'centralised decision-making, a leadership style which is pace-setting, driving, rather than devolved' – is seen as promoting purposeful liaison between managers. Change is being used positively, to improve the environment for management.

Differences between role-holders

One of the questions addressed in the research is whether the roles of different middle managers were perceived differently, whether one role had more status or authority than another. A practical answer was offered by a Senior Manager: 'Salaries are different: Heads of Service may not be on the same salary . . . there is far less chance of career progression . . . it is difficult to imagine one being a senior manager.' Further insight was offered by another Senior Manager: 'Those with cross-college roles [Heads of Service and Student Service] may have more contact with SMT.' Heads of subject may seem more powerful 'downwards' and by the Senior Manager who commented that as teaching is the prime function of the college – 'the student is our product' – the quality systems apply more rigidly to Heads of School than other Heads, and that this might give the message that the college values its Heads of School more.

These answers indicate the retention of power – in terms of salaries, career progression and nearness to the primary function of the college – by Heads of School, but a closeness to the heart of decision-making – also an indication of power – by the Heads of Service and Student Service.

A respondent in another case study in this series commented that the 'professionalisation' of service functions is comparatively recent in colleges; this was mirrored in this case study by the fact that only recently have Heads of Service and Sudent Service met regularly with Heads of School and Senior Managers: previously the group meetings were for Heads of School and Senior Managers only. There are echoes here of the 'professionalism/managerialism' debate (Randle and Brady, 1997), with the joint meetings enabling the college management to blur any remaining distinctions between those for whom 'primacy of student learning' might be paramount and those whose concern was 'primacy of student through-put and income generation' (Randle and Brady, 1997: 128). Data from the focus groups indicate that middle managers do perceive their roles differently, but that there is no entrenched hierarchy of roles.

Factors Facilitating and Impeding the Middle Manager Role

Another of the key questions for the research was to seek generic factors which facilitate or impede middle managers in role. After further analysis, these will be incorporated with data from the other case studies in order to model the middle manager role. A preliminary analysis of the current data is presented in Table 13.1.

Table 13.1 *Factors facilitating and impeding the middle manager role*

Facilitators	Impediments
Senior manager perspective	
Culture of support – positive environment	Lack of training for management
Performance-related culture – targets	Complexity of role
Clarity of systems	Tension between innovation/devolution and control/centralisation
Quality agenda	Differential performance of middle managers
Strong communication	Communication not fast or far-reaching enough
Robust data	Data access still difficult
Co-operation between middle managers	Difficulties of large, multi-site college
Career progression encouraged	More personal development needed
Team spirit between Heads & SMT	Middle managers unfamiliar with unit structure
Middle manager perspective	
More clarity than in the past	Need for further role clarity
Having authority	Being on everyone's agenda
Team expertise	Performing management across sites
Team co-operation	Lack of resources, especially admin support
Proactive senior management team	Senior management workload
Having a champion at senior management level	More training needed for middle managers
Team perspectives	
Middle manager skills – communicators, approachable, open to ideas	Poor interpersonal skills
Positive attitude	Not suitable for this stressful job
Experience, extensive knowlegde	Too many roles and responsibilities
Support from college: finance, admin support	Overload – not enough time or resources

Facilitators	Impediments
Support from senior management	Senior managers out of touch with client group
Hardworking, co-operative staff	Unfriendly, unco-operative staff
Having time for teams	Lack of interest in students and staff
Knowing the people they line-manage	Not understanding staff problems

Three perspectives emerge clearly: the senior management preoccupations are with the cultures and systems; the middle managers concerns focus on role: its clarity, authority and the perceptions and support offered by members of the role set; the team are concerned with the skills, experience and attitude of 'their' middle manager, as well as their level of support he or she receives from senior management. In practice, middle managers will be affected by all three sets of perceptions, as all will contribute to their received role.

Although the elements in Table 13.1 were assembled from comments by different respondents, individuals were often well aware of issues which they raised as being elements in a continuum. To take some examples: the same Student and Senior team members who cited support from senior management as a factor in their managers' success in carrying out their role, also listed the attitude of senior managers as impediments. The Heads of Service focus group who applauded the move to greater clarity was well aware of the impediments caused by lack of clarity in role. The Senior Manager who applauded the 'strong communication' within the college expressed discontent when the communication did not flow fast or far enough. Valuing a factor at the facilitating end of the continuum appeared to increase awareness of potential impediments caused when college operated at a different point in the continuum.

Most of the impediments were not seen as fixed; often they were on the agenda for change. It is not clear from the range of replies received what training will be offered to middle managers in the future, but there is a consensus that present provision is not adequate. The planned move toward greater autonomy for centres – itself a response to the difficulties of multi-site operation for middle managers – and the intention to draw more upon the innovative skills of middle managers would seem to provide a useful focus for a re-definition of the role and an agreed programme of development.

The most 'immovable' impediment would appear to be that of workload, 'being on everyone's agenda' and the perception by middle managers and their teams of a need for greater resource, especially administrative support. This might be addressed by greater clarity of role; there is little in the data from this case study or the others in the series that colleges are looking to offer greater administrative support to middle managers. This may be because the middle managers themselves are seen as the administrators, the facilitators, the people who 'make things happen'. A respondent from one of the other case studies commented that the more the middle manager role had to do with students, the more unpredictable and potentially 'unmanageable' it was: the number of human interactions and the range of human needs to be satisfied is naturally increased when large numbers of students are added to the equation.

A further strand of argument running through the middle manager and team data is a need for people elsewhere in the hierarchy to 'understand' their needs, their agendas, their day-to-day work and the needs of students and other clients. This would seem to be a feature of the size of the institution: as most of the senior and middle managers have held positions through the hierarchy, been students themselves and had direct contact with students and clients, it is probably not experience which is lacking. More likely there is simply not the opportunity to empathise – or even to talk regularly – with those occupying different functions in the college. Remoteness is then perceived as a lack of care and understanding: this is even seen in team members whose middle manager is sited at a different centre: 'somebody who becomes unavailable' is taken as somebody out of touch with student and staff need. Calls for middle and senior managers to spend more time in the classroom as evidenced in the team questionnaires, could be seen as a symptom of this malaise, rather than a practical solution to remoteness.

Conversely 'having a champion', a leader, an expert, someone with time for you, at the next level of the hierarchy was highly valued and strongly evidenced. One Senior Manager commented that technology of further education is strongly staff centred, that staff are the key to efficiency and performance, and that therefore the middle manager role in managing staff is crucial. Data from the middle managers and their teams indicate that whilst a lack of social 'connection' can cause frustration and impede middle management, interpersonal skills, both in the middle managers themselves and in their senior managers, are highly prized.

Environment for Management: Summary

The data analysed in the case study to date are all contributory elements of the environment for management: the formal context of management structures and styles, mediated by the attitudes, perceptions and expectations of staff at all levels which impact upon the management role. It would appear that there is at this college a clear structure for management within which the different groups of middle managers operate. This structure is regularly interrogated, and changes are made as necessary. The current round of changes – to a more Centre-based management – should help to remove some of the impediments identified in this study. Where the clarity is less secure is over the involvement of middle managers in strategy: at present their capacity to engage with strategy is limited, yet there is an expectation that they will contribute usefully to strategic discussion.

Leadership styles of senior and middle managers have yet to be analysed in detail but there is a self-evidenced intention to move from greater central control towards a more devolved model, giving more scope for innovation. It may be that the success of the devolved model depends upon the understanding and practice which is current in the 'control' model: as time progresses, either the devolved centres may develop their own custom and practice, or there may need to be strong direction from the senior management in order to keep a 'whole college' culture.

The attitudes and perceptions which go to make up the received role of middle managers are too complex to be adequately summarised here, but key features include the expectation of team leadership – a form of transformational leadership which values people, uses their skills to best advantage and empathises with difficulty. There is also a strong expectation of transactional leadership: staff at all levels expect the middle manager to set up and monitor the frameworks by which the fundamental work of the college is done, and thereby to translate vision into action. There is both respect for the middle manager – as expert, as facilitator, as performing a key role – and a wish to see them function better, for example through receiving more support or training. Both of these attitudes indicate that the role is valued. Being valued has its disadvantages: the problems of workload are largely caused by 'being on everyone's agenda'. Greater role clarity might seek to alleviate this situation, but the problem may be an inherent feature of middle management.

Implications for the Remaining Case Studies

The three other case study colleges include one other large, multi-site college. It will be valuable to examine the structures and management styles at the two multi-site colleges to see whether they impact differently upon the middle manager role. Of the two further colleges, one operates on a single site, whilst the other has one main and one secondary site. Once the complexities for management imposed by multi-site operation are removed, do other complications take their place? Once the potential for allegiance to site is removed, is there a stronger tendency for allegiance to department or college function? In the case study college reported here, there was relatively good liaison between middle managers occupying different roles, and a largely positive attitude towards other role holders: will different environments for management produce different attitudes and practice?

One aspect which this report has only touched upon is the difference in perception of the middle manager role by staff at the various levels of the college, and by the role-holders themselves, a factor noted by Lumby (2001: 19). Further analysis of this difference, both within individual colleges, and across the colleges, will provide valuable insight into generic features of the role.

Conclusions

This case study is one of a set, from which features of the environment for middle management of middle managers in the case study colleges will be modelled, in order to identify generic features which enable and impede middle managers in role. Analysis of the data so far has made use of a number of frameworks from the literature. Bennett's (1995) concept of the manager's 'assumptive world' or 'theory in use' is particularly evident in managers who have learned 'on the job', often by progressing through a number of roles in the college. The work offered by Busher and Harris (1999), drawing upon the work of Glover *et al.* (1998) of the four dimensions of middle management: transactional, transformational, supervisory and representative is particularly useful. Preliminary analysis of the data indicates that, whilst all the managers occupied all dimensions to some degree, middle managers occupying different roles are operating more strongly in some dimensions than others. The debate over the extent to which middle managers are concerned with strategy formation, discussed, among others, by Earley (1998) and Lumby (2001) is another useful focus through which to assess the role. The various aspects of role, set out by Kahn *et al.* (1964), subsequently developed by themselves and others, are particularly valuable in analysing factors which facilitate and impede role effectiveness.

It is anticipated therefore that these frameworks will underpin the analysis of data across the four case studies; the emergent factors will then be further analysed in order to present conceptual models of middle management in Further Education.

References

Bassey, M. (1999) *Case Study Research in Educational Settings*, Buckingham: Open University Press.

Bennett, N. (1995) *Managing Professional Teachers: Middle Management in Primary and Secondary Schools*, London: Paul Chapman.

Briggs, A.R.J. (2001) Academic middle managers in further education: reflections on leadership, *Research in Post-Compulsory Education*, 6(2):219–32.

Busher, H. and Harris, A. (1999) Leadership of school subject areas: tensions and dimensions of managing in the middle, *School Leadership and Management*, 19(3): 305–17.

Earley, P. (1998) Middle management: the key to organisational success? In, Middlewood, D. and Lumby, J. *Strategic Management in Schools and Colleges,* London: Paul Chapman.

Glover, D., Gleeson, D., Gough, G. and Johnson, M. (1998) The meaning of management: the developmental needs of middle managers in secondary schools, *Educational Management and Administration*, 26(3): 181–95.

Hughes, C., Taylor, P. and Tight, M. (1996) The ever-changing world of further education: a case for research, *Research in Post-Compulsary Education*, 1(1): 7–18.

Kahn, R.L., Wolfe, D.M., Quinn, R.P., Snoek, J.D. with Rosenthal, R.A. (1964) *Organisational Stress: Studies in Role Conflict and Ambiguity*, New York: Wiley.

Lumby, J. (2001) *Managing Further Education: Learning Enterprise*, London: Paul Chapman.

Mintzberg, H. (1990) The manager's job: folklore and fact, *Harvard Business Review*, March–April, 163–76.

Randle, K. and Brady, N. (1997) Managerialism and professionalism in the 'Cinderalla service', *Journal of Vocational Education and Training*, 49(1): 121–39.

Shain, F. and Gleeson, D. (1998) Managing ambiguity: between market and managerialism – a case study of middle managers in further education, *Sociological Review*, 47(3).

14

Managing through Teams

John O'Neill

Introduction

The concept of 'the team' is now firmly embedded in the educational management literature and appears at first glance to have suffered none of the tissue rejection difficulties which have afflicted many other attempts to transplant approaches from mainstream management into the working processes of schools and colleges. Part of the reason may be that 'team' status is awarded unconditionally by practitioners to any number of different functioning groups within the institution (the course team, the senior management team, the learning support team, the office team). Yet, the little research which has been conducted in this area within education suggests that, if the group dynamics and achievements of these self-styled 'teams' were evaluated according to normative descriptions of 'teamwork', many would not qualify as such (e.g. Tansley, 1989; Walker and Stott, 1993).

In contrast, theoretical definitions of teams tend to be succinct yet extremely challenging (for a review of the literature, see Coleman and Bush, 1994) in terms of the demands they make on team members. The issue is that these definitions, many of them expressed as taxonomies of behaviours or norms, are merely frameworks which need to be given organisational contexts and specific management issues if we are to gain meaningful insights into the extent to which the working patterns of professional teacher-managers are being enhanced through teamwork.

Since the mid-1980s in England and Wales, a succession of education and broader employment Acts have served to redefine the official relationships between laity and professionals with regard to governance (Grace, 1995), and

Source: Bush, T. and Middlewood, D. (eds.) (1997) *Managing People in Education*. London: Paul Chapman Publishing. Edited version.

between senior staff and other professionals in terms of management (Ball, 1993). Seen through a political lens, the moves represent a realignment of power and authority in education. Moreover, financial autonomy in the staffing of schools and colleges, combined with a growing government insistence that public sector pay increases shall be funded predominantly by 'productivity gains', has led to the widespread use of part-time and temporary contract staff within educational institutions together with a blurring of the historical occupational divide between teaching and support staff (Mortimore *et al.*, 1992).

At site level, the trends combine to generate a problematic management context in which issues of status, remuneration, commitment, time, access, responsibility and accountability all inform individual staff members' perspectives and actions in any number of 'team' settings. Is it equitable, for instance, to encourage classroom support staff or hourly paid course tutors to attend staff meetings for which they may receive no pay and at which their voice is largely without influence?

The intention, through teamwork, to increase staff commitment via greater involvement in decision-making processes is laudable but remains a double-edged sword in practice. On the one hand, Sinclair (1992), for example, cuttingly refers to the unfettered and unethical application of this management approach as the 'tyranny of a team ideology'. Her pessimistic assessment is given some justification by reports of research conducted in England and Wales (Mortimore *et al.*, 1992) and Aotearoa/New Zealand (NZEI/Te Riu Roa, 1995) which confirm that many primary and secondary schools make unrealistic demands on the goodwill of their support staff. On the other hand, Hopkins and Ainscow (1992, p. 299), commenting on their work with a number of institutions in a school improvement project, observe that 'organisational structures such as senior management teams and the use of school-wide task groups seem at times to have a dramatic impact on development activities'.

Four specific issues are addressed in this chapter. First, there is an analysis of the role of conflict in team development. Secondly, I provide a brief critique of the canons of team literature, namely the models developed by Tuckman, Adair and Belbin. Thirdly, we explore a number of the potential benefits and pitfalls of teamwork in schools and colleges by drawing on some of the evidence provided from empirical studies in education. In the concluding part of the chapter a tentative 'model' for teamwork in educational settings is discussed.

Conflict in Teams

Let us begin with a working definition: 'A team is a small group of people who recognise the need for constructive conflict when working together in order for them to make, implement and support workable decisions.' This description of a team is unconventional inasmuch as it highlights the notion of conflict as an integral feature of effective teamwork. Stephenson (1985, p. 105) argues that conflict is present in all organisations and is 'the inevitable outcome of interdependence linked with the scarcity of resources.'

As a result of the curriculum reforms of the last decade, schools and colleges are clearly made up of a number of increasingly 'interdependent' subject areas and staff teams. Moreover, these groups are frequently required to compete actively against each other for their slice of a shrinking resource cake, be it in terms of personnel, materials, room allocation or timetable space. Arguably, then, educational managers are now more likely to encounter conflict within the institution than they did ten years ago.

However, Stephenson also makes an essential distinction between 'constructive' and 'destructive' conflict. In the former, managers attempt to use inevitable differences of opinion and values to seek better solutions to problems. In the latter, such differences are by-passed or ignored. The positive potential of conflict is elegantly summarised by the Scandinavian academic Per Dalin who was, for a number of years, involved in a structured school improvement programme (IDP) throughout northern Europe:

> Instead of avoiding conflicts, the IDP 'uses' conflicts as opportunities for understanding the reality of the school, for raising key issues related to participants' perceptions of reality, and for exploring ways in which energy 'stored' in conflicts can be released for the benefit of the school. Conflicts offer opportunities for learning because they often provide a chance for clarifying issues, for putting unresolved issues on the table and for helping to understand another point of view.

> (Dalin and Rolff, 1993, p. 28)

Dalin's observations consider conflict in general terms and at the whole-school level yet similar conclusions have been drawn from focused studies of smaller groups and teams in educational settings. Knight (1993, p. 293, emphasis added), for example, analyses the process of curriculum policy development by a school council in Melbourne, Australia:

> This mix of parents and staff empowered to make curriculum decisions immediately ran into traditional forms of antagonism . . . From the outset, the formation of school curriculum policy at Duke Park High was not going to be a consensus model of decision-making. '*It stayed and still remains, four years later, a conflict model, though this does contain some advantages*'.

In one sense, this antagonism between community and staff members on the school council is not surprising. Traditionally, professionals are reluctant to cede control over their activities to 'outsiders'. None the less, Knight's conclusion implies that the quality of curriculum decision-making was enhanced because of, not in spite of, the way in which conflict was used to confront entrenched professional positions: 'Parents and community representatives on the school council brought a pluralist perspective to issues and provided links to diverse and minority community opinion. Well-managed conflict can provide a healthy mechanism for problem-solving (*ibid.*, p. 298).

Conversely, a study of teams by Harrison and colleagues (1995) demonstrates the negative consequences of conflict that remains unacknowledged or is avoided altogether. They document (*ibid.*, p. 55) the experience of one respondent who, when reflecting on his regular meetings with the school's senior management team, '. . . identified the sometimes bland response that he encountered, when offering constructive criticisms or proposals to the team, as the "we all work very hard" reaction. Senior managers had established and encouraged this culture as a means of fending off uncomfortable ideas'.

Thus, in my definition articulated above, conflict is accepted as endemic but, to elaborate on Stephenson's distinction, is viewed as a means of constructively challenging the status quo rather than destructively stifling open discussion. I recognise that, in choosing to describe teams in this way, I have omitted four of the most frequently invoked criteria in this field. Typically, effective teams are described as having

■ defined tasks
■ inclusive processes
■ deep commitment
■ collective expertise.

Often, these are overlaid with an emotional gloss which maintains that teams are as much about socialising and developing individual members as they are to do with meeting task objectives (e.g. Schein, 1988; Bell, 1992). In such definitions, the presence of conflict is rarely acknowledged in any meaningful way, yet the manner in which inevitable differences are handled is essentially what distinguishes a team from the looser notion of a 'group': 'The new senior management team is working well as a team. There is a good balance of personalities and experience. *We are now comfotable enough to disagree with each other and it is very productive*' (Bolam *et al.*, 1993, p. 96, emphasis added).

In short, according to my understanding, a team is, or becomes, confident in its ability to exploit conflict as a vehicle for making better decisions. Effective teams assume that members will hold different and, occasionally, irreconcilable views on certain issues. In the two senior management teams they studied over the course of a year, for example, Wallace and Hall (1994, p. 190) 'were aware of some difficult moments when consensus could not be reached, soaking up time; or when grappling with new ideas, which, for most members, posed a threat to the existing culture of teamwork'. A group, however, is more likely to be concerned with merely avoiding such conflict altogether or, alternatively, with either socialising or excluding from the group those who are perceived to have different values and norms.

■ Theories about Teams

Nearly forty years ago, whilst working for the US navy, Tuckman (1965) constructed a model of team development which has proved remarkably enduring in many other occupational sectors. Based on an analysis of the extant literature, Tuckman suggested that teams go through several basic stages of growth. These have since been labelled, in mnemonic fashion,

- forming
- storming
- norming
- performing.

The key point is that a period of 'storming' or turbulence is essential if the team is to establish shared norms which will enable it to function effectively. A further developmental option has since been added to the model suggesting that performing teams go on either to 'underperforming, if they become too complacent or outlive their usefulness, or to 'grieving' if a team member leaves and the group thus reforms.

With regard to team development, new policy areas, time constraints and competing priorities are all examples of the sorts of routine pressures which impact on professed team norms and thereby produce the potential for conflict. Indeed, it appears naive to imply, as many models do, that the process of developing team norms in schools and colleges can be readily isolated from external accountability constraints and the internal pressures induced by

- limited resources;
- the cultural and historical context within which the team works;
- and its relationships with other teams within the institution.

To acknowledge the presence of conflict, latent or active, within teamwork is implicitly to make a case for astute, creative orchestration of the relationships, work and membership of the team. Adair's model of leadership (1988) is frequently cited to illustrate the three areas of concern for team leaders; namely, the need to balance their wish to get things done with the development of individuals and that of the team as a whole. As with many other traditional leadership models, Adair embodies these activities in terms of an individual – the leader.

This singular form of leadership is now regarded as dated in many occupational sectors. Nevertheless, in permanent work groups in schools and colleges such as departmental, key stage or senior management teams it is relatively easy to envisage similar 'leadership' and associated 'deference' expectations being tied to the formal authority of a postholder as designated team leader.

This person clearly has a vested interest in balancing the three domains identified by Adair. One difficulty, though, is that permanent teams are likely to have settled work and social patterns, norms which are highly resistant to change even on the part of an active leader. Hence, the leader's freedom to act is subtly constrained by the habitual actions of other members of the team.

Groups formed to address *ad hoc* tasks, crosscurricular issues or whole-school projects, however, begin life as embryonic teams, in the early stages of evolution, and are unlikely to possess these idiosyncratic shared norms from the outset. Consequently, such groups are possibly more vulnerable, or amenable, to radical leadership action. In a similar vein, *de facto* 'leadership' activity, exercised by one or more individuals, may emerge informally from within the group in such situations as members 'form', 'storm' and 'norm'. Conversely, as Paechter (1995) reveals in her report on interdisciplinary coursework initiatives in 29 schools and colleges, without sufficient time set aside at the outset for the clarification and acknowledgement of participants' different purposes and viewpoints, these crosscurricular groupings may never achieve a worthwhile, workable consensus: 'Carrying on as if everyone had the same motives, however, is likely to lead to dissatisfaction on the part of those whose agendas are not being addressed, with a consequent failure of commitment' (*ibid.*, p. 101).

In education, individuals frequently belong to more than one established team; staff members may teach in several subject areas, and often have pastoral duties as well. Senior management staff routinely have some classroom delivery responsibilities, and heads of department are usually members of a middle management group which has whole-curriculum considerations as part of its brief. As a result, those working in schools and colleges can expect to have to adopt a number of different roles each of which imposes discrete expectations. In a reference to primary school headteachers, Yeomans (1987) describes this dualism as 'leading the team and belonging to the group'. Equally, with many teams consisting of a fluid mixture of full-time, part-time and temporary staff, experienced and inexperienced teachers, and professional, para-professional and lay members, it is reasonable to assume that team development is a fragmented, non-linear process and considerably more complex than many normative models imply.

The importance of having team members who are capable of making different but complementary contributions was identified and developed by Belbin (1981; 1993). Belbin discovered that teams made up solely of high-achievers were unlikely to work productively together. He suggested that a more considered mix of team roles was necessary. For example, he identified the need for someone who could 'shape' or 'chair' the work of the team. Equally important was the presence of a 'completer-finisher' to keep the team focused and on-task. His model was originally derived from observations made in artificial situations, yet in terms of its potential for analysis and development of teams the taxonomy continues to enjoy great currency in many occupational sectors, and as Wallace and Hall (1994, p. 67) observed, it has gained credibility in education:

Four heads had been influenced by the work of Belbin on complementary team roles, and sought to achieve heterogeneity in teamworking styles within the SMT. The head at Underhill was unique in being able to create a team from scratch. He used a typology of complementary team roles to assess candidates during the selection process for both deputies, having become aware of his preferred team role as a result of his recent training.

In short, Belbin's work is helpful because it

1 allows individuals to identify their own preferred or natural team role; and
2 enables teams to identify gaps in the range of natural roles amongst team members.

More challenging, however, is the notion that members need to take on unaccustomed roles according to the demands of the task in hand in order to keep the team functioning effectively. This dictum applies especially to small functioning groups and institutions where the nine possible Belin roles may significantly outnumber the actual membership of the team!

Teams, Teaching and Management

In this part of the chapter, I wish to explore some potential limitations on the use of teams in school and college settings and, in particular, the assertion that teams are an ineffectual medium for developing classroom teacher expertise. We also examine the impact of feminine management perspectives on our analysis of teams in education. Finally, some likely difficulties within cross-curricular teams are identified.

The limitations of teams

In attempting to develop team structures, educational managers need to take into account two characteristic features of teaching:

■ Teachers spend most of their working day physically isolated from colleagues.
■ Teachers value authority and the ability to exert control.

My view is that these two factors militate strongly against the successful adoption of team approaches by classroom teachers.

According to their champions (e.g. Everard and Morris, 1990; Jenkins, 1991; Bell, 1992; West-Burnham, 1992; Caldwell, 1994) the considered application of team approaches in education would appear to have immense potential to break down the traditional 'egg crate' (Lortie, 1975) or cellular pattern of teachers' work. I want to proceed with considerably more caution, however, and argue that there is one historical 'no-go' area in schools and colleges where team models have yet to make any real inroads; namely, the classroom. Teaching is almost invariably a solitary activity.

Despite an apparent move towards more collegial and collaborative forms of management in schools and colleges, the underlying, deeply entrenched occupational culture of teaching continues to value strongly the notion of 'control'. This reification of authority appears pervasive in schools and colleges. It is manifested most clearly both in respect for formal status – most notably that of the headteacher or principal – and in the expectation that individual teachers must develop the ability to 'control' their students (see Nias, 1992; Brown and McIntyre, 1993; Court, 1994). Indeed, until the introduction of compulsory teacher appraisal and a national inspection regime in England and Wales, achievement of control traditionally conferred the right to enjoy autonomy in one's classroom and, in doing so, reinforced the idea of teaching as an activity practised in isolation by 'self-managing' professionals.

Burgeoning external accountability demands and the requirement to provide a seamless learning experience for students have created pressures for collaborative planning, resourcing, delivery, assessment and evaluation of the official curriculum. Teams are thus easily seen as a ready solution to the intensification of teachers' and managers' work in schools and colleges. At the level of institutional practice, however, staffing structures, demarcations of responsibility and salary scales all remain predominantly hierarchical and, as such, constitute a powerful organising framework within which those working in education continue to conceptualise 'the natural order'.

According to Clement and Staessens (1993, p. 147), an additional, persitent difficulty is that the practice of teaching and the process of teamwork may simply be incompatible bedfellows:

> . . . there is a fundamental difference between a team of football players and a team of teachers. The core events in the two professions differ entirely in nature. For a football team, the core event is a collective event: a football game. Of course, the individual players have to be well trained for this collective event. The core event for a team of teachers is what happens in the classroom between teacher and pupils. This is not a collective event, although teachers can benefit from good collegial relations and support. By denying this state of affairs, one denies the fundamental nature of teaching and being a teacher.

On the basis of their study of teacher development in a number of Flemish primary schools, the authors argue that both collegiality and autonomy are necessary. However, the way in which schools choose to manage this tension between the various forms of collegiality and autonomy is crucial in terms of stimulating or stunting the growth of opportunities for professional development. We can usefully apply this argument to our present discussion and suggest that team approaches, used selectively, provide an appropriate and important context in which curriculum and teacher development might be nurtured. However, asking teacher-managers to adopt routinely 'authentic' team approaches may undermine the basic tenets of their workplace culture and, consequently, these approaches may not be readily attainable through the management structures currently in place in the vast majority of schools and colleges.

Teams and teacher development

The literature suggests that formal team approaches have succeeded in education where the focus is removed from the domain of individual teacher development priorities and is concerned with arguably less sensitive administrative or management issues. This would make sense inasmuch as many management activities are, sooner or later, capable of reduction to rational processes and procedures in a way which is problematic for those intuitive, spontaneous and highly individualised facets of the art or craft of classroom teaching.

I want to suggest that mandated team approaches are too threatening and demanding a vehicle for the development of individual teaching expertise in many schools and colleges.

The idea that 'wanting to' is a necessary precondition for collaboration or teamwork amongst teachers is given credence in empirical studies conducted by Nias *et al.* (1989) and Wallace and Hall (1994). In their study of successful primary schools, Nias and colleagues observed that effective teamwork, including the open and good-humoured discussion of classroom successes or failures, became possible only when colleagues already liked each other on a personal level. Similarly, Wallace and Hall (1994, p. 198) concluded, from their analysis of SMTs in secondary schools, that 'the culture of teamwork is no stronger than individuals' commitment'.

By implication, collaborative management models such as quality circles (FEU, 1987; Stewart and Prebble, 1993), which are intended to encourage team approaches to enhancing classroom practice, may only experience the essential early success where individuals can elect to work on the basis of existing friendship groups or where they feel that they personally will gain more by collaborating than by acting in isolation. Indeed, Brown and McIntyre (1993, p. 115) are absolutely forthright on this point: 'The benefits of such attempted sharing of expertise are likely to be realized only if an exclusively positive perspective is taken on the observed teaching and if time is set aside and used for post-observation discussion of the observed teacher's thinking.

Teams and feminine management styles

In their analysis of primary school staff teams, Nias *et al.* (1989) raised the issue of whether the 'culture of collaboration' they identified could be attributed directly to gender factors. Was this less structured version of teamwork, based on closely interwoven personal relationships, an example of feminine management and thus a unique manifestation of the preferred work styles of women? At the time, Nias *et al.* were content simply to ask the question. However, there is now an emerging body of theory and research in the field of educational management which has as its central argument the idea that feminine management approaches are distinguished by their concern with empathy and negotiation and their lack of emphasis on role and status. More significantly, they are claimed to offer a more educationally appropriate, holistic alternative to traditional, masculine educational management approaches. The latter are perceived to depend on compartmentalised understandings of rationality and authority.

In her study of a middle-school syndicate (year group) of women teachers, Court (1994) recounts the effects – on the three participants, on the principal and on other syndicates within the school – of an atypical leadership model in which the responsibilities and additional remuneration of the former senior teacher postholder were shared equally amongst all three teachers. Court draws two particularly insightful conclusions from her study of this team at work:

1 Unlike their male counterparts, women tend not to distinguish between team teaching and team management but, consistent with other research on women administrators, see the two as 'similar and part of the same field of endeavour' (*ibid.*, p. 41).
2 While the three women found this 'official' team arrangement a natural extension of the way they liked and needed to collaborate as teachers, the shared leadership model had little impact on existing hierarchies elsewhere in the school. Indeed, the principal made a unilateral decision to discontinue the 'trial' after less than a year. Court observes that a principal's official 'sovereign' status continues to limit the development of non-hierarchical management approaches throughout an institution.

Tensions in cross-curricular teams

Court's second finding is consistent with those derived from other studies (Earley and Fletcher-Campbell, 1989; Bolam *et al.*, 1993; Wallace and Hall, 1994; Paechter, 1995) of larger schools and colleges which have examined the relationships between, and within, groups in the same institution. A conclusion to be drawn from these studies is that in essence, establishing an inclusive, collaborative management approach in the subject department 'team' is generally unproblematic, given appropriately sensitive and tactful leadership. In contrast, it is much more difficult to develop true teamwork characteristics in middle management or crosscurricular groups where sectional interests may take precedence. The difficulties appear to be twofold:

1 These groups are reluctant to accept ownership of decisions concerning initiatives which are perceived to have originated elsewhere.
2 With regard to the group's authority to act, designated areas of responsibility and accountability are often vague.

Not surprisingly, the participants within such groups may remain fiercely partisan and consequently are unable to develop either the whole-school or college perspectives necessary for informed decision-making, or the sense of altruism needed to turn an essentially amorphous group into a fully functioning team.

To summarise my argument thus far, there is an important caveat to be applied to the introduction of off-the-shelf team approaches in schools and colleges. Resistance to the analysis of individual teaching practice in a formally constituted team forum may be attributable more to the inappropriateness, and lack of intimacy, of the approach itself than to the recalcitrance of teachers. If team approaches are to begin to influence the analysis and development of individual teacher practice, perhaps they will do so more readily with greater acknowledgement and proliferation of feminine styles of collaborative management.[1] Finally, whilst the process of developing a team ethos within discrete subject, pastoral or management teams may prove comparatively straightforward, attempts to create whole-school or college teams tend to be less successful.

■ Conclusion: Towards Effective Teams

Despite these various caveats, however, it is clear from studies which have been carried out in educational contexts that a team model does offer a feasible, challenging and supportive means of enhancing *management* practice – and here we must include the teaching-*related* activities of curriculum design, assessment and evaluation. It does so by encouraging norms of openness, interdependence and a clarity of focus together with a clear task-driven purpose and an explicitly collaborative process. Gillborn (1989, p. 78), for example, writes of 'an increasing interdependence between headteachers and their senior staff' in the secondary schools he researched. Similarly, the authors of the one major study which deals specifically with teams in education (Wallace and Hall, 1994) are cautiously optimistic in their assessment of the potential teams have for enhancing management effectiveness. Furthermore, Bolam *et al.* (1993) also identified effective team norms operating within their self-selecting sample of schools. The more significant point is that team approaches can help challenge existing, conventional management structures through their focus on collective rather than unitary sources of authority and responsibility. Bolam *et al.* (*ibid.*, pp. 95–6) describe the steps taken by a newly appointed special school headteacher to dismantle the previous management structure:

> The restructuring consisted of an enlarged senior management team [seven] with new people and new roles; all staff working in three curriculum groups [primary/secondary/FE]; six administration teams and cross-curricular co-ordinators. The headteacher pointed out that the new structure gave a flattened hierarchy so that in addition to the school teacher management team, eleven of the twenty four staff had leadership roles. Each of the groups and teams had a devolved budget and took on decision-making roles.

In this extract we have some indication of the major preconditions for effective management teams in education. First, and most importantly, the revised management structure serves the actual working priorities and organisational arrangements of the school; it is not a historical anachronism. Secondly, and related to this, is the principle that these reconstituted groups, with newly defined roles and briefs, have power and authority to act autonomously; they also possess the financial resources necessary to help implement any decisions they make without, one assumes, having to refer decisions back for approval. Thirdly, there is a clear attempt to provide functional curriculum groupings of staff with administrative support, and to link their work by using cross-curricular co-ordinators. Finally, the notion of distributed or collective leadership is evident in the assertion that a large number of staff are expected to take on leadership roles. Interestingly, the positive staff feedback on the effectiveness of this revised management structure, as reported by Bolam *et al.*, fully supports the headteacher's claims of involvement, commitment and autonomy.

However, not all schools and colleges are in a position to undertake major restructuring along these lines; and therein lies the difficulty for teacher-managers who wish to operate on the basis of teamwork. To a certain extent, historical staffing, responsibility and remuneration structures can be modified on paper, and nominal teams can be created, but habits and attitudes are relatively immune from such simple panaceas. Thus, a more pragmatic assessment of when and where to encourage teams is needed. This assessment may lead to the realisation that team approaches need to be cultivated in piecemeal fashion when the conditions are favourable. The analysis undertaken in this chapter suggests that management through teams is likely to succeed only where all members are committed to the process. This commitment requires team members to acknowledge and value differences of opinion and to recognise that consensus may not always be possible. Similarly, there is a real possibility that different teams within the one institution may have incompatible priorities and, particularly in larger schools and colleges, that team members may have conflicting loyalties. These too need to be taken into account.

Equally, I have argued that a team approach is an inappropriate vehicle for the collective analysis of classroom teaching practice. Thus, a team structure needs to be leavened with other management approaches, such as induction, mentoring and appraisal, for individual teachers. Finally, if the ultimate purpose of all this management activity is to enhance the quality of learning for both staff and students, then senior staff in schools and colleges need to recognise and have faith in the benefits which derive from continued teacher autonomy together with informal collaborative initiatives which are based on friendship groups; in effect, a valuing of the enduring occupational culture of teaching itself.

Note

1 Currently, in Aotearoa/New Zealand, an understanding of Maori 'manage-ment' approaches is also contributing to a questioning of the universal applicability of conventional management structures in education. Parallel with the growth of Kohanga Reo and Kura Kaupapa Maori, which provide education in Maori, by Maori, for Maori, there has emerged an awareness of the need to organise these institutions in the same way as the extended family groupings they serve. This cultural awareness has been articulated recently by one secondary school head of department:

I do not see myself as the 'head' of my department. Being a Maori institution implies that the way the Maori Department functions should reflect the cultural values found on the marae. In our situation, there is what I call the 'Tatou tatou' concept. This means that we operate as a whanau or family unit. The managerial and leadership roles are shared. Who takes the lead depends on who is best qualified to do the job. Furthermore, another key concept which underlies what we do and how we do things in our Department is the notion of 'Tautoko'. Tautoko means that we collectively help one another to perform our tasks. This also implies that we share the accountability of our department (Tibble, n.d.).

References

Adair, J. (1988) *Effective Leadership*, London: Pan Books.

Ball, S. (1993) Education policy, power relations and teachers' work, *British Journal of Educational Studies*, Vol. 41(2), pp. 106–21.

Belbin, M. (1981) *Management Teams, Why they Succeed or Fail*, London: Heinemann.

Belbin, M. (1993) *Team Roles at Work*, London: Butterworth-Heinemann.

Bell, L. (1992) *Managing Teams in Secondary Schools*, London: Routledge.

Bolam, R., McMahon, A., Pocklington, D. and Weindling, D. (1993) *Effective Management in Schools*, London: HMSO.

Brown, S. and McIntyre, D. (1993) *Making Sense of Teaching*, Buckingham: Open University Press.

Caldwell, B. (1994) Structural reform in a global context: an international perspective on self-managing and self-governing schools and their potential for improving the quality of schooling, paper given at Loughborough University, March.

Clement, M. and Staessens, K. (1993) The professional development of teachers and the tension between autonomy and collegiality, in Kieviet, F. and Vandenberghe, R. (eds.) *School Culture, School Improvement and Teacher Development*, Leiden: DSWO Press.

Coleman, M. and Bush, T. (1994) Managing with teams, in Bush, T. and West-Burnham, (eds.) *The Principles of Educational Management*, Harlow: Longman.

Court, M. (1994) *Women Transforming Leadership*, Palmerston North, NZ: ERDC Press.

Dalin, P. and Rolff, H. G. (1993) *Changing the School Culture*, London: Cassell.

Earley, P. and Fletcher-Campbell, F. (1989) *The Time to Manage? Department and Faculty Heads at Work*, Windsor: NFER/Nelson.

Everard, B. and Morris, G. (1990) *Effective School Management* (2nd edn), London: Paul Chapman.

Further Education Unit (FEU) (1987) *An Evaluation of Quality Circles in Colleges of FE, Planning Staff Development*, No 7, March, London, FEU.

Gillborn, D. (1989) Talking heads. Reflections on secondary headship at a time of rapid educational change, *School Organisation*, Vol. 9(1), pp. 65–83.

Grace, G. (1995) *School Leadership, Beyond Education Management*, Lewes: Falmer Press.

Harrison, B., Dobell, T. and Higgins, C. (1995) Managing to make things happen: critical issues in team management, in Bell, J. and Harrison, B. (eds.) *Vision and Values in Managing Education. Successful Leadership Principles and Practice*, London: David Fulton.

Hopkins, D. and Ainscow, M. (1992) Making sense of school improvement: an interim account of the 'Improving the Quality of Education for All' project, *Cambridge Journal of Education*, Vol. 23 (3), pp. 287–304.

Jenkins, H. (1991) *Getting it Right, a Handbook for Successful School Leadership*, Oxford, Blackwell.

Knight, T. (1993) Setting a democratic base for effective schooling, in Crump, S. (ed.) *School Centred Leadership, Putting Policy into Practice*, Melbourne: Nelson.

Lortie, D. (1975) *Schoolteacher, a Sociological Study*, Chicago, IL: University of Chicago Press.

Mortimore, P., Mortimore, J. with Thomas, H., Cairns, R. and Taggart, B. (1992) *The Innovative Uses of Non-teaching Staff in Primary and Secondary Schools Project, Final Report*, London: Institute of Education.

Nias, J. (1992) Introduction, in Biott, C. and Nias, J. (eds.) *Working and Learning Together for Change*, Buckingham: Open University Press.

Nias, J., Southworth, G. and Yeomans, R. (1989) *Staff Relationships in the Primary School*, London: Cassell.

NZEI/Te Riu Roa (New Zealand Educational Institute) (1995) *Breaking New Ground, Support Staff in Today's Schools*, Wellington, NZ: NZEI/Te Riu Roa.

Paechter, C. (1995) *Crossing Subject Boundaries, the Micropolitics of Curriculum Innovation*, London: HMSO.

Schein, E. (1988) *Organizational Psychology* (3rd edn), Englewood Cliffs, NJ: Prentice-Hall.

Sinclair, A. (1992) The tyranny of a team ideology, *Organisation Studies*, Vol. 13 (4), pp. 611–26.

Stephenson, T. (1985) *Management, a Political Activity*, London: Macmillan.

Stewart, D. and Prebble, T. (1993) *The Reflective Principal*, Palmerston North, NZ: ERDC Press.

Tansley, P. (1989) *Course Teams, the Way Forward in FE?*, Windsor: NFER/Nelson.

Tibble, K. (n.d.) Unpublished MEDAmin assignment, Massey University.

Tuckman, B. (1965) Developmental sequences in small groups, *Psychological Bulletin*, Vol. 63, pp. 384–99.

Walker, A, and Stott, K. (1993) The work of senior management teams, some pointers to improvement, *Studies in Educational Administration*, Vol. 58, pp. 33-40.

Wallace, M. and Hall, V. (1994) *Inside the SMT, Teamwork in Secondary School Management*, London: Paul Chapman.

West-Burnham, J. (1992) *Managing Quality in Schools, a TQM Approach*, Harlow: Longman.

Yeomans, R. (1987) Leading the team, belonging to the group, in Southworth, G. (ed.) *Readings in Primary School Management*, Lewes: Falmer Press.

15

Senior Management Teams: Creating a Team in their own Image?

Mike Wallace and Lynda Huckman

This chapter is based on an analysis of four case study senior management teams (SMTs) encountered over a specific period in their team history. The focus of these case studies is on the dynamics of developing team approaches to management. First, factors are examined which stimulated the heads to opt for a team approach and to set about creating one or, alternatively, to reinterpret evolving practice in terms of teamwork. A different mix of school-level and national influences contributed in each case. An important task for heads was to bring together a group of staff to form the SMT. Various constraints denied heads an unfettered chance to select their 'dream team', though they sought room to manoeuvre where possible. As governing bodies now held the balance of authority over selection of staff, a high premium was placed on heads' ability to use influence with governors. The opportunity to select new team members was a comparatively rare event, because these were permanent teams whose membership related as much to individuals' status and salary levels as to their management responsibilities. Second, consideration is given to how heads fostered a supportive culture of teamwork that accorded with their beliefs and values, and how they met with a varied response from other members, depending on elements of their professional culture. Finally, the way team members learned to work together is explored, whether through planned induction and development opportunities or everyday experience. Participation in a team approach to management, as the model of the SMT role suggested, could constitute an individual professional development experience for every member.

Source: Wallace, M. and Huckman, L. (1999) *Senior Management Teams in Primary Schools*. London: Routledge. Edited version.

Putting together the SMT at Winton

Experiences in her first headship at one of the schools which merged to become Winton had brought home to this headteacher the value of teamwork. At that time she had inherited a deputy with whom she had found it difficult to work, but when this person left the school, she had been able to a appoint a deputy who shared her professional beliefs and values, and the head–deputy partnership became what she described as 'an instant team'. When an opportunity arose to create a senior post, the experienced teacher appointed proved able to work closely with the head and deputy, this threesome constituting a team 'almost before we knew what a senior management team was – before it had been invented'. Belief in the notion of an SMT had here followed practice:

> It was never a conscious decision, 'I am going to have a senior management team', I had two people who were wholly competent and capable who I got on well with personally, and it was a natural and normal way of working. Therefore when it came to the new school it didn't occur to me to work in any other way.

The head's positive account of their working relationship suggests they had succeeded in developing a strong culture of teamwork. When the school was scheduled to be merged with two others, the prospect of being interviewed for the headship of what would become Winton presented the head with the occasion to develop her ideas about a management structure which would be effective in that context. When asked at interview how she would ensure good communication in such a large school, she answered in terms of her vision of a management structure which would include an SMT. Her success in securing the post as headteacher-designate of Winton enabled her to use influence with governors over appointing other staff: 'I was in an unusual position in that I had to invent a complete management structure for a new school . . . and then interview for it.' Her deputy from the pre-merger school was appointed as the juniors deputy and her senior teacher was promoted to the post of special needs co-ordinator, forming the nucleus of the present SMT: a group whose members had already developed a shared culture of teamwork, though based on experience in a relatively small school. The juniors deputy reflected on the contrast between the possibility of the whole staff in the pre-merger school operating as one team and the need for a matrix of teams imposed by the size of the merged institution. She perceived the head to have been preoccupied with the issue of

> how we would make such a large school work. And there was very much an overriding idea of having to have teams because in the past, in a small school, you are a team. You have smaller teams within it, but you are a working team. With so many, we deduced that it would be very difficult to have a whole workable team [of all staff] except on very, very few occasions. So the whole

ethos behind it was to have a team approach right through. And obviously people would have dual links with various teams, the idea being that it would then bring everything together. Starting with the senior management team, the curriculum teams, the year group teams and the departmental teams.

This account supports the contention that increasing size of institutions virtually dictates that management structures must be based on staff subgroups. The pre-merger school had twelve teaching staff, but Winton had two and a half times that number and staff meetings were no longer practical as a setting where all staff views could be aired. It also highlights how the SMT was integral to the design of the complex matrix management structure at Winton.

While the head had influenced governors over appointing projected SMT colleagues whom she already knew would share her beliefs and values about teamwork, she also had to operate within significant constraints. First, the LEA's 'ring-fencing' policy for appointing staff other than deputies to the merged school put her under pressure to accept staff whom she would not ideally appoint to management positions. An unexpected opportunity to bring an outsider into the new team was presented when a second deputy appointed from one merging school resigned before taking up post and the head and governors perceived that there was no suitably experienced replacement within the merging institutions. The infants deputy was appointed from a nearby school where she already had deputy headship experience, and the head was satisfied from evidence gathered by visiting her at work and from the interview that she shared key beliefs and values about teamwork, management and education. Second, ring-fencing, coupled with a tight LMS budget, limited the potential for allocating salary increments to staff. The head's preferred team structure would have consisted of five members, including a teacher with three salary increments responsible for the nursery and reception classes. A teacher who already had a similar brief in one pre-merger school, but whose post carried two salary increments, was interviewed but the governors decided not to appoint at the more senior level. While this teacher remained in post, it would not be possible for the head to engineer the intended position, and the SMT was confined to four members.

That all members of the SMT turned out to be women had been a side effect of the selection process. Governors and the present head had given priority to selecting the strongest candidate on professional grounds, gender being much lower on their list of criteria. The chair of governors would have preferred, ideally, to appoint a man to the SMT as he perceived that fathers among the parents might react better to a man. However, he perceived that no male applicants had matched up to those appointed.

The head adopted a strategic stance towards staffing, making contingency plans in case anyone left the school and retaining a mental wish-list of potential replacements whom she might seek to appoint from within the school or to attract from outside. Her conception of the SMT was never static, although its membership had not changed in three years. She balanced commitment to its present form with a vision of possibilities for future development through changes in membership.

One design consideration for the head had been to have a small team, in line with her belief in a relatively egalitarian mode of operation where all members could take initiatives and engage fully in debate. She wished to avoid the strongly hierarchical approach that she perceived might follow from creating a large one:

> I have always stuck out against a larger team because I couldn't see how I could make it workable on a regular basis. I couldn't imagine how I could have regular and meaningful meetings with seven or eight people. So it didn't just become a token thing – 'We have got a senior management team, we meet once a fortnight, and I bring things to them and say, "This is what I want us to do!", and they rubber stamp it.' I don't think you can have genuine discussions in a group that size.

It is notable that the hierarchical approach she had rejected as 'tokenism', where a head would essentially seek support for his or her agenda, was close to that embraced by other case study heads.

▌ Remodelling the SMT at Pinehill

Applying for a second headship in a school double the size of the one experienced in his first headship was also a major event for the head at Pinehill. His decision to go for a team approach was informed by his positive first headship experience of teamwork and what he witnessed on his pre-interview visit to Pinehill:

> I had developed a team approach to managing my last school and had seen the benefits and successes of it, and so when I applied for this job . . . it jumped out at me that a team approach was the way forward. Because a school this size can't really function unless there is a structure of some sort, and that structure would seem to be a team structure which actually empowers all the members of the team and that includes all members of staff. That seemed to me something that this school didn't really have properly . . . it was there in name only; it really wasn't working in practice. That was very clear to me on the day before the interview. That night I went home and structured my presentation very much around the need for a team approach.

There is no guarantee that an externally appointed head will find that other staff share her or his beliefs and values about teamwork, and this head perceived he was going into a situation where the staff did not operate according to his conception of a team structure. As senior members they had been in a position, in the absence of the previous head, to express their beliefs and values about their preferred way of working. It seems likely that they would not fully share the culture of teamwork to which the new head subscribed. The head reiterated the belief he had expressed at interview: 'I was appointed because of my commitment to a management structure which is rational, that empowers people, and encompasses a team approach.' He used his authority to act unilaterally in real-locating staff responsibilities. However, he had much less room to manoeuvre than the head at Winton since he inherited the full complement of other staff, and was also constrained by his inability to revise (especially downwards) the status and salary levels which individuals already enjoyed.

If the SMT was to extend beyond the deputy, the assumption that the SMT should represent the most senior staff within the management hierarchy meant that three teachers, each with three salary increments, would be in the running for team membership. These individuals had experienced substantial management responsibility in recent years when, as the head put it: 'They had done their best, basically, to run the school for some time.' At interview, several other members confirmed this account, their view of the team history prior to the arrival of the new head including the enduring story or myth that they had been empowered to operate as equals in managing the school. As he did have authority to change individual management responsibilities, his compromise design solution was to allocate to each senior teacher the responsibility of leading the team of staff in a department. He also created a parallel curriculum management team of subject coordinators led by a curriculum leader. His priority was to introduce a revised management structure, incorporating a team approach, to give existing staff differential levels of managerial responsibility and workload within the parameters of their current hierarchical levels of salary and status.

The gender balance was equal among staff whom the head included in the SMT on grounds of their salary and status, which he perceived to be fortuitous because he was concerned not to perpetuate the national shortfall in promoted posts for women:

> In primary schools . . . gender is quite an issue, especially in senior
> management. It's a complete embarrassment. It's a balance [in this team] that I
> feel very comfortable with because it is roughly equal and there is certainly a
> feeling of valuing individuals. Gender, in a sense, is irrelevant to the
> professionalism that we're looking for.

He was aware of a tension between wishing to achieve equal representation among women and men in senior posts while putting top value on relative individual merit among candidates in specific situations:

> 'Gender is an issue that we're conscious of; certainly from a management point
> of view I'm conscious to trying to get that balance right. But the bottom line
> has to be the best person for the job, whatever the gender.'

A design flaw in the new management structure had soon become apparent:

'The fault at the moment, which I think is becoming fairly clear, is communication between curriculum management and senior management. It is certainly something I would want to develop, how we could improve that communication.'

In addition, the head believed that cross-school responsibility for special needs coordination should ideally be incorporated into the SMT. He faced a dilemma over the possible negative consequence of a decision to expand SMT membership to incorporate the curriculum leader and special needs coordinator. There were two constraints. First, as the head stated, 'If you make a management group too big, it becomes unwieldy'. Large size, as the head at Winton had implied, militates against full participation in teamwork during meetings. Further, a financial cost of expansion would be to increase the amount of teacher cover required to enable two more members of staff to attend SMT meetings.

During the year, the head took the plunge by first inviting the curriculum leader onto the SMT, then the special needs coordinator. The former soon gained promotion to another school and the deputy took over curriculum leadership responsibility, providing a permanent link between the curriculum management group and the SMT. Problems with the team structure, its location within the management structure, and individual responses to team membership prompted the head to make incremental adjustments in the attempt to align its contribution to management more closely with his vision of a team approach. He continued to rely heavily on his coalition with the deputy, a team within the team built firmly into the management structure. After eighteen months in post, the head had retained his vision for the SMT, but had yet to resolve his dilemma over how to promote a more egalitarian way of working while protecting his position at the top of the management hierarchy:

What we want is a collaborative leadership . . . I've got to have the overview of that leadership, but I've got to be able to let go a bit.

Evolution of the SMT at Kingsrise

The origin of the two other case study SMTs was less clear-cut. Their establishment reflected a shift in awareness about team approaches to management and re-labelling of practices that were developing over a period of time. Experienced staff had worked together, mostly over several years, according to their present division of management and teaching responsibilities. The idea that they constituted members of a team surfaced gradually, rather than the heads consciously choosing a team approach, then assembling its members. The head at Kingsrise had become aware of her increasing dependence on other senior staff when, in 1981, she was appointed as head of the primary school created by merger of the junior school of which she had hitherto been the head and an adjacent infant school. The head noted how a management structure incorporating staff from both sites 'evolved slowly'.

The head had been instrumental in both shaping the management structure and selecting staff over the years. An important criterion for selecting senior staff had been to ensure that, between them, they had intimate knowledge of all pupils, their families, and the local community. She viewed the composition of what had come to be conceived as an SMT in terms of her belief in creating a 'balance' of length of service in the school and management experience.

Gender was a potential criterion for selection which she had rejected, and she particularly resented the sexist view relayed by the media that only men could maintain discipline:

> I don't think we should look at gender in terms of positives, although we have ended up with almost completely women in the management structure. That was on merit. I am not a subscriber to the view that we should have special all-women lists. I think it is positively patronising and we don't need it . . . We do have it often quoted on radio by the politicians that they need men to control the discipline. This is regarded as one of the most difficult areas of the city; if I walk into the hall it will go quiet. They [the children] know who's boss.

Governors' approach to filling vacancies for more senior posts had varied, sometimes supporting the head in inviting a teacher to take on a new responsibility, at others advertising a post outside the school. Present team members other than the head had all achieved internal promotion either because they were perceived to be the most suitable person in the school to do a particular job, or because they had beaten external competition. Internal appointments had the advantage for the head that she knew how far those concerned shared her beliefs and values about management. There had been considerable turnover among senior staff as individuals gained promotion elsewhere, their individual success causing difficulty for the head in developing consistent management and teaching practices:

> 'If the head is the only constant figure over a five-year period, how on earth do you get your management team going, your systems working, and your children responding to continuity and structure?'

There had been several selection opportunities in recent years. Involvement of existing SMT members in selecting staff who would join the team was limited, ordered in line with the management hierarchy. Where internal candidates had applied, the head gave them an open reference, consulted the deputy and the assessment coordinator about their view on the suitability of these candidates, and made her recommendations to the governing body. The latter took the final decision after an interview which, according to the chair of governors, was likely to include attention to candidates' ability to contribute as a member of an SMT whose head was a strong personality: 'Their capacity to stand up to the head and express a view that was not the current orthodoxy in the school . . . looking at their capacity to coordinate and lead a team, as well as hold their own within the senior management team.'

The department two leader, the most recently appointed SMT member, noted how criteria for selection were made explicit in the job description and person specification sent to applicants, and how 'they just chose the person, hopefully, who was going to be best at the job and to fit in, and had the expertise'. The notion of 'fitting in' implies that a newcomer to the team should share much of the professional culture of other members.

Emergence of the SMT at Waverley

The seeds of what became this team were sown in the early 1980s when the present head was appointed. He inherited a rudimentary management structure where posts carrying major management responsibility were restricted to the deputy and head of the infant department (both of whom had since left the school) and there was no tradition of meeting to develop school-wide, policy. He wished to impact on other staff according to his vision of good practice, reflected in the restricted form of transformational leadership which culminated in the establishment of the present SMT. His perception that he must involve colleagues in the process of developing the school if they were to come to share his beliefs and values about education and management was symptomatic of his dependence on them. He had used his authority as head to make incremental changes to the management structure which would create conditions fostering a staff professional culture embracing regular debate and shared decision making:

> From the day I came, I felt there was a need for it . . . for several reasons. First of all, the world was changing – not as rapidly as it has done subsequently. There were not just entrenched attitudes towards management but also quite entrenched attitudes towards curriculum and teaching and learning. I felt the only way to take people with me was to have a structure in place in which they were involved and in which they could make a contribution. If they didn't contribute, I could write all the schemes and policies in the world, and they wouldn't have had the ownership of them.

He had proceeded incrementally, working to gain acceptance for more participation in management across the school. Initially, he had instituted regular staff meetings which he had later made more frequent:

> It took about four or five years to start getting it as I wanted it. I inherited a
> situation where staff meetings weren't a regular feature; I did that on a softly softly
> basis. I introduced them on a fortnightly basis to begin with, and then as issues
> arose and the need to move forward in different areas occurred, they were increased
> to weekly. Gradually the structures you see in place now began to evolve.

A strong partnership was soon forged with the original deputy (and subsequently her successor), and he was opportunistic in making external appointments whenever vacancies arose. He established the principle that individuals appointed to senior posts in the management hierarchy would be required to attend regular management meetings of senior staff which had originally comprised just himself and the deputy.

The juniors leader testified to the gradual development of what was now labelled as an SMT. When he had been appointed in 1989, there were meetings of the most senior staff including the juniors and infants leaders, but they were held infrequently when the need arose. SMT meetings had become formalised only in the last two or three years. At his appointment interview, the focus of questions about management had been more concerned with his departmental leadership than membership of a senior staff team. Similarly, the deputy, appointed two years later, noted that her interview had focused on deputy headship responsibilities: 'I don't think the management team was actually mentioned.' The head's concern to share the management load had been given added impetus by his realisation that his curriculum expertise amassed during his class-teaching days was becoming outdated and a consequence of education reforms. Successive curriculum reforms have increased dependence of primary school headteachers on their colleagues. He could no longer expect to be omnipotent in terms of educational knowledge.

The head's criteria for seeking to recruit staff able to contribute to the SMT included extensive 'experience, both on the management side and on the leadership front . . . they've got to have that experience for credibility with colleagues . . . and a range of curriculum expertise and experience'. He was concerned that the credentials of SMT members should be regarded by other staff as appropriate and acceptable. Another criterion was complementarity in the span of SMT members' combined expertise, the head noting how he had unique knowledge about the LMS budget, but looked to colleagues' strengths in curriculum that he could not realistically possess. Involvement of other SMT members in the process of appointing individuals who would join the team had been limited. The deputy had been consulted about candidates but had not served on the interview panel. The strictly hierarchical principle for inclusion in the SMT linked with prior management experience had been relaxed to allow other staff the opportunity to gain some of this experience through team membership.

One such change had been to invite the English and IT coordinator to join the team. The head had suggested it might benefit her to join the SMT, subject to colleague members' approval, to gain the management experience she desired to enhance her promotion prospects. Supporting members' individual professional development could also have less positive consequences for building towards a team approach to management. The juniors leader had sought a development opportunity of a different kind which had taken him out of school on second-ment for a term, and no other member of staff in the junior department had been willing to stand in for him. The head had become acutely aware of the lack of representation of junior department staff within the SMT during this time. To maintain the juniors leader's sense of involvement in the SMT, the head sent him a copy of SMT meeting minutes throughout his secondment.

Shaping the Culture of Teamwork

It is evident from the above accounts that reasons why the heads had insti-gated some form of team approach to management differed according to site-specific circumstances, beliefs and values they brought to their second headship born of previous experience, and what had happened since. Heads wished to involve other staff, though they varied in how far they sought to empower colleagues to take initiatives, as at Winton, or sought to empower themselves through harnessing others' support to realise the personal vision they had brought to the post. The reforms had also exerted a diffuse influence, mainly by imposing new management tasks which increasingly fell to mem-bers of the teams. Mounting pressure on the teams' agenda was coming from the requirements imposed by forthcoming inspection of the schools. Emphasis on selecting an SMT member specifically to provide a staff development oppor-tunity was confined to Waverley and, even here, it was seen as a preparatory experience rather than one of learning how to contribute to the present SMT.

The contrasting modes of operation of the SMTs were a result of interaction between the heads and the other members they brought into the team, whether by choice or inheritance. The heads' authority to create the team and establish its working practices gave them a strong hand in promoting a culture of teamwork to which colleague members would subscribe whether leaning towards the egalitarian or the hierarchical. In three teams, the head had played a major part in selecting other members and most or all of the present SMT members had worked together for several years. A large measure of satisfaction was expressed among members with the composition of the team and the abil-ity of the group to engage in fruitful teamwork. Observation of team meetings confirmed that interaction within them was largely harmonious and comple-mentary, indicating that members had internalised sufficient shared beliefs and values about teamwork to conduct the business of the SMT as they conceived it. The impact of the heads in forging a cohesive culture of teamwork was indicated as much by what did not happen as what did. For example, arrangements for managing the meeting process, such as setting the agenda, chairing, turn taking, dealing with interruptions, keeping to task, keeping a record of discussions or reaching decisions were universally accepted within these teams and so went unremarked and unchallenged.

A shared culture of teamwork was not so well established at Pinehill, where the arrival of the new head and his use of authority to make unilateral moves to change individual members' responsibilities and the working practices of the SMT had impacted on a team culture already fragmented by past lack of formal leadership. Here, interviews with SMT members revealed some dissatisfaction with the composition and operation of the team among the three department leaders. Observation suggested that, at first, there was not universal acceptance about some aspects of the head's view of 'the way we do or don't do things around here', both inside the team and in relation to other staff. One department leader reportedly felt undervalued by the new head because he had unilaterally drawn tighter boundaries around individual management responsibilities, stating when interviewed that: 'It used to be a totally equal team . . . I used to feel equally valued as everyone else in the group. And I think the new management structure's more top down.' The new head and the deputy were perceived to have formed a hierarchically dominant group within the team.

The initial level of fragmentation did not last; during the next year there was evidence of transition as individuals made mutual adjustments, beginning the process of cementing a more widely shared culture of teamwork. Reflecting back on the first year of his present appointment, the headteacher commented on a shift in his belief about involving colleagues in developing practice as a result of his experience:

> If I have learned anything since I have been at Pinehill, I am learning to shut up. Sometimes you have to know when to keep quiet and let other people have their head. This is hard; I have a very clear vision of where we ought to go and what we should end up looking like, but we are not going to get there if I impose it all the time – it's got to be a shared vision.

Like the head at Waverley, he had wished to implement his vision through other staff, but had attempted to introduce it much more rapidly. He had since slowed the pace, and was now working towards a more widely shared vision by empowering colleagues to make a greater input. One department leader had noted this shift with approval, suggesting that the team was on the way towards greater cultural accord: 'We are on the right road. I feel that people are valuing what other people say, that we're not being lectured at so much; I think what is going to happen now is more corporate management.'

Another potentially potent means of team culture building for heads – extensive involvement of existing SMT members in selecting their future team colleagues – was not employed in Kingsrise and Waverley where the opportunity had been presented. Even informal consultation here did not appear to reach beyond the deputy, consistent with the hierarchical orientation of the heads and reinforced by the formal authority of governors to make appointments.

Structured and Unstructured Team Development

Members of each team were learning to work together productively through a process of team development which was almost entirely subliminal and fortuitous, an outcome of shared experience in doing the job where they focused on management tasks rather than team development itself. Little use had been made of *structured development activities* like teambuilding exercises for the whole SMT (see Wallace 1991a). Such heavy reliance on learning through job experience alone related to factors affecting some or all teams: limited awareness of possibilities for structured development; paucity of external provision; priority given to developing individuals' ability to lead teams of other staff over their ability to be an effective SMT member; the low priority for team members of making time for team development activities when they were already very busy; and an assumption that, when individuals were appointed to the SMT, they should already be competent to fulfil the requirements of the job description, including their contribution to the team.

Existing members had received no formal induction where they joined an established team. The head might introduce externally appointed staff to the school, but not more specifically to the team and its operation. When the SMT at Winton was formed, induction was deemed unnecessary as three members had previously worked together. The head had planned to provide a day's induction for the externally appointed infants deputy, but her attempts had been overtaken by events as she and her SMT colleagues were heavily stretched with getting the new school up and running.

The head at Pinehill was the newest member of his team, and all members of the SMT at Kingsrise had been internally appointed, so were familiar with the school. The head made a point of having an occasional 'chat' with new team members: 'Talking with them and guiding them in what I think the role should be and then feeding back how they think it's working, what they feel comfortable doing and what they are not yet confident enough to do with their own colleagues.' The focus of these discussions apparently lay primarily on colleagues' performance of their individual management responsibility rather than their contribution as members of the SMT. A need for induction support was expressed by the department one leader, who had just been promoted to this position. She had found the transition from class teacher to department leader difficult at first, being 'used to managing children but not grown-ups'. It was taking time to win department colleagues' acceptance of her as their leader, having had equal status with them until now: 'People are used to you being on one level and then suddenly you're doing something else. If a person comes from outside the school into the management team, then staff are only used to that person being one thing – a manager.' At Waverley there was no tradition of formal induction; in the words of one member, 'It's literally come in, sit down, get on with it!'

Management training had also played little part in development of the teams. Most consisted of off-site courses provided by the LEA for individuals in their own role, not shared opportunities for the team as an entity. Both deputies at Winton attended a management course designed for deputies, but it had not dealt with teamwork or team-building. The head and deputies, however, had been together on an LEA course more directly focused on head–deputy partnerships. A more directly relevant activity for the whole SMT had been organised by the head in collaboration with the heads of five other local schools. They had been away with other members of their teams on a residential weekend programme, where there had been opportunities for each SMT to do team-building activities as a group.

Several members of the SMT at Pinehill had experienced some kind of management training but, ironically, not together. The head had completed a master's degree programme at a higher education institution, and two department leaders reported having done team-building activities led by a consultant in school during the days of the previous incumbent. The present head looked to LEA management courses to meet needs of individuals identified through staff development interviews, and to the opportunity for each SMT member to develop management skills during the regular non-contact time awarded to staff. Team members received non-contact time at different points in the week. It seems probable that individuals focused more on their individual responsibility within the management structure for leading other staff than on their contribution as a member of the SMT.

Team members at Kingsrise had least involvement in structured development support. No member had received any management training. The head stated that the only LEA management course available was for deputies, the focus of which was confined to managing the curriculum. It is noteworthy that all members of this team conceived of training solely in terms of external courses for individuals. In contrast, every SMT member at Waverley had completed or was currently taking an external management course. The link with teamwork was indirect, however. Each course was for individuals, ranging from a 'one-term training opportunity' that the head had experienced in the late 1980s to short LEA courses on 'management skills' attended separately by the head, deputy, and English and IT coordinator. The head was looking to his local 'cluster group' of schools set up by the LEA to introduce shared training activities.

An informal but nevertheless structured development activity of a very different kind featured only at Winton, where SMT members occasionally met up for a semi-social occasion intended both as part of team development and as a means of doing uninterrupted SMT business. Commitment to a team approach here extended to ceremonial occasions which helped to bond team members while working on their agenda. According to the head: 'The social side is part and parcel of teams because we are usually doing school business, but there isn't necessarily an agenda, or it is a very loose agenda like discussing ideas for building of the new school over an Italian meal.' In the other case study schools, SMT members did not deliberately mix their shared business with shared pleasure in a relaxed setting away from the school.

Since structured activities had been little used in most SMTs, members' ability to work together was very largely (and for Kingsrise entirely) a product of *unstructured development*. The different levels of complementarity among contributions achieved in the SMTs grew with experience of mutual support among heads and their team colleagues. The passage of sufficient time for mutual adjustment was a critical factor. Development of trust was gradual, resting on consistent experience of support and colleagues' effective fulfilment of their individual responsibility and contribution to teamwork in the SMT. Almost a year since the arrival of the new head at Pinehill, a department leader reflected that:

> If you don't trust the responses of others within the team, you are unlikely to say what you think. We are still in the process of learning to trust one another and I don't feel completely comfortable with the situation we find ourselves in. It will take time to counteract and get rid of that feeling.

An important component of team development is connected with individuals' emotions, such as a sense of being valued or of confidence in contributing to the team, or even of learning to subjugate an impulse to control. Shared humour, though not necessary for team performance, could help SMT members to form a bond, rendering teamwork an intrinsically valuable experience and fostering a positive attitude towards working together. Humour featured in all the teams and particularly strongly at Winton. The head's view was that members had developed a close but informal working relationship underpinned by shared commitment to teamwork: 'It is a team with skills, knowledge, good attitude, commitment, conscientiousness and loyalty and support. The loyalty is incredible, the support is second to none, and we have lots of laughs.' Reflecting on an all day off-site SMT meeting she noted how, not only, had team members worked hard, but 'we did enjoy ourselves'. Jokes often turned on irony, making light of serious issues while taking them seriously. The head and special needs coordinator had turned up late to one such meeting because of having to deal with a break-in at the school overnight when the head's computer had been stolen from her desk. The special needs coordinator announced to other members the good news that: '[The head's] desk has been cleared.'

Unique to Winton was non-work-related social contact between team members. At the other schools, socialising was confined to a few individuals who had become friends outside their work context, or to formal occasions for the whole staff as at Pinehill, where staff had an evening meal out together twice a term. The purpose of this form of socialising was simply to enjoy each other's company, but there was a spin-off for SMT members at Winton that these occasions furthered the bonding which had come to underpin their close and mutually supportive working relationship.

Multiple images of development

This account has shown how the heads of the four case study schools variably employed their power of decision to embark on a team approach to management, subject to promises to governors that might have been made at interview, or to reinterpret evolving management practice as embodying an SMT. Yet, within the dialectic of control among team members, influence held greater sway than authority over developing the shared culture of teamwork required to undergird the capacity to work together productively. Heads could count on their ability to establish structures and give the group of senior managers a team label. They certainly could not guarantee development of close collaboration through complementary contributions of team members, whether on a relatively equal or more hierarchical basis, since they were dependent on colleagues' willingness to work together in this way.

The strong cultural accord characteristic of three teams was a product both of selecting like-minded members who would stand a good chance of sharing the management and educational beliefs and values of the head, and of nurturing a way of operating which suited all members, largely through unstructured development experiences. Selection opportunities narrowed the parameters for transformational leadership in respect of SMTs in that, where colleagues shared key beliefs and values, it was unnecessary to transform this culture. The difficulty over developing a shared culture of teamwork at Pinehill highlights just how significant opportunities to select members can be for heads seeking to develop their preferred version of teamwork. Equally, the cultural gulf between the initially hierarchical approach adopted by the head and the belief among department leaders that they should be treated more as equals illustrates how incompatible images of team approaches pursued by different members may inhibit team development.

The variable but, in all cases, limited use of structured team development activities indicates that they are not vital for teamwork to develop and flourish in favourable circumstances. On the other hand, those that involve all team members getting together to focus on improving their ability to work as a team may provide a setting for opening up intractable issues like the disjunction between expectations of the head and colleague SMT members at Pinehill. Such concerns may not otherwise be easy for members other than heads to voice, especially where heads operate with a strong hierarchical emphasis. Such activities may have potential to speed the development of a team. The constraint imposed by limited availability or affordability of such support for all four teams was bolstered in three cases by the shared belief that training meant traditional off-site courses for individuals. In contrast to Winton, there was little evidence of initiatives in the other SMTs to engage in structured whole team development work.

The heads' employed different strategies for promoting development of a team approach. Forms of unstructured and structured development at Winton were more wide ranging, reaching beyond the professional arena. This breadth of development effort was, arguably, linked to the more equal and therefore more extensive commitment to teamwork sought by this head in comparison with the other three. For strongly hierarchical operation reflecting a restricted form of transformational leadership, they required less of their colleagues: to accept a subordinate position in line with the management hierarchy; to support the heads' initiatives to meet their agenda; and to carry out their individual management responsibility.

Reference

Wallace, M. (1991a) *School-Centred Management Training*. London: Paul Chapman Publishing.

16

Managerialism, Collegiality and Teamwork

Franziska Vogt

Introduction: An Ethnographic Multi-Case Study Involving two Swiss and two English Primary Schools

This chapter is based on ongoing research which investigates teachers' perceptions and experiences of policy change, teamwork and organisational culture in relation to new managerialism in Switzerland and England. It focuses on how education policy established at the macro level of the country or canton is enacted and experienced at the micro level of day-to-day work of primary school teachers, including their experience of teamwork and organisational cultures.

First, the research design and characteristics of the schools are outlined; then teachers' spontaneous perceptions on what makes a good team are explored. Finally, the question of possible links between policy change at the macro level and teamwork is addressed.

'New managerialism' and 'new public management' are concepts that are used to refer to a set of values and practices which have been part of recent changes in public services and education in many countries. The comparison between England and Switzerland enables exploration of the interplay of a discourse invoking globalisation and local organisational culture and traditions. Changes in public sector organisation identified as new managerialism do not follow a single model, nor are the resulting organisations completely 'new' or changed. There are few international comparative studies on new public management except within Anglo-Saxon culture, for instance, Pollitt (1993) compares new public management in Britain and the USA. Reference to education policy in other countries has often been made in order to justify policy; Gonon (1998) uses the term 'international argument' to highlight how

Source: Commissioned.

international comparisons are often used as an instrument for local or national debates. Halpin and Troyna (1995) refer to 'policy borrowing', whereby aspects of policies from one country are transferred to another country without analysis of the conditions, similarities and differences of these and their local context. The starting point for this research is that, within the context of a global discourse, international comparisons are needed.

New managerial policy has been interpreted and introduced differently in the two countries involved in this study. In the Swiss debate, the rhetoric of new public management in education is closely linked with the promotion of teachers' teamwork and organisational development of local schools. For that reason, teachers' experiences and perceptions of teamwork in the context of the school are taken as the focus of the research. Policy changes informed by new public management are a matter of public debate throughout Switzerland, such as changing the role of headteachers, partly devolved budgets, more autonomy for local schools, quality assurance and performance-related pay for teachers. Reforms that have an impact on all schools have been implemented in a number of Cantons, amongst them Luzern, where the schools in the sample are located.

In the English education system, a number of aspects of new managerialism have been implemented over the last two decades. These have included parental choice and representation on governing bodies, abolition of the negotiating procedures for teachers' pay and conditions, the National Curriculum and league tables, and local management of schools. More recently, performance management and performance-related pay have been among the most controversial aspects. Research investigating the impact of recent policy change on primary schools has often focused on the effects of the National Curriculum (Campbell and Neill, 1994; McEwen and Thompson, 1997; Galton *et al.*, 1999), of inspection regimes (Peatfield, 1995; Jeffrey and Woods, 1998; Hopkins *et al.*, 1999) and of open enrolment (Menter and Muschamp, 1999). The focus of the research reported in this chapter is teachers' teamwork in connection with policy change.

Four primary schools in Switzerland and England were selected for this multi-case study. An ethnographic research strategy was employed. The sample consists of a small primary school, with around hundred pupils, and a larger school, with around 250 pupils, in each country. The schools are identified as English large (El), English small (Es), Swiss large (Sl) and Swiss small (Ss). All schools are state schools and have a similar management structure, with a headteacher and a governing body responsible for the school. At this stage of the research, all four schools have been visited in three or four fieldwork phases of three to five days each. In addition, shorter visits have been made for one-off events or meetings. Although the ethnographic fieldwork also includes tape-recorded semi-structured interviews and the analysis of documents, this chapter draws only on participant observations in school and notes from informal conversations. All names are pseudonyms and anonymity is ensured.

Teachers' perceptions of what makes a good team

The schools involved are aware that my research is about teamwork and this encourages spontaneous comments about the team and teamwork and their view of what makes a good team. Many teachers feel that a good mix of personalities contributes to a good team. The following extracts also illustrate how difficult it is to determine what really makes a good team: is it a similar mindset or the diverse mix of personalities?

> *Katie*: Teamwork is going well also because we have a similar frame of mind.
> *FV*: What do you mean by that?
> *Katie*: There is nobody with a fixed idea. And everybody works first for the good of the children. And there is a good mix of personalities.
> *FV*: How would you describe that mix?
> *Katie*: There are people who are bubbly and bring ideas and others who are quieter and willing to go along with other people's ideas. Creative people, and people who are good in organising, around the school. And there are those who dot the i's and cross the t's. Everybody respects what the other person can do, nobody is frightened to ask for advice (field notes, Es, December 1999).

Nora had even taken 'the mix' in the team as a reason to apply and accept the post at the large Swiss school:

> Nora. . . and also, because it is a mixed team, there are teachers, who have been here for a longer time, and new teachers, and also a mix in terms of age, and not everybody lives in the village' (field notes, Sl, March 2000).

Teachers' first reactions about teamwork are linked with the people involved. A good team and good teamwork are first of all interpreted as a result of a good mix of personalities: a balanced team. This first reaction might lead to the impression that teamwork has not much to do with new managerial policy change. However, there are reasons to think otherwise. First, that interpretation can be seen as a general process of social cognition resulting from the 'fundamental attribution error', as casualty tends to be attributed to people rather than the impact of the situation (Ross, 1977). Secondly, teachers also comment spontaneously about changes in teamwork.

Changes in teamwork

Teachers often mention how their work has changed and how teamwork has increased:

> On the way out, the supply teacher asks me what the research is about. She then says: teamwork has definitely increased. Before, everybody would do their own things, now it is all planned in teamwork. She finds it good, as it takes the workload off each other (field notes, El, May 2000).

Traditionally, teaching is not seen as a team job. The cultural construction of teaching involves an adult working with a group of children on her or his own. The isolation of teachers' working arrangement has been widely commented on (Huberman, 1993; McLaughlin, 1997). Teamwork can go against some teachers' preferences, and the breaking of the isolation of one adult (the teacher) working with a class of children in a room is not always welcomed:

> Rose bursts out, something like: I prefer working on my own rather than in a team, and then starts saying that she did not have bad experiences with people coming in, but she needed to get used to them, also with the support staff (field notes, Es, December 1999).

Teamwork is celebrated in some of the literature on teacher professional development as well as in new managerial approaches. Teamwork is advocated as part of new management techniques, both in the public and private sectors. For example, teams are seen to be 'powerful learning entities' (Murgatroyd and Morgan, 1992, p. 142): 'the new rule for organizational design and effectiveness is team work' (ibid.). In Switzerland, teamwork in education has been closely linked with the rhetoric of new public management. In a vision of educational change for the canton of Zürich, teamwork is positioned prominently, with pupils needing to learn teamwork as a necessary skill for future employability, as well as teachers being asked to develop stronger teamwork within the school (Buschor, 1998).

In the British context, new managerial policy change is often understood as changing or undermining collegiality. There is a 'significant shift of time in meetings into administration and away from professional development' (Campbell and Neill, 1994, p. 56), and 'de-socialisation' of staff relationships occurred to a certain extent, as 'staff relations, were changed and narrowed, with an emphasis on businesslike and procedural exchanges' (Ball, 1997a, p. 325). Hoyle and John (1998) think that, as a result of policy changes, teachers have become more collaborative, but at the same time have experienced a decrease of professional autonomy. The findings from the large English school would support that analysis. Some teachers at that school view the joint planning in phase groups as a decrease of their professional autonomy.

Joint Planning – a Result of Policy Change?

In this section I will focus on the case study of the large English school and their practice of teamwork in phase groups where they undergo joint planning on a weekly basis. Joint planning is perceived both positively and negatively by the teachers at the school. The teachers also reflect to what extent the practice of joint planning is a result of policy change or the initiative of the headteacher.

Responses to the pressure to adhere to plans and schemes of work are examined and interpreted in relation to issues of power and resistance. Issues of power become very apparent in the context of industrial action, where the unions called for a reduction in meetings. Finally, the case of joint planning at this large English school is compared to the processes at the other schools in the sample.

Positive and negative perceptions of joint planning

In the responses to questions about teamwork in the large English school, teamwork was often referred to in the context of joint planning. It seems that, for many teachers, my research questions about teamwork and policy change were interpreted as being about joint planning. Opinions about joint planning vary from the very positive through to the very negative:

> After the meeting [joint planning meeting Key Stage 1], Val and Ann are saying to me that teamwork has definitely increased. Val says that everybody used to shut the door and do their own thing. She identifies the changes with the National Curriculum as having brought more teamwork, because everybody has to teach the same thing at the same time, so it makes sense to share.
> *FV*: Does it help with the workload?
> *Ann*: Oh yes the workload is huge, and you can only manage by exchanging materials (field notes, El, June 2000).

In contrast to this positive view of the effectiveness of joint planning, there are also critical voices. Mary is also teaching in Key Stage 1 and she expresses her negative view of joint planning:

> Mary . . . thinks that teamwork has definitely been affected by the changes. Mary says: 'you did your own thing.' Mary had been working at this school for her whole professional career, 20 years now. Mary explains how everybody did the things they liked and they were good at, and when the weather was good 'you would do sunny things, but you can't do this now.' You wrote down what you did, but you did not have to write these planning sheets. The work is now much more planned and one cannot do things differently or spend more time on something, or develop things in a particular way. The phase groups plan together . . . These planning meetings are led by a member of the senior management, and it becomes clear that teachers cannot do things differently, and I also get the feeling that the senior management member [Ann] wishes to impose her own teaching style. When I asked about where the restrictions come from, Mary says a lot comes from central government, but there is also a lot from within school (field notes, El, January 2000).

The different people involved have very different perspectives on joint planning at Key Stage 1. Whereas Ann is emphasising the positive outcome of sharing the work, Mary is unhappy about the lack of flexibility and freedom and sees joint planning as restricting her professional autonomy. Kiley, who is in the same phase group, is critical about Ann's style of expecting the others to teach the way she wants:

> Kiley thinks teamwork has increased a lot. Now every lesson is planned beforehand, there is no flexibility. Kiley seems to miss a bit of that freedom saying how one could always choose the themes one liked and thought were appropriate for the particular age group. On the other hand, she also sees advantages in the new system, as it ensures the children all get the same education. In the last OFSTED report, she says, it was positively mentioned that the reception classes did give the children exactly the same experience (field notes, El, May 2000).

The teachers' different views on joint planning will be analysed further as they highlight issues of power in organisations and responses to it. I will first address the question of whether joint planning is part of a wider policy change or whether the conflict is rooted in the particular management of that school.

Is joint planning a result of policy change?

The teachers have different views on the joint-planning practices at their schools. The question arises as to whether joint planning is a result of a wider policy change or whether it is a characteristic of the headteacher's policy approach. Mary and Kiley, in the extracts above, interpret the practice of joint planning, first, as something implemented by the headteacher and enforced by the member of senior management but also refer to the wider context of policy change. Mary says these changes are coming from government policy as well as the headteacher's management approach, and Kiley refers to the inspection regime as the reason for the tightening up of joint planning. Is it policy or is it the headteacher's interpretation? I put the question to Ann (a member of the senior management):

> *FV*: Having been here for so long, you have experienced different heads as well?
> Ann laughs, oh yes, 3 heads, an acting head in between, and even more deputy heads. She then recounts: the first head was an old fashioned head, it was his last years before retirement and you could tell. The second head was very strong on innovation and in pastoral care. Tina is strong on whole school issues, and on planning and teamwork. She brought in these planning meetings, the planning sheets etc.
> *FV*: Is it her special focus or does it reflect wider policy changes?
> *Ann*: That is the question, isn't it, that's what you are looking at. I don't know, it has been introduced by Tina, but it might well be it is also because of the requirements. You can't really tell that (field notes, El, June 2000).

The headteacher herself sees teamwork and joint planning as something she has worked hard to get started at the school:

> *Tina*: With what you're looking at, performance-related pay will have a knock-on effect on teamwork. We have done so much to get it off the ground, but it will not continue in the same way. All the teamwork we have started to build up will go.
> *FV*: What will change?
> *Tina*: People will still have to plan together, but they will no longer share the resource to the same extent (field notes, El, February 2000).

The initial reaction attributes the reason for the practice of joint planning to people – the headteacher (Tina) and the phase group leader (Ann). The role of the headteacher within new managerial policy change has been widely acknowledged: 'In the education sector the headteacher is the main "carrier" and embodiment of new managerialism and is crucial to the transformation of the organisational regimes of schools' (Ball, 1997b: p. 259). Without negating the role of the headteacher for the team culture of a school, it is also important to take situational factors, in this case educational policy, into account.

The teachers are also aware of policy influences and they identify a change of practices overall, interpreting policy change as initiated by central government, as well as considering the influence of OFSTED. A characteristic of Ethnographic policy research is that it constantly deals with such a change of perspectives, moving between the particular case, between the particular actors involved within a particular organisational culture and the wider context of policy change. A practice such as joint planning can therefore be conceptualised as an enactment of new managerial policies: the decrease of professional autonomy (less flexibility and freedom) and a culture of accountability (work schemes, planning sheets, OFSTED).

Responses to the regime of joint planning

Three types of responses to the regime of joint planning at the large English school can be identified. Mary has developed a mode of self-regulation because she took the hint that 'bending' the topic is not approved of and, therefore, she now follows the joint plans. Some teachers take a rebellious stance, making suggestions of their own or not following the plans closely. Kathleen is taking the stance that she has to adapt things for her class. The headteacher is furious that she does not always adhere to the planning agreed in the phase group. Kathleen faces a lot of pressure from the headteacher to adhere to joint planning:

> Kathleen . . . finds it very difficult with Ann [phase group leader], because she and Ann have such different approaches . . . Kathleen worries, because Tina [headteacher] had given her planning time on Friday mornings, for her to plan with Ann, and Kathleen is frustrated because no reason was given for it, and she suspects it is because they think she is not doing it right or not how Ann wants it. Kathleen feels however she cannot adopt the same approach (field notes, El, May 2000).

A third response to the regime of joint planning is the reduction of effort and commitment from some teachers. Kathryn, a member of senior management and a phase group leader at Key Stage 2, noticed the effects of Ann's approach on the teachers at Key Stage 1:

> *Kathryn*: I am team leader and I find it difficult that some people, not everyone, seem to expect that you do certain things for them.
> *FV*: Can you give an example?
> *Kathryn* : They expect that you do – well they expect you take a leading role which I presume is okay and I am doing, but – they expect that you give it to them more on a plate. I know that they are doing that in Key Stage 1, they get it more on a plate.
> *FV*: Why are you doing it differerntly?
> *Kathryn*: I think everybody is intelligent enough by themselves, they're all teachers, have the same skills, they have all been long enough in teaching (field notes, El, June 2000).

The regime of joint planning is linked with institutional micropolitics and new managerial education policy; teachers careers and the nature of teaching are 'intertwined in a complex process of changes' (Ball, 1994, p. 64). The development of teachers' careers over the last half year within this school could be seen as part of the complex processes of institutional micropolitics: the teacher engaging in self-regulation had been off with stress and depression for half a year; the teacher resisting openly has come under a lot of pressure from the headteacher; and the teachers resisting through non-commitment have left the school for other posts.

Critical organisational event: industrial action and joint planning

Critical organisational events highlight ongoing issues and cultural change. In relation to joint planning, the call of some teachers' unions to take industrial action was such a critical organisational event. It revealed teachers' views, the power dynamic at that school and the change in organisational culture. The industrial action was aimed at reducing weekly meetings to one hour. The staff of the school agreed to do more ($1\frac{1}{2}$ hours) and suggested they still do the joint-planning meetings in the phase groups and to skip the staff meeting. Ann explains the motivation behind this deal:

> Ann says that they now don't want to miss the planning meeting with the industrial action, because 'we feel we have more work if we don't have the planning meeting' (field notes El, June 2000).

At the unions meeting (called over lunchtime in the union representative's classroom) the industrial action is discussed. Present is Bethan (the deputy head), Ann (member of the senior management), a supply teacher (Tamara), the union representative and Kathleen:

> They discuss the issue of meetings, the union wants them to only do one hour per week, they suggest one and a half, because of OFSTED maybe coming up in September. It was agreed to propose one hour planning meeting and half an hour staff meeting as an action (field notes, E1, June 2000).

Although the industrial action is targeted at meetings, those teachers who decided on the industrial action at that school did not target the joint-planning meetings as such. The policy changes and practices resulting from such policy change as joint planning might not be liked, but the threat of an OFSTED inspection coming up soon leads to them accepting joint planning meetings as necessary. The decisions taken might illustrate how the teachers have internalised the pressures of the system. The critical event of industrial action reveals how in the view of the teachers, there is not much alternative to the regime of joint planning, although a considerable part of the teaching staff do not like it. In addition, the union meeting is dominated by members of senior management who both emphasise the function of meetings: Ann does not want to lose joint planning; Bethan sees staff meetings as crucial for teachers to participate in decision-making. After the meeting in the staffroom, Tamara presents the decisions to Tina, the headteacher:

> Tamara says to Tina: I need to tell you, when should it be? Tina, laughingly: depends what you decided! Then she says she needs to know as soon as possible really, 'so go on'. Tamara passes her little piece of paper with her notes over to her . . . On the issue of meetings, the staff seem to have decided to do one and a half hour meetings per week rather than the recommended one hour. They decided to do an hour planning meeting and a half hour staff meeting. Tina says: 'this is not for you to decide. You decide, how much meeting time you give, and I appreciate you are doing more, but it is for you to only say we are doing one and a half hours and for me to decide which meetings you should go to for that amount of time' (field notes, E1, June 2000).

Tamara (in passing over her notes) permitted the headteacher to know who was opposed to what; later, the union representative shared information with the headteacher. When Tamara discussed the outcome of the meeting with Tina, all the teachers present in the staff-room listened and observed what was happening. The issue of meetings and industrial action shows the power relations at the school, the headteacher taking the opportunity to state that it is she who decides about teachers' directed time. The headteacher is also adamant that those teachers who are not members of the two unions that are taking industrial action are working the full amount of directed time.

No joint planning in the other schools

Having analysed the 'regime of joint planning' in the large English school, it is necessary to compare it briefly with the practices in the other schools in the multi-case study. Neither of the small schools are engaging in joint planning. This is probably due to the fact that no two teachers teach the same year group. In the small English school, some form of joint planning focuses on curriculum areas. Each teacher is a co-ordinator for at least one subject and is responsible for planning that subject. The teachers at the school do not interpret these activities as a decrease in professional autonomy. At the small Swiss school, teachers informally help each other out with ideas for lessons, but each teacher is solely responsible for teaching the curriculum. The Cantonal curriculum sets some guidelines and, within these, the teachers have considerable freedom to plan. None of the teachers at the small Swiss school plans with other colleagues outside the school. In contrast some of the teachers at the large Swiss school do engage in joint planning. Joint planning depends on the initiative of the teachers: a few teachers at the school plan together and some teachers have planned with their year group colleagues in the past. It is also quite common in that school for teachers to plan with colleagues at other schools. The teachers decided at the last team development day that they want to co-ordinate some curriculum areas within the school. At the large Swiss school there seems to be no pressure to institutionalise joint planning. Nevertheless, cantorial policy-makers seek to encourage teamwork at schools, and joint planning is one of their suggestions (Bischof *et al.*, 1998).

▌ Informal and Formal Teamwork

Throughout the fieldwork, the distinction between informal and formal teamwork emerged as a significant issue. After the first week of fieldwork in the small English school, just before Christmas when the teachers were working intensively together to set up the two nativity plays, the deputy headteacher brings up the distinction between two aspects of teamwork, informal and formal:

> *FV*: What do you think I did not see?
> *Katie*: You have seen a lot of informal teamwork, it will be important to see more formal settings like the Monday staff meeting. Also a meeting with the governors might be useful (field notes, Es, December 1999).

Formal teamwork – how much is right?

In three of the sample schools, the amount of time necessary for staff meetings and other meetings is an issue of concern to many teachers. Many teachers express the opinion that they feel staff meetings are taking up too much time. Bettina says:

Parents meetings would be okay, but team meetings. The time used for school development needs to be taken from somewhere. I have to take notes of working times again, to see how many hours I am working really (field notes, Ss, March 2000).

New managerial policy change in Switzerland has been closely linked with increased teamwork and school development amongst the teachers (Dubs, 1996; Bischof *et al.*, 1998; Bucher, 1999). Nadja comments critically about that development:

They behave at the cantonal authority as if team and team development would be the most important. For me, the essential is still teaching, working with the children (field notes, Ss, March 2000).

As part of new managerial policy change in Switzerland, some guidelines have been given on teachers' working hours. The headteacher of the large Swiss school explains at a governing body meeting what school development tasks could be expected from teachers as part of their duty. He tries to convince them that teachers working on a steering group (soon to be introduced) should be paid for their attendance. The headteacher's statement is interesting as it uses new managerial terms, such as 'core business', to make its argument:

Christoph explains to the governors that 5% of working hours are for team meetings and team development, besides that there are meetings with parents, meetings about special needs, preparation time, and the core business of teaching. The steering group would place demands exceeding the time set on Tuesdays for team development (field notes, Ss, May 2000).

At the small Swiss school, team meetings are not as structured throughout the school year compared with the large Swiss school, and the teachers tend to see team meetings as an additional burden.

At the large English school, the demands of 'directed time' in coming to staff meetings and planning meetings are accepted as routine. Nevertheless, when the headteacher expects the teachers to stay for longer in exceptional circumstances, teachers react with frustration. Because of an imminent inspection, the teachers were expected to stay for half an hour or an hour longer:

Kyra mentions that monster staff meeting tomorrow, how this is getting difficult, because they usually have staff meetings, which used to be on Tuesdays, finished at 4.30 or 5.00, but now it has been moved to Wednesday and it has only been said last week that it will go on for two hours until 5.30. This makes people angry, because they have made arrangements. Kyra says if you wanted to go to a class or something, and Nancy says, yes and when you have to pick up the children, and also when they have to drive a long way, you get into the traffic when you leave at that time and so it gets very difficult. Kyra is also implying that they have not been informed early enough (field notes, El, May 2000).

Teacher's statements about the increasing demands on their time for meet-ings are often based on the perception that the time needed for team meetings has increased through policy changes in recent years. The kinder-garten teacher at the small Swiss school suspects that there are meetings for the sake of having meetings:

> Tita: I have worked here for 13 or 14 years now. At the beginning, the others certainly have told you already, things were very different. There was only Andi, Nadja and I. There was little teamwork, and I had more contact privately with Nadja . . . There were no team meetings, just for the three of us it was not needed . . . During break, everything was discussed and there wasn't that much to discuss. The essential was teaching. Now so many things have come on top of it . . . What was different is also that we all did not work for so long in the evenings. Half an hour after school finished, the school was empty. I ask myself now and again whether the additional work does really bring any benefit. Also, what is there, what needs to be discussed every Thursday [team meeting day]? It is unbelievable! (field notes, Ss, June 2000).

What builds a team – formal or informal teamwork?

New managerialism in education in Switzerland is linked with an emphasis on teamwork. In the Canton of Luzern, a project introducing new manage-rial approaches was designed as a team development process. Teams could obtain the help of external supervisors to coach them in their team-building processes. Some teachers of the large Swiss school think that the supervision and team building processes have become too much. They are critical about the team development days, where conflicts in the team should be addressed with the help of an external supervisor. Some teachers feel this more psycho-logical approach does not really help and prefer team-building in their day-to-day working together along with banter in the staffroom:

> Markus says that he sometimes finds the team processes arduous because old stories and tensions are discussed. During supervision, it was all about two teachers who did not get on, and who split the team a little bit into two. The two teachers have now left and since then things are better. The external supervision has not contributed much in Markus' view. He defines himself as a bit conservative in relation to supervision and team development. He thinks that social events benefit the team more (field notes, Sl, March 2000).

Similar to Markus' critique, Nadja at the small Swiss school feels that team-work is misunderstood as formal teamwork. What really counts in her view is informal teamwork on a day-to-day basis in the staffroom. She criticises the fact that recent policy change has shifted the emphasis to formal teamwork and paperwork:

The team is not when one has a team meeting, team is sitting together in here [staffroom], sharing with each other, helping each other (field notes, Ss, March 2000).

From all the schools, I had the impression that many teachers place an emphasis on informal teamwork. The very basic notions of getting on with each other, pulling together and supporting each other are seen as very important:

Nina finds teaching year 1 demanding and the children had been unruly in the last weeks. Nina says that the team, the colleagues here, they are very good otherwise work would be demanding.
FV: What kind of support do you think is most important for you?
Nina: Mostly the support for your morale, you know, that I can go to the staffroom and share, that it is demanding, that I can complain about it.
FV: How important is sharing teaching materials?
Nina: Gregor helps me now and again, as he taught year 1 last year, and I could get material from him. However, teaching material and preparation is not the problem really (field notes, Ss, March 2000).

Emotional support can be crucial for teachers at certain times. At the small English school, Rosemary was off for some time because of the illness and death of her father. When she came back, she told me:

people have been very supportive, and she adds: that's it about the team isn't it? Brian in particular had rang her up, to see how she is, and encouraged her to come back (field notes, Es, June 2000).

The expectation of support and camaraderie is seen as important even in schools where some teachers feel controlled and under pressure. Three extracts from the large English school paint a complex picture:

They are talking about the advisors and joking, and Nancy, Kyra and Beatrice are saying . . . what would happen if they put a sign up at the door, no visitors, or they let them in and tell them to teach the class? Beatrice says to me: You know what I thought inspection would be? That these inspectors come in and teach your class and you could watch them and learn! (field notes, El, May 2000).

FV: How did you experience OFSTED and how does it affect the team?
Beatrice: During OFSTED, that pulled us together really. We came in late, and put all the displays up, and the school was made to look perfect, and so forth, but it pulled us together, a kind of camaraderie (field notes, El, June 2000).

FV: Did you get support in the time you did the year 6?
Beatrice: Yes, Tina was asking what I wanted to do, and so forth. However you don't really give support in the same way. You had time to care for each other before, and

it is strange to think that teachers who should be caring cannot care for each other because of all this paperwork and workload. Everybody is so busy with their own things. And you think about what to say, how would it be seen if you, say, send a child to another teacher because they were not behaving. You did that, you would tell others before, but now you could think that it means you were not able to control them (field notes, El, June 2000).

Although camaraderie is emphasised and experienced, it is mixed with a feeling that one should not share one's difficult or weak moments as this could give the management a negative impression. The need to be able to share stressful moments and to get support from colleagues seems to be essential for teachers' satisfaction with the organisation's culture. Policies aimed at controlling teachers' performance could have a negative impact on this basic motivational factor of team support.

■ Conclusion: What is Important about Teamwork?

In this chapter I have noted some of the aspects surrounding new managerial policy and teamwork:

- The mix of personalities – the balance of the teams – is often seen as the basis of a good atmosphere in the team. Getting on well with each other is seen as important. This is experienced in day-to-day banter in the staffroom, in socialising and in being able to share and receive emotional support. These aspects can be understood as informal teamwork. Formal aspects of teamwork, however, are described with less enthusiasm; informal teamwork is crucial.
- Teachers in both countries tend to think that teamwork has changed and that there has been an increase in teamwork in relation to policy change. Many 'before' and 'now' comparisons are made when discussing teamwork.
- The practice of joint planning in the large English school highlights how teamwork is linked with new managerial policies. Joint planning decreases professional autonomy and increases control in the school. Some teachers are very positive about joint planning whereas others have a very negative view.
- Regimes such as joint planning evoke a variety of responses. Processes of self-regulation, open resistance and a reduction of commitment have been found. Teachers' responses to such policies are intertwined with their personal career histories.
- As a first reaction, individual teachers attributed causes to people rather than the situation and the policy context. Policy analysis needs to examine carefully these perceptions and take both perspectives into account: the micropoiitics and power relations at the school and the context of teaching within policy change.

In this chapter teachers' views about formal and informal teamwork have been discussed. To highlight the very different opinions, I would like to present the two images as a juxtaposition of what is important about teamwork.

■ Is it the elaborate organisational structure of team meetings, subteam meetings, management of special needs and planned social activities like this (Sl, year plan of team meetings)?
■ Or the day-to-day banter and giving each other little treats like this?

Petra placed the left-overs from her meeting on the staff room table, together with a note saying: The cakes are given to the team free for consumption (field notes, Sl, June 2000).

References

Ball, S.J. (1994) *Education Reform. A Critical and Post-Structural Approach*. Buckingham: Open University Press.

Ball, S.J. (1997a) Good school/bad school: paradox and fabrication. *British Journal of Sociology of Education* 18(3): 317–36.

Ball, S.J. (1997b) Policy, sociology and critical social research: a personal review of recent education policy and policy research. *British Education Research Journal* 23(3): 257–74.

Bucher, B. (1999) 'Schulen mit Profil'. Volksschulentwicklung im Kanton Luzern. Paper presented at the OECE-CERI Regionalseminar, Rheinfelden.

Buschor, E. (1998) Vorwort des erziehungsdirektors. In P. Zürich (ed.) *Fortbildung*. Zürich: Pestalozzianum.

Campbell, R.J. and Neill, S.R.S.J. (1994) *Primary Teachers at Work*. London: Routledge.

Deem, R. and Brehony, K.J. (forthcoming) Educational policy-making and analysis. In M. Ben-Peretz *et al.* (eds.) *International Encyclopeadic Dictionary of Education*. London: Routledge.

Dubs, R. (1996) *Schule, Schulentwicklung und New Public Management*. St. Gallen: Institut für Wirtschaftspädagogik.

Galton, M., Hargreaves, L., Comber, C., Wall, D. and Pell, T. (1999) Changes in patterns of teacher interaction in primary classrooms: 1976–96. *British Educational Research Journal* 25(1): 23–37.

Gonon, P. (1998) *Das internationale Argument in der Dikdungsreform*. Bern: Peter Lang.

Guy, P. d. and Salaman, G. (1992) the cult(ure) of the customer. *Journal of Management Studies* 29(5): 615–33.

Halpin, D. and Troyna, B. (1995) The politics of education policy borrowing. *Comparative Education* 31(3): 303–10.

Hopkins, D., Harris, A., Watling, R. and Beresford, J. (1999) From inspection to school improvement? Evaluating the accelerated inspection programme in Waltham Forest. *British Educational Research Journal* 25(5): 679–90.

Hoyle, E. and John, P.D. (1998) School teaching. In M. Laffin (ed.) *Beyond bureaucracy? The Professions in the Contemporary Public Sector*. Aldershot: Ashgate.

Huberman, M. (1993) The model of the independent artisan in teachers' professional relations. In J.W. Little and M.W. McLaughlin (eds.) *Teachers' Work. Individuals, Colleagues and Contexts*. New York: Teachers College Press.

Jeffrey, B. and Woods, P. (1998) *Testing Teachers. The Effect of School Inspections on Primary Teachers.* London: Falmer Press.

Little, J.W. (1990) The persistence of privacy: autonomy and initiative in teachers' professional relations. *Teachers College Record* 91(4): 509–36.

McEwen, A. and Thompson, W. (1997) After the National Curriculum: teacher stress and morale. *Research in Education* 57: 57–66.

McLaughlin, M.W. (1997) Rebuilding teacher professionalism in the United States. In A. Hargreaves and R. Evans (eds.) *Beyond Educational Reform.* Buckingham: Open University Press.

Menter, I. and Muschamp, Y. (1999) Markets and management: the case of primary schools. In M. Exworthy and S. Halford (eds.) *Professionals and the New Managerialism in the Public Sector.* Buckingham: Open University Press.

Murgatroyd, S. and Morgan, C. (1992) *Total Quality Management and the School.* Buckingham: Open University Press.

Peatfield, J. (1995) Coping or managing? Assisting primary schools to prepare for, manage and exploit the potential of the OFSTED inspection system for internal development through in-service. *Teacher Development* May: 48–52.

Pollitt, C. (1993) *Managerialism and the Public Services* (2nd edn). Oxford: Blackwell.

Ross, L. (1977) The intuitive psychologist and his shortcomings: distortions in the attribution process. In L. Berkowtih (ed.) *Advances in Experimental Social Psychology* (Vol. 10). Orlando, FL: Academic Press.

Zahorik, J.A. (1987) Teachers' collegial interaction: an exploratory study. *The Elementary School Journal* 87(4): 385–96.

Part 4

A Case Study of Leading in Action

17

The Attrition of Change: A Study of Change and Continuity

Dean Fink

This chapter represents a summary of a study of the 25 year history of a new and purposefully innovative school, Lord Byron High School. It opened in 1970, and quickly gained a reputation as one of Canada's most innovative schools. In its first 3 years of operation, it averaged over 7000 visitors per year, many from outside of Ontario. Gradually, however, the school lost much of its innovative zeal. Lord Byron High School today looks very much like a regular Ontario secondary school. The emphasis on creativity and experimentation in the 1970s has been replaced by a focus on continuity and survival in the 1990s. This pattern raises the essential question of why did a school, which started out with more advantages than virtually any other secondary school in Ontario and Canada, lose its innovative momentum, and experience an 'attrition of change'.

The organizational literature as well as my own observations led to the following research questions:

- is there a 'life cycle' to new and innovative schools which leads to the attrition of change? If such a life cycle exists, what are its stages and characteristics?
- are there identifiable danger points or turning points and forces, internal and external to the school, which contribute to the attrition of change?
- how appropriate is the establishment of an innovative or 'lighthouse' school in promoting change in a school system?

Source: School Effectiveness and School Improvement, Vol. 10, no. 3, 1999, pp. 269–95. Edited version.

Methodology

The retrospective nature of the topic and its 'boundedness' necessitated a qualitative case study. Since the researcher is the key methodological instrument in qualitative studies (Anderson, 1990; Woods, 1986), I adopted Ball's (1993) suggestion of a research biography to describe the processes used to develop the Lord Byron case. To this end, I have avoided what Goetz (1988) has called the 'pseudo-objectivity' of using the third person in science writing by using a first person, 'researcher-as instrument' (Ball, 1993, p. 46) stance. To investigate the case in some depth required methodologies from three research traditions. The historical aspect of the case led to a search of relevant documents from the province of Ontario, the South Board of Education, of which Lord Byron was a part, and from the school itself. An ethnographic approach was used to search for factors which led to the attrition of change. To this end, I interviewed over 70 present and past Lord Byron staff members as well as key respondents from the South system. The vast majority of these interviews were conducted with people who were teachers at Lord Byron at various junctures in its evolution.

The third source of data was from my investigation of the relationship of Lord Byron to the professional and personal lives of the respondents. My review of the change literature convinced me of the importance of investigating teachers' work and lives as part of the larger conceptual framework (Ball and Goodson, 1985; Goodson, 1992; Goodson and Walker, 1991). I, therefore, augmented my scripted interview questions with in-depth probes into the question of Byron's relationship to respondent's professional and personal lives.

Conceptual Framework

To develop a conceptual framework for my interviews and the subsequent analysis and reporting of the research on Lord Byron, I sought to view the school as an integrated whole rather than the sum of its parts. To this end, I originally identified the concepts of change, context, culture, teachers' work, and teachers' lives as the components of my conceptual framework. My own background, reading (Telford, 1996), and interests suggested that leadership is crucial to change in schools and should also be a distinct category for analysis (Fullan, 1993; Stoll and Fink, 1996). Moreover, after the first few interviews, it became obvious that the structure of the school and the school's meaning and purposes were key constructs which required elaboration. It became equally apparent that it was virtually impossible to separate teachers' work from teachers' lives (Hargreaves, 1991). Since change is a concept which runs throughout my analysis I concluded that it should be integrated into each category. I finally settled on six interrelated lenses or frames through which to view Lord Byron High School: context, meaning, leadership, structure, culture, teachers' work and lives (for an elaboration of each construct consult Fink, 1997).

A Brief History of Lord Byron

Years of creativity and experimentation: 1970–1975

The early 1970s was a unique era in the educational history of Ontario and the South Board of Education, the school district in which the school was located. For those who joined the staff of Lord Byron with a view to effecting change in the 'deep structures' (Cuban, 1988) of Ontario schooling, the times could not have been more propitious. Ontario was in the midst of a progressive era in education which created a context for the South Board and its reform minded Director of Education (CEO), Jim Sizemore, to initiate Lord Byron as an experimental 'lighthouse' school. Lord Byron High School opened with the expressed purpose of not only challenging the structures of secondary education in Ontario, but also the curriculum, the teaching, and pupil assessment methods. Perhaps what was most innovative for the times was the philosophy espoused by its first principal, Ward Bond, and in large measure adopted by the original staff. In a formal document of the period, the philosophy was stated as, 'Our aspirations for Lord Byron are the development of a humane educational environment for students: a situation in which conduct and growth will develop from *reason* and *mutual respect* and *trust*'.

The creation of Lord Byron coincided with the publication of a revolutionary (at least for Ontario) report on education entitled *Living and learning* (1968), more commonly known as the Hall–Dennis report after its co-chairmen. This report advocated a radical rethinking of education in Ontario. It savagely criticized the prevailing system as inflexible, dehumarizing and elitist. The report asserted that, 'the child should not be treated as an isolated, entity, but educated for life in a society which respects his individuality' (p. 67). In the Hall–Dennis world, teaching strategies would be more child-centred, the curriculum less subject-centred. The needs and interests of the pupils rather than the narrow prescriptions of a curriculum would determine their learning. It challenged just about every structure in existing schools.

Lord Byron's innovations reflected the Hall–Dennis report and many of the ideas current in 1970. Byron was the first semestered school in Ontario. The Byron programme enabled students to take a broad programme from a wide diversity of courses. The organization of the school was designed to allow pupils to broaden and deepen their programmes. Each pupil was allowed one free period each day. Periods were lengthened from the conventional 40 minutes to 60 minutes. The longer period enabled teachers to use a variety of teaching strategies to engage pupils.

Byron teachers, however, spent more time with classes than teachers in other schools. This realized a savings in teacher allocation at Byron. Some of these savings were allocated for extra counsellors and to provide time for chairpersons. The remainder was given in cash to the school, to hire extra secretaries, teacher aides, lab assistants, artists to work with pupils in class, professional musicians to support music classes, and audio-visual specialists to ensure equipment was available and ready when required. While the work load was heavier for teachers, there was considerable support available.

Byron's departments were organized into cross-disciplinary units such as Social Sciences, the Arts, Mathematics, Science and Technology with a department chair in charge as opposed to a department head. The number of formal leaders was therefore reduced from as many as 22 in some schools to 10. I was one of these chairmen and a rather vocal regional and provincial spokesman for the school and its organizing principles. The major role of the chairmen was to support the classroom teachers. They also formed the principals' cabinet to work out school policies and procedures and make sure that teachers were informed and had input on school issues. Guided by the creative and charismatic Bond, the school's first principal, the chairmen (they were all men until 1975) worked out policy and procedures, but the actual approval was a staff decision. Staff members recalled the exhilaration, the tremendously hard work, and the public scrutiny of the thousands of visitors who came to this school of the future in its first 5 years.

Years of overreaching and entropy: 1975–1985

No sooner had the recommendations of Hall–Dennis made their way to policy than forces within the province attempted to modify the document's perceived openness and lack of rigour. The teachers' federation, universities, and many in the public at large joined in questioning practices which were quite different from their own experiences and therefore suspect (Stamp, 1976). As long as the economic times were good the challenges were muted, but that too changed rapidly. The provincial government in time responded to the criticisms. The Ministry tightened the curriculum, increased the number and range of mandatory credits, restricted textbooks to those approved by the Ministry, and in general, communicated a conservative message.

At the same time, events in the South Board changed Byron's context dramatically. Jim Sizemore, the Director who had helped to create and sustain Lord Byron, retired. His replacement saw it as his role to treat all schools equitably and as a result Byron no longer enjoyed the special interest of the CEO. Subsequent local elections produced single issue candidates for the School Board who were less co-operative with each other and certainly with administration. Previous boards had been content to allow schools to evolve in different ways. The school boards of the late 1970s wanted policies which could be applied across the system. The special advantages enjoyed by Lord Byron in Sizemore's time, such as differentiated funds, were affected by this trend. The severe school board budget difficulties of the mid 1970s, the renewed protectionism of the teachers' federation, and the Board's swing to a more conservative stance, combined to curtail or at least circumscribe the spirit of innovation which had characterized the Sizemore era.

The departure of Ward Bond was a major turning point in Byron's history. He was aware of the need for succession planning because he required chairmen to train their successors in the event of their departures. Succession planning for principals, however, was a system responsibility, and in this it miscalculated. Ward was such a revered and admired figure that his successor would have to be uniquely prepared.

Overreaching

The new principal, Bruce Grey was 34 years of age in 1974, when he was assigned by the system to Lord Byron High School. He had been a successful vice principal in a very large traditional school and he embraced his conception of the Byron philosophy enthusiastically. His greatest difficulty was that he was not Bond. Grey's appointment coincided with renewed aggressiveness from the teachers' Federation over the chairmanship structure and differentiated staffing, which they argued cost teachers jobs and opportunities. The Board in Grey's view, allowed the Federation to win the differentiated staffing issue. My one year as Grey's deputy was a useful learning experience. I found myself interpreting the school to Grey and explaining Grey to the staff. Inside the school there was a feeling among staff members that Grey used the rhetoric of Byron but he did not really believe in its philosophy because he was not a 'Byron person'. Many people on staff felt that liberty had become license and blamed the new principal, when in fact most of the problems which ensued could be traced to a dramatic increase in pupil enrollment – from 900 pupils in 1970 to over 2000 in 1976. Tendencies which were evident in the first 4 years became manifest in the 'Grey era'. The halls were often littered. Pupils would sit in front of the school smoking. Some rather unconventional staff were hired. As the size of staff increased, communications tended to be through department meetings as opposed to staff meetings. Some placed the blame at Grey's door, others more charitably saw school size, the promotion of many of the key players, lack of regional support, and attacks by other professionals in the system as factors in Byron's losing its way.

By 1977, when Grey received a promotion and moved to another school board, Byron was one of the largest schools in the system. In addition to record growth, Grey felt that a number of people on staff had difficulty transferring their loyalty from Bond to the 'Byron concept'. As Grey said, for some people on staff, change got personified in the originating principal rather than becoming part of the structure and culture of the school.

When Grey left in 1977, Byron was a large, well-resourced, and ostensibly successful school, but the seeds of its decline were evident to people in the school. Many teachers felt the school had been so caught up in issues like differentiated staffing, adult education, community outreach, and adding programmes such as an outdoor education immersion, that the essential Byron vision had become blurred. In essence, Byron suffered from 'innovation overload' – too many new approaches added before previous changes had been consolidated.

Entropy

Concerns that the original Byron concept had been lost resulted in the assignment of Graham Clark, the former vice principal to Bond, as principal to replace Grey. It was felt that he might be able to capture something of the essential Byron approach. Clark's arrival coincided with a number of logistical and organizational changes over which the school had no control. He inherited a school of nearly 2000 pupils and 100 teachers and 135 staff in total. The school's enrollment declined by 150 each year of his 3 year tenure. This meant that each year the most junior teachers were declared surplus to the school. Since Byron had only known growth, this was an important psychological turning point for staff. The drop in enrollment coincided with two mandated organizational changes which further undermined the initial concept of Byron.

In 1977, the Ministry of Education for Ontario required Byron and other experimental schools to conform to the diploma requirements of the rest of the province. Byron adopted the standard semestered timetable which was used by all but three schools in South. This arrangement effectively ended the free period for most pupils. This new timetable arrangement also largely eliminated the savings in teachers which had led to differentiated staffing funds from 1970 to 1977. Since differentiated staffing was a source of irritation to the Federation, the system's leaders agreed to its elimination.

During Grey and Clark's tenures there was considerable staff mobility. By 1978 only 23 of the 135 staff members had been at Byron in its first 3 years. Only five of the original 10 chairmen remained. The five who had left, all for promotions in the system, were considered by Bond to be the heart of his original group.

When Clark was promoted, his replacement was one of the original chairmen George Owens. He had been one of the most powerful intellectual and creative forces within the original group and was well-liked by pupils and staff. In spite of Clark's and others' best efforts however, Owens found a school which had changed profoundly from the one he left in 1974 and was now little different from other South schools.

Byron's rapid decline in enrollment not only forced staff reductions, it also meant significant curtailment of pupils' programmes. Compounding the problem was an exodus of pupils to the neighbouring school, Roxborough, whose numbers were remaining relatively stable. Many of these pupils were high performers who left to get more specialized courses or to participate in Roxborough's elitist programme for the gifted. The flow of optional attendance was creating great imbalance between Roxborough and Byron. This further erosion of the student base through optional staff attendance made public relations and not educational issues the main school priority. Staff members felt betrayed by the Board, by the administration, and by the school's community. They believed they were 'fighting ghosts'. Owens saw his role in those years as 'to maintain and contain'. With so much needed in the school, he felt he had little left 'to fight the ghosts'. When the Ministry offered him a secondment to review provincial policies in his subject field, he accepted the opportunity. I arrived on the scene as Byron's superintendent (inspector) in Owen's last year. The school was a shadow of its former self. The staff was disheartened and Owens was overwhelmed by the enormity of the problems. His departure enabled me to facilitate the appointment of a completely new management team.

In 1984, a new principal, Patrick Garner and vice principal Betty Kelly were assigned to the school. Neither had ever taught at the school, but both had requested this assignment. They admired Byron's innovative reputation and welcomed the opportunity to restore some of Byron's past 'glory'. Their major challenge was to restore public confidence and rebuild a staff which had been buffeted by the debilitating effects of declining enrollment, and the inchoate criticisms of colleagues in other schools and their own community.

Survival and continuity: 1985–1995

To ensure the school's viability the new principal agreed to add two regional special education programmes to the school. Other schools also had space but Byron offered a caring philosophy which had persisted through good times and bad. The addition of special education programmes, while laudable, did not stem the outflow of the more academically talented pupils to Roxborough. Throughout their tenures as principal, Garner and Kelly after him, sought to balance the traditional egalitarianism of Byron with the very real community and social pressures for excellence and elitism. To retain their higher achieving pupils, they convinced staff to support the addition of a French Immersion programme as well as segregated gifted programmes. Their approach to the community was to use every opportunity to say 'Byron has changed'. In practice, though, the substantive changes were minimal. Garner and Kelly recognized that Byron's programmes were still as good if not better than most schools and worked energetically to alter public perceptions of the school, which they achieved with considerable success. They, with the support of their teaching staff, succeeded in ensuring Byron's survival by accepting the structures and cultural norms of the other secondary schools in South.

▌The Life Cycle of New Setting

This brief history of the school suggests that there was a very definite, and definable cycle in Byron's evolution. From its creative and experimental origins, it evolved through a phase of overreaching and entropy, to a third stage, survival and continuity. Like all new schools, Byron was an act of creation and establishment, which as Hargreaves and his colleagues (Hargreaves, Fullan, Wignall, Stager, and Macmillan, 1992) indicate is 'very different from changing a school from one state to another' (p. 105).

Overreaching

The very act of creation at Lord Byron had within it the 'seeds' of organizational difficulties. In a sense a dialectic emerged. Forces which promoted the new organizational order, paradoxically contained within them forces which could result in disorder and instability. The challenge for Bond's successor was not only to encourage staff to transfer loyalties from the originating principal to the innovative meaning and concepts of the school, but also to establish his own credibility to ensure that the seeds of discord never germinated. The following discussion uses the analytic framework used in the study to collect and analyze the data for this study.

Context

Context has a powerful effect upon change in schools and classrooms in particular, and especially in new schools that are challenging the educational and parent communities' perceptions of how a 'real school' should function (Metz, 1991). Context may be defined as the whole situation, background, or environment relevant to some happening' (Grossman and Stodolsky, 1994, p. 18l)

At Byron, the leadership and staff continued in the second 4 years of the school's life to add innovative programmes, while at the same time they attempted to consolidate the initial innovations. This overload or 'overreaching' placed pressure on the creative structures which harboured these 'seeds' of disorder which eventually blossomed into serious and in some cases irresolvable difficulties.

Byron benefited from the favourable provincial and Board climate for innovation. The Hall–Dennis report still enjoyed public support in the early 1970s and Sizemore as Director in South at the time encouraged innovation and used his considerable influence to support Byron politically. By the middle 1970s, that favourable climate had changed. The province was in full retreat from the progressivism of Hall–Dennis, and Sizemore had retired to be replaced by less supportive leadership at central office. The opposition of colleagues at Roxborough, and throughout the system, began to have an impact on public opinion. Byron's initial prominence and community efforts had kept this undercurrent quiet. The growing tide of professional criticism, however, changing contextul factors, and internal problems at the school related to enrollment increases created a climate for the expression of this unrest. Lord Byron continued to institute new programmes, while attempting to resolve the problems of a dramatic increase in school population. The climate had changed but the school had not.

Meaning

Bennis and Nanus (1985) state: '. . . all organizations depend on the existence of shared meanings and interpretations of reality, which facilitate action . . . an essential factor in leadership is the capacity to influence and organize meaning for the members of the organization' (p. 39).

Over time what people considered to be the purpose or mission of Lord Byron changed as its context shifted. Byron was intended to be a 'lighthouse' or model school. It publicized, and some might even say flaunted its uniqueness, its innovativeness, its 'newness'. It put the pupils, not content, first. It espoused caring, humane relationships, challenging but individualized programmes, and democratic decision making. In the 1970s, in the minds of most people, this philosophy and its supporting concepts were not those of a 'real school'. Roxborough, the neighbouring traditional school, was a 'real school'. Critics waited to find evidence of flawed implementation to demonstrate a flawed philosophy. By overreaching, the school put pressure on structures such as pupil free time that led to abuses by pupils which provided ammunition to the critics. Stories of perceived laxness, lack of discipline and rigour were repeated so often that they become part of the Byron 'folklore'. The staff's conception of a 'good' school and the community's definition of a 'real' school increasingly conflicted.

Leadership

The importance of the leader in the management of meaning in an organization is one of the few concepts in the management literature about which there is fairly consistent agreement (Bennis and Nannus, 1985; Fullan, 1993; Stoll and Fink, 1996). In recent times, this literature has referred to managers as people who do things efficiently and leaders who do things effectively (Bennis and Nannus, 1985). Others have described transactional leaders as those who use conventional, rather than political means to get the job done, and transformational leaders as those who unite their associates through a shared vision to achieve organizational goals (Burns, 1978). Bond was clearly a transformational leader. Conversely, staff perceived Grey as a transactional leader.

The 'overreaching' phase was in some ways a function of these conflicting leadership images. Bond, the first principal, was, as most people commented, a hard act to follow. His departure after only three and a half years created a succession problem for the school Board. Its choice of a very young, ambitious and innovative principal who intended to push the Byron approach even further proved to be a questionable choice for that particular period of Byron's life cycle. While hindsight is '20/20', it would appear that a consolidator and not another innovator was needed. The delicate decision making balance between management, department chairs, and staff gradually eroded which complicated the micropolitics of the school. The positive politics of the early days became pathological in the 1980s.

Structures

For purposes of this study structure refers to the use of time and space, and the functioning of roles and responsibilities. Some structures which worked well for 900 pupils proved inadequate for 2000 pupils, but Byron persisted because these structures were part of the original organization. The most glaring example was pupil free time. The seeds were planted for misuse in the early days, but became a significant problem in the late 1970s. Rather than modify the policy for perhaps the younger pupils, Byron persisted. The misuse of time by pupils was a major community concern. The teacher workload which permitted differentiated staffing became intensified as the school grew. The architectural flaws in the building were exacerbated by the rapid increase in pupils. Simply stated, the school's reluctance to alter structures which enabled the school to prosper in the early years contributed to the 'attrition of change'.

Culture

The evidence indicates that in its early years Byron could well have been described as a 'collaborative culture' (Hargreaves, 1994). It was also pointed out that criticism, even in the early days, had contributed to Byron becoming 'balkanized' as a school in relationship to the rest of the region (Fullan, 1993). In addition there were signs of 'balkanization' within the school as well. The rapid increase in pupil and teacher population led to a more fragmented and less cohesive staff. Perhaps more harmful for the school was the introduction to the staff of a few teachers who pushed the Byron ideals to the 'extreme' and irreparably damaged Byron's reputation. In the words of one of my teacher respondents, a few of them did some 'dumb, dumb, things'. The need to continue to be new, unique, and innovative resulted in these questionable selections.

Teachers' work and lives

Byron, like all new and innovative schools placed tremendous pressure on people's energy levels and personal lives. After 5 years of constantly being under public scrutiny many teachers felt a need for some respite. There was a significant exodus of original staff in the mid 1970s. Rather than a pause to consolidate, more changes, and more innovations ensued to the point that by 1980 the incoming principal felt that many people were 'burned out'. As a result there is considerable evidence that the staff was unprepared to cope with the difficulties of declining enrolment and contraction of programmes in the late 1970s and early 1980s. Many of the difficulties described were masked in the mid 1970s by the growth, availability of money and the 'overreaching'. The problems surfaced, however, once the pupil population began to decline. The school turned inward for protection and initiated a period which I have described as entropy ensued.

Entropy

In response to disorder, systems become closed to their environment and lose energy which in scientific terms is called entropy. Systems that remain closed ultimately expire. From the mid 1970s until the mid 1980s, the staff sealed itself off as a school, and within the school in their departments. They expended inordinate energy solving problems inherited from earlier days. Simultaneously, they faced the image problem, shrinking resources, loss of key staff members, internal divisions, to mention a few of the issues. They looked inward for comfort and tended not only to shut out the critics but also new learning.

1983 was the low point in the school's life cycle. The principal was ill, rumours of imminent school closure abounded, and Byron was losing over 60 pupils a year to Roxborough. Questions of the school's survival did surface periodically. The time had come for a totally new direction.

Survival and continuity

The appointment of a new leadership team in 1984 coincided with a leveling off of the enrollment decline and the school moved into a third phase. This enabled the new principal and vice principal with the support of staff, parents and senior system's managers, to move the school in a more conventional direction while at the same time ensuring the school's survival by inviting regional programmes to be housed in the school. In this way, the innovative past was merged with the conventional present to help create a more stable environment for succeeding years. The result of the work of Garner and Kelly was to place Byron very much into the mainstream of schooling in South.

Many of the factors which contributed to this 'attraction' were conditions over which the school had very little, if any control – the 'givens' (Mortimore, Sammons, Stoll, Lewis and Ecob, 1988). There is no question that contextual factors were powerful and pervasive. For schools of the future the unpredictability of these forces will increase. What is important, therefore, is to learn from this experience of how a school like Lord Byron responded to these forces. By looking at Byron in a multi-dimensional way, it seems clear that preventing the 'attrition of change' requires attention to a complex interrelationship of many factors which influence structures and cultures in schools. Some factors like rapid growth or decline in pupil population may exacerbate pre-existing conditions which result in retrenchment and the 'attrition of change', but to suggest that this caused a school like Byron's problems is too simplistic. The complexity of the factors described, and their connections and relationships, make it virtually impossible to determine causation, and therefore impossible to *predict* with certainty that attending to this factor or that will ensure a school's continuing growth and development. The best that can be said is that schools that are aware and attend to these factors will *probably* continue to retain their innovative edge and be 'moving' schools.

The 'attrition of change': its dual meaning

This study suggests (as do others in the case study literature) that the hopes and dreams of the initiators of 'lighthouse' schools will prove disappointing in the long run. As previously noted, there does indeed appear to be a life cycle to new and innovative schools. With careful planning, a reasonably stable context, and a little good fortune, however, the stages of the 'attrition of change' might be delayed by avoiding 'overreaching and entropy'. Simply stated, new schools such as Byron will, over time, look and sound like the other schools in the system. This view that 'attrition of change' for new and innovative schools is probable, if not predictable, is somewhat pessimistic. Looked at another way, however, the strategy of 'model' schools can be considered a positive influence for change over time in the larger system. In many ways, the schools in South came to look and sound like Byron. The system's acceptance of change as an integral part of practice has been well documented (Giles, 1998; Stoll and Fink, 1992, 1994, 1996). Over its 25 years, Lord Byron has contributed significantly to the gradual 'attrition' of barriers to change in the South Board – thus a second meaning of the 'attrition of change'.

Leadership

Leadership at various levels played an important part in this, and other similar studies of new and innovative schools (Smith *et al.*, 1987). At the system level Byron experienced unique benefits and suffered undue criticism because of the initiating CEOs enthusiasm for its innovations. In addition, the choice of an outstanding, charismatic leader for the school's first principal made his replacement very difficult. Loyalty to the person as opposed to the concept was a particular problem in both the Byron study and Smith and his colleagues' research (1987). These circumstances raise a number of questions of policy and practice. What type of person should be chosen as the first leader of a new and innovative school? What commitments should the formal school leaders make to ensure some stablity in the first few years? What processes will ensure appropriate succession planning?

The role of the system

Throughout this study I have connected Lord Byron to the South system, and in turn to the province of Ontario. There is an increasing effort in Canada and other countries to allow market forces to determine educational polices (Barlow and Robertson, 1994; Gerwitz, Ball, and Bowe, 1995; Robertson, 1996). Governments, through various policy initiatives like direct funding to schools, changes in taxing responsibilities, and direct and overt restructuring of school districts, have often limited the role of the local educational authorities. Such intermediary levels of governance are usually viewed as impediments to governments' change agendas. School districts are depicted as unnecessarily bureaucratic and inefficient. While there are no doubt districts which fit this description, the Lord Byron story suggests an alternative picture which indicates that school districts (LEAs) can and do play an important role in trying to ensure a quality education for all children, not just those of the influential middle class. The South Board and Jim Sizemore created the opportunity for the creation of Lord Byron which attempted to respond to the needs of all pupils. Throughout the difficult times, the Board through its administrative support, ensured the continuing viability of Lord Byron. The selection of principals in the mid-1980s, the addition of regional programmes, and the efforts to balance enrollments between Roxborough and Byron are examples of the system's intervention to protect the quality of programmes for all pupils. In a pure market approach, Roxborough would have accepted the most academically suitable pupils which would have left Byron as a repository for lower socio-economic, non-academic and special education pupils (Whitty, 1997). As a result of the Board's intervention, however, Byron maintained a comprehensive pupil population that enabled it to offer a breadth of programmes to meet a wide variety of pupil needs. While the market might promote quality for some schools (although even this is doubtful, see Stoll and Fink, 1998), the Lord Byron experience suggests that governments need to reassess the role of the district in maintaining equitable education for all pupils. In their rush to eliminate the intrusive effects of local government bureaucracy, national and regional governments may also end up removing invaluable forms of co-ordination and support.

Conclusion

The literature on change has grown significantly in recent years. Most of it however, attends to strategies to change ineffective, or in Rosenholtz's (1989) term 'stuck' schools into effective or 'moving' schools. Such organizations are characterized as learning organizations which can respond to the vicissitude of a rapidly changing context (Garratt, 1987; Senge, 1990; Stacey, 1995). Very little, however, has been written on how innovative or 'moving' schools can maintain their momentum in the face of an increasingly complex, diverse and unpredictable world. While this chapter does not address this issue directly, it has shown how one school struggled to maintain its essential meaning, while confronted by forces over which it had little or no control. In the process, this study provides a number of possible 'warning lights', which, depending on a school's context, has the potential to help 'moving' schools to stay the course.

The cases of new and innovative schools (Fletcher *et al.*, 1985; Gold and Miles, 1981; Smith *et al.*, 1987) have the stuff of classic tragedy – heroic leaders laid low by often unfair criticism, exciting visions of new educational worlds blinded by people's timidity and fears, and promising organizations and institutions destroyed or significantly diminished by internal and external discord. Lord Byron has many of these qualities – a gradual 'attrition' of its innovative ethos after the departure of its revered leader, aggressive opposition from the people it was trying to serve, and internal divisions and conflicts precipitated by forces over which the school had little control. Unlike the other stories, however, this study views the school over a 25 year period, and also focuses on the school's relationship to its district context. Looked at from this perspective, we have a more romantic picture of a school with a powerful vision of educational change, which produced a generation of leaders who carried the school's message to more traditional settings, and used their Byron experience to initiate processes to speed the attrition of barriers to change in these other settings. While the internal manifestations of the Byron experiment have eroded over time, the power of its essential meaning can be seen in every secondary school in the South Board of Education, as each day they attempt to respond to the diverse needs and interests of *all* their pupils.

References

Anderson, G. (1990). *Fundamentals of educational research*. London: Falmer Press.

Ball, S. (1993). Self doubt and soft data: social and technological trajectories in ethnographic fieldwork. In M. Hammersley (ed.), *Educational research: current issues* (pp. 32–48). London: Paul Chapman Publishing.

Ball, S. and Goodson, I. (1985). Understanding teachers: concepts and contexts. In S. Ball, and I. Goodson (eds.), *Teachers' lives and careers* (pp. 1–26). London: Falmer Press.

Barlow, M. and Robertson, H. (1994). *Class warfare*. Toronto: Key Porter.

Bennis, W. and Nannus, B. (1985). *Leaders*. New York: Harper and Row.

Block, P. (1993). *Stewardship: choosing service over self interest*. San Francisco, CA: Berrett Kohler.

Brouilette, L. (1996). *A geology of reform: the successive restructuring of a school district*. Albany, NY: State University of New York Press.

Burns, J.M. (1978). *Leadership*. New York: Harper and Row.

Byrne, B.M. (1974). Burnout testing for the validity, replication, and invariance of causal structure across the elementary, intermediate, and secondary teachers. *American Educational Research Journal*, 31(3), 645–73.

Crump, S.J. (1993). *School-centred leadership*. Sydney, Australia: Thomas Nelson.

Cuban, L. (1988). A fundamental puzzle of school reform. *Phi Delta Kappan*, 70(5), 341–44.

Fletcher, C., Caron, M. and Williams, W. (1985). *Schools on trial*. Milton Keynes: Open University Press.

Fullan, M.G. (1993). *Change forces: probing the depths of educational reform*. London: Falmer Press.

Garratt, B. (1987). *The learning organization*. Glasgow: Wm. Collins Press.

Gerwirtz, S., Ball, S.J. and Bowe, R. (1995). *Markets, choice and equity in education*. Buckingham: Open University Press.

Giles, C. (1998). Control or empowerment: the role of site-based planning in school improvement. *Educational Management and Administration*, 26(4), 407–15.

Goetz, J. (1988). Review of membership roles in field research. *The International Journal of Qualitative Studies in Education*, 1(3), 291–94.

Goodson, I.F. (1992). Studying teachers' lives: an emergent field of inquiry. In I.F. Goodson (ed.), *Studying teachers' lives* (pp. 1–17). New York: Teachers College Press.

Goodson, I.F. and Walker, R. (1991). *Biography, identity and schooling: episodes in educational research*. London: Falmer Press.

Grossman, P.L. and Stodolsky, S. (1994). Considerations of content and the circumstances of secondary school teaching. In L. Darling-Hammond (ed.), *Review of research in education* (Vol. 20, pp. 179–221). Washington, DC: American Educational Research Association.

Hargreaves, A. (1984). *Classrooms and staffrooms* (pp. 303–29). Milton Keynes: Open University Press.

Hargreaves, A. (1986). *Two cultures of schooling*. Lewes: Falmer Press.

Hargreaves, A. (1991). Curriculum refom and the teacher. *The Curriculum Journal*, 2(3), 249–580.

Hargreaves, A. (1994). *Changing teachers, changing times*. London: Cassell.

Hargreaves, A., Fullan, M., Wignall, R., Stager, M. and Macmillan, R. (1992). *Secondary school work cultures and educational change*. Toronto: Ministry of Education.

Hargreaves, D.H. (1995). School culture, school effectiveness and school improvement. *School Effectiveness and School Improvement*, 6, 23–46.

Metz, M.H. (1991). Real school: a universal drama amid disparate experience. In D.E. Mitchell and M.E. Goetz (eds.), *Education politics for the new century* (pp. 75–91). New York: Falmer Press.

Miles, M.B. and Huberman, A.M. (1984). *Innovations up close: how school improvement works*. New York: Plenum Press.

Mortimore, P., Sammons, P., Stoll, L., Lewis, D. and Ecob, R. (1988). *School matters: The junior years*. Somerset, UK: Open University Press.

Oakes, J., Wells, A.S., Yonezawa., S. and Ray, K. (1997). Change agentry and the quest for equity: lessons from detracking schools. In A. Hargreaves (ed.), *Rethinking educational change with heart and mind: the 1997 ASCD Yearbook* (pp. 43–72). Alexandria, VA: ASCD.

Ontario Department of Education (1968). *Living and learning: report of the Provincial Committee on Aims and Objectives of Education in the Schools of Ontario*. Toronto: Newton Publishing.

Robertson, S. (1996). Teachers' work, restructuring and post fordism: constructing the new professionalism. In I.F. Goodson and A. Hargreaves (eds.), *Teachers' professional lives* (pp. 11–44). London: Falmer.

Rosenholtz, S.J. (1989). *Teacher workplace: the social organization of schools*. New York: Longmans.

Senge, P. (1990). *The fifth discipline: the art and practice of the learning organization*. New York: Doubleday.

Segiovanni, T. (1992). *Moral leadership*. San Francisco, CA: Jossey-Bass.

Smith, L.M., Dwyer, D.C., Prunty, J.J. and Kleine, P.F. (1987). *The fate of an innovative school*. London: Falmer Press.

Stacey, R. (1995). *Managing chaos*. London: Kogan Page.

Stamp, R. (1976). *The schools of Ontario*. Toronto: Queen's Printers of Ontario.

Stoll, L. and Fink, D. (1992). Effective school change: the Halton approach. *School Effectiveness and School Improvement*, 3, 19–41.

Stoll, L. and Fink, D. (1994). *Voices from the field. School effectiveness and School Improvement*, 5, 149–177.

Stoll, L. and Fink, D. (1996). *Changing our schools: linking school effectiveness and school improvement*. Buckingham: Open University Press.

Stoll, L. and Fink, D. (1998). The cruising school: the unidentified ineffective school. In L. Stoll and K. Myers (eds.), *Schools in difficulty: no quick fixes* (pp. 189–206). London: Falmer Press.

Stringfield, S., Ross, S. and Smith, L. (eds.). (1996). *Bold plans for school restructuring: the new American schools design*. Mahwah, NJ: LEA Publishers.

Telford, H. (1996). *Transforming schools through collaborative leadership*. London: Falmer Press.

Whitty, G. (1997). Creating quasi-markets in education: a review of recent research on parental choice and school autonomy in three countries. In M.W. Apple (ed.), *Review of research in education* (pp. 3–47). Washington, DC: American Educational Research Association.

Woods, P. (1986). *Inside school: ethnography in educational research*. London: Routledge and Kegan Paul.

Index

academic achievement, 109
academic excellence, 109
academic leadership study, 43–55
  conceptual framework, 45–7
  conclusions, 55
  discussion, 53–4
  findings, 48–53
  method, 47
acceptance, school relations, 179–81
accountability
  headteachers, 99–101
  middle managers, 202–3
achievement, SQH, 65
acquisition metaphor, learning, 32, 39
Adair model, leadership, 219–20
administrative workload, of headteachers, 94
affirmation, need for, SQH, 65
alienation, school relations, 175
ambiguity, middle managers' role, 203
androgogy, ideal jobs, 144
answerability, 99–100
antagonism, school relations, 175–6
Antal, A., 74
anthropological studies, learning, 37
application, professional knowledge, 31
approachability, female headteachers, 117
aspirational aspects, SQH, 65–6
assertive leadership, 92
assessment
  of leader's influence on development, 127–8
  SQH, 63
assumptive world, 200
authority, middle managers, 206
autocratic/directive style, of management, 108
autonomy
  teachers, 152–3
  see also departmental autonomy; professional autonomy

Barrett, F.J., 76
basic trust, 173
behaviour
  mentoring, 77
  in organisations, 18
Belbin, M., 220–1
benevolent leadership, 92
Bennett, N., 200
Bennis, W. and Nannus, B., 87, 91, 271
Benton, Sue, 94
Bettis, R.A. and Prahalad, C.K., 75
Blatchford, Roy, 89, 90, 97, 98, 99, 101
Bolam, R. *et al.*, 118, 225–6
Bolman, L. and Deal, T., 85, 87
Bottery, M., 18
boundary management, 187–8
bounded instability, complex systems, 76
bounded non-systemic thinking, 157, 158–61
  see also systemic thinking
Bovair, Keith, 92, 96, 97, 98, 101
bridging and brokering role, middle managers, 201